# Conversations
# with Arrau

# Conversations with

# ARRAU

# Joseph Horowitz

ALFRED A. KNOPF

New York 🐎 1982

Copyright © 1982 by Joseph Horowitz
Discography copyright © 1982 by T. W. Scragg
All rights reserved under International and Pan-American Copyright Conventions. Published in the United States by Alfred A. Knopf, Inc., New York, and simultaneously in Canada by Random House of Canada Limited, Toronto. Distributed by Random House, Inc., New York.

Grateful acknowledgment is made to the following for permission to reprint from previously published material: Doubleday & Company, Inc.: Excerpt from a song by Hermann Allmers from *The Ring of Words*, translated by Philip L. Miller. Reprinted by permission of Doubleday & Company, Inc. *High Fidelity:* "A Performer Looks at Psychoanalysis," by Claudio Arrau. February 1967. All Rights Reserved. Reprinted in its entirety. I.H.T. Corporation: Excerpts from the *New York Herald Tribune*. © New York Herald Tribune. Reprinted by permission of I.H.T. Corporation. *Newsweek:* Excerpts from "Arrau's Arrival." Copyright 1943 by Newsweek, Inc. All Rights Reserved. Reprinted by permission. *The New York Times:* Excerpts from *New York Times* reviews. Copyright © 1923, 1936, 1941 by The New York Times Company. Reprinted by permission. Pantheon Books: Eugen Herrigel, *Zen in the Art of Archery*. Copyright © 1953 by Eugen Herrigel. Pantheon Books, a Division of Random House, Inc. Time, Inc.: Excerpts from "Arrau Makes Hay." Copyright 1942 by Time. Inc. All rights reserved. Reprinted by permission from *Time*.

Picture Credits: 1955—Arnold Newman; with Colin Davis—Tom Schippers; in Douglaston—Virginia Liberatore; hands—Virginia Liberatore; in performance—from *Claudio Arrau: A Life in Music*, A Robert Snyder Film / Masters and Masterworks Productions, Inc.; 1978—Wherner Kruten. All pictures not otherwise credited are from Claudio Arrau's private collection.

Library of Congress Cataloging in Publication Data
Horowitz, Joseph, 1948–    Conversations with Arrau.
Discography / T. W. Scragg: p.
Includes bibliographical references and indexes.
1. Arrau, Claudio, 1903–   2. Pianists—Interviews.
I. Arrau, Claudio, 1903–   II. Title.
ML417.A8H7    786.1'092'4    82–47817
ISBN 0-394-51390-8    AACR2

Manufactured in the United States of America
First Edition

# Contents

## Contents

### III. Conversations about Arrau

### IV. "A Performer Looks at Psychoanalysis"
*by Claudio Arrau*
239

### V. Conclusion: Arrau on Records
251

### Appendices

### Index

# Acknowledgments

Nancy Zannini was the person who at the right moment prodded me to write a book about Claudio Arrau. Robert Gottlieb of Knopf was enthusiastically supportive from the start; no aspect of my project, including the numerous musical examples and photographs, was ever suspected of being too lavish. Materials for the book were assembled from libraries and private collections as well as from memorabilia in the Arrau household. Among those who helped furnish documents, photographs, oral memories, and hard-to-find recordings, I am especially indebted to Agustin Arrau, Mrs. Ruth Arrau, Daniel Barenboim, Arturo Carvallo, Peter Clancy of Philips Records, Mrs. Lucrecia van den Daele, Sir Colin Davis, Elba Fuentes of the Chilean Consulate in New York, Loretta Goldberg, Herb Helman of RCA Records, Ludger M. Hermanns of the Deutsche Psychoanalytische Vereinigung, Marcos Klorman, William Melton, Garrick Ohlsson, John Pfeiffer of RCA Records, Earl Price of CBS Records, Heidrun Rodewald, Friede Rothe, Gerard Schwarz, T. W. Scragg, and Peter Warwick. Help in translations from French, German, and Spanish was provided by Steven Gleason, Jacob Horowitz, M.D., Kathleen Hulser, and Virginia Liberatore. Some vital sources and ideas were suggested by Daniel Pincus and Wil Tanenbaum, M.D. Philip Lorenz, a close Arrau associate for many years, unstintingly shared his knowledge with me. Two people who helped in a general way were my agent, Robert Cornfield, and Kathleen Hulser, who was always ready to read what I had written and to offer sound advice. Finally, my greatest debt of gratitude can only be to Claudio Arrau, for being as generous with his trust as with his time.

# The Chilean Mozart: Claudio Arrau Leon

*The following article, signed by Antonio Orrego Barros, appeared in the November 1909 issue of* Selecta, *a magazine published in Santiago. The English translation is by Steven Gleason.*

I feel as if my heart were singing. As this child performs his marvels on the piano, I think I hear a mysterious voice whispering in my ear, telling me that Claudio Arrau Leon is one of those beings whom nature has favored with an overabundance of gifts, that the world will bow down before him as if in the presence of a god.

But in the joy and the pride I feel, as an artist and a Chilean, to watch this wonder reveal itself on our very soil, there is mixed a melancholy foreboding that will take deeper root in me each day, for I know that people lose their way in this world; their talents are wasted and come to naught; the gifts of the soul are neglected and forgotten. . . .

And if we add to this the potent force which today rears its head like a viper, threatening society because it recognizes birthrights and God because He bestows the privilege of genius, threatening Nature because she denies her gifts to one and lavishes them on another, and the ocean, I suppose, because it keeps its waters forever uneven—then does the spirit truly shrink from the thought of what might befall one who spoke up in the name of something not cast in the common clay. . . .

I don't know whether it was the child at the piano or the harmonies of Beethoven that stirred these murky meditations, but that is what I thought as I sat before the prodigy.

And that child with the unruly head of hair and the pensive eyes has it all: refinement, elegance, good looks. He never loses the freshness and candor of a child who delights in toys and candies, yet his gaze bears the intense and luminous expression of someone who is able to penetrate the mysteries of art.

He passes from candies to the piano, from the piano to candies, with the same ease and cheerfulness. He amazes but does not frighten; you are aware of genius but not the freakishness genius sometimes carries with it. He is in all respects a child, even when he's playing: you almost get the feeling the piano is a child's toy. But this is a child whose gaze is alluring, whose movements are captivating, whose very being hints at something unspoken and marvelous.

Dressed in white, seated at the piano, with his moppish head of hair, his eyes riveted to the music, he is for me the very image of the young Mozart.

It wasn't his execution that surprised me the most. What astonished me was his artistic instinct, that this child should lose himself in the profound harmonies of Beethoven, prizing them above all other music. I grant you, his child's heart cannot fathom the great human passions, the emotions, the pathos, and the anguish those harmonies embody, but it divines them, it senses and comprehends them with the clairvoyance that lies at the heart of artistic inspiration.

Blessed inequality, thought I, that we who feel no resentment at having to clear the path for one bound for glory should savor the joy of having something on this earth to admire.

What the boy most enjoys is not to show off with a polished performance of a piece he already knows, but rather to play at first sight. Every time he discovers a new composer of merit, or comes upon a work he doesn't know by one of his favorites, Beethoven, Mozart, and Liszt, you can't drag him away from the piano. . . .

On the evening we watched him play, he first encountered the music of Bach. The master appealed to him, and it was a wondrous thing to witness the efforts the child made to overcome the difficulties of those arduous works. The task was all the more formidable because his right hand could not even span an octave, so that he often had to bring over his left hand to complete a chord.

A woman's voice behind me was saying, "Good Lord! That child is sight-reading a piece that brought me to tears when I studied it . . . and I never did get it right. Just look how he's playing!"

I turned around to discover that the voice belonged to a celebrated concert pianist!

A while later, my neighbor opened a book of music and showed it to him, asking, "What is this?"

Claudito looked, his eyes lit up, and he exclaimed, "That's Beethoven!"

Then he took the book and began to turn the pages enthusiastically. In one group of pages, a title passed by and the music of another composer began.

Claudio could tell there had been a change just by looking at those signs which to the average person on the street look like so many little black marks on a ruler, and he said, "That's Liszt."

"How do you know?"

"Because that's the way Liszt is," he answered simply.

And he was right: it was Liszt.

This child is as intimate with the great masters of the musical art as we are with the members of our family. To know who has passed by or who is speaking, we need only hear the sound of the steps or the echo of the voice. For him a few chords are sufficient to distinguish among the composers.

"Shall I transpose this piece, Mommy?" he whispers in his mother's ear.

She tries to dissuade him, but he keeps imploring, like a child asking permission to play. Finally his mother gives in; he sits down at the piano and transposes an entire composition to another key. He's discovered a new game!

He'd first been asked to transpose just two days before, during a test our musicians Paoli and Guiarda gave him. He got through the exam in a breeze, leaving the teachers a bit astonished.

And the boy had yet another surprise in store for us. He got down from the piano stool to eat some candy and, between one treat and another, the musicians played chords to him, up to ten notes at a time. With his back to the music, he identified the chords perfectly, note for note, the way you and I name household objects.

How long ago had this talent for music revealed itself? An idle question perhaps, but one we all asked his mother nonetheless.

"When he was two," she told us.

At the age of two he already knew Beethoven and could distinguish his music from that of all the other masters.

"That's so pretty . . . keep playing!" he would say to his mother when he heard her intone the harmonies of the tragic deaf master from Bonn.

And that music, profound revelation of the mysteries of the human heart, soon enveloped the child's soul in its melancholy mists. Claudito learned Beethoven's biography by heart, and would exclaim in a sorrowful voice, "Poor Beethoven . . . he couldn't hear!"

By then he could distinguish the masters from the run of the mill, and no sooner would his mother start to play the work of a lesser composer than he would walk away, saying, "No, Mommy, not that. That's ugly."

At four years of age he was confusing his mother with questions about the value and meaning of musical symbols. Once he had tired her out, he would turn to his older sister, who explained them to him with the patience children have for one another. That was how he learned theory.

In his eagerness to learn how to play, he would copy down the works of the masters and play them over and over until he'd learned them by heart.

Thus it came to pass that at five he played the music of his favorites, Beethoven, Mozart, and Liszt, at a charity concert in his native town of Chillán. Now that he is six (he was born on February 6, 1903), he has taken up the tradition of Mozart, who as a child was the wonder of the world: he has learned to perform those marvels which we witnessed with the exhilaration and dread one feels in the presence of the extraordinary.

We all said "He's a genius" in the detached voice so expressive of our cold and indifferent national character. And we said it almost in a whisper for fear of making fools of ourselves by appearing to exaggerate.

Yet just as we called him a genius in the privacy of our homes, and just as they called him a genius in his mother's salon, so was he deemed a genius, without the word being pronounced, in the chambers of the Palacio de la Moneda, where he arrived without fanfare and demonstrated, to the delight and amazement of His Excellency the President of the Republic and a few members of the diplomatic corps, the wonder of his extraordinary precocity.

Soro Barriga, the young composer who is now the pride not only of Chile but of all Latin America, had a chance (albeit in passing) to see and hear the boy, and he, who had also been a precocious child, marveled at the talents Claudito displayed.

He told me that though he never put too much stake in the ability to play well at an early age, for it wasn't such an exceptional thing, in this case the child had certain gifts he found awesome, such as his ability to read music the way he did. It's not surprising that Soro Barriga wasn't overly impressed by Claudito's other talents, for, as he told me, he'd hardly had a chance to see the child. . . .

As for Paoli, Amelia Cocq's old teacher, he told me that Claudio was a child of extraordinary natural abilities; among other things, he couldn't imagine how the boy could have developed such hands, for they seemed to have spent more time on the keyboard than the child had years. Searching for a comparison, he recalled his disciple Amelia Cocq and said, "Her hands had to be trained." What most attracted the teacher's attention, besides Claudito's perfect ear for music, was the incredible reading ability that Soro Barriga had already pointed out to me.

"Naturally," Paoli said to me, "he would make a great conductor, because I've seen him accompanying the voice and the violin, and arranging at sight to introduce the notes of the vocal part into the accompaniment. That is impressive.

"As for his becoming a great musician," he continued with the skepticism of an old teacher, "those are abilities still dormant in him. But they're manifest in his taste for good music, his perfect grasp of the art form, and, when you look at him, in those eyes that speak volumes."

Then he emphasized once again the boy's extraordinary facility for reading music, how he could take in a whole chord and play it at a moment's glance.

And here I cannot but return to that theme which must cast a shadow amidst all this light. The reception at the presidential palace was a triumph for Claudito; in his enthusiasm, the President took a book from his library and gave it to the boy after writing a flattering description that took up a whole page. The foreign minister picked him up, lowered him from the piano stool, and hovered around him with the enthusiasm felt only by true lovers of art. Such was the admiration Claudito evoked in the minister that a few days later he brought the boy home to introduce him to his family, thus giving him a further taste of encouraging approval. At about the same time, a curious anecdote was making the rounds.

Claudito had been enchanted to hear Premyslav play a piece by Godard, so he asked his mother to buy the music for him. She brought him to the music store, where he asked for works by Godard.

"But which piece do you want?" asked the store owner.

"Show them all to me," replied the boy, and he began to read them.

The store owner, marveling at this curious child, went to tell Premyslav, who happened to be there at the time, what was going on. Meanwhile, Claudio had picked out the piece simply by scanning the music and recalling the performance.

"Shall I play it?" the boy asked.

Premyslav, aglow with enthusiasm, brought him to the piano, where he performed at first sight, and impeccably, the music for which the great violinist was renowned.

The astonished Premyslav declared that he had never seen or hoped to see such a prodigy.

Wherever the boy went, anecdotes of his amazing feats followed him. Every indication was that his name would be taken up by the press and his prodigious talents hailed from the rooftops. Alas, the true story was written on the faces in the crowds at the horse shows and the soccer matches; the avid interest aroused by headlines announcing the great triumphs of this or that show horse could not be diverted to bring to the public's attention a young boy whose feet were just like everyone else's and who wasn't even precocious enough to know how a soccer goal was scored.

No headlines, no pictures in the daily papers to let the public know about the child prodigy. Only our photographer Vera (and I mention his name because the portraits he's made of the boy are a credit to him as an artist)—only he sought the child out to capture his image on film for posterity.

I told a journalist, a practical man, about Claudio Arrau and he said to me, "It's a good campaign you're waging; you have to make a sensation of the child so the government will give him a scholarship to study in Europe."

I do not say let us make a sensation of this child, but rather, let us not neglect our national heritage.

While that journalist, that practical man, was speaking to me of creating a sensation, the names of Beethoven and Mozart came to mind, and I contemplated the shame of those nations that gave them life but were not able to appreciate them. I thought of how the child prodigy who'd played at the court of Francis I at the age of six, and later filled the world of art with his genius, had no more to live on than the pittance the Archbishop of Salzburg gave him as a church musician. I thought of the shame Austria must feel in hearing the bitter closing words of Mozart's biography:

> His funeral was a disgrace for the Emperor, for the Court, for the public, and for society itself. On the evening of December 6, 1791, his body was hurriedly transported to a paupers' cemetery, and because it was raining, his friends Swieten, Süssmayr, and three others turned around and let him go alone to his final resting place.

And I thought of the satisfaction the English deservedly feel, and the shame that Germany must feel, each time the story of Beethoven's life is told, the story of the greatest of all musicians, in those words no Englishman can forget:

> It must fill the heart of every Englishman with pride to know that it was the Philharmonic Society of London which most relieved Beethoven's suffering on his deathbed, with a generous gift, and that practically the last words of the dying man were to thank his friends and admirers from that country.

All of this was written and said simply to express outrage at nations that had had the good fortune to produce a genius and the disgrace of denying him their esteem. Today we have among us a prodigy who at this early stage in his life can be compared to Mozart. A page of history is about to be written: will it be one of pride or of shame for Chile? Let us learn the lesson and honor our artists.

# PART I

# Introduction

Not long after meeting Claudio Arrau for the first time, in 1976, I was invited to watch him rehearse Beethoven's Third Piano Concerto at New York's Avery Fisher Hall. Dapper in a three-piece suit and gravely composed, Arrau at the keyboard made the nonchalant New York Philharmonic seem a vulgar backdrop to affairs of the soul. Afterward, in Arrau's dressing room, there were complaints about the listlessness of the orchestra. They will play better for the concert, Arrau said; in rehearsal, the musicians are always casual. Does Claudio Arrau ever play casually? someone asked. "I *can't!*" he answered, his eyes aghast, his face burning with feeling.

This glimpse of the artist at the mercy of his emotions has been renewed many times in the course of our acquaintance. His mere salutations are delivered with devouring honesty. He seems as incapable of lapsing into mere amenity as into rudeness. Notwithstanding his eminence, and the ponderous undertow of his visceral energies, he is an endearingly gracious man.


Neither his English, which bears traces of Spanish and German, nor his changeable physiognomy defines his origin. In fact, Arrau made his way strangely into the world. Chillán, Chile, where he was born in 1903, was a small city many hours from Santiago. His mother, who was already forty-three and had been married twenty-one years, taught piano. He never knew his father. He seems to have learned to read music mainly on his own, and before he could read words. When he was eight, he went abroad to study, supported by a stipend awarded by the Chilean Congress. In Berlin, where he settled with his mother, brother, and sister, he became the favorite pupil of Martin Krause, an imperious pedagogue who himself had studied with Liszt. His early

3

celebrity continued: he played for kings and queens, and under Arthur Nikisch and Fritz Steinbach. Then, in 1918, Krause died, and Arrau's progress halted. Abandoned in postwar Berlin, he lacked the cunning to promote his career, even to support himself and his family. An abbreviated American tour in 1923–24 sent him home penniless. On the verge of giving up, he sought help in psychoanalysis. Gradually, his reputation was remade, and his adulthood consolidated. In 1935–36, in a heralded feat of memory and endurance, he performed the complete solo clavier works of Johann Sebastian Bach in twelve recitals. In 1937, he married Ruth Schneider, a mezzo-soprano from Frankfurt, and moved out of the flat he had shared with his mother and sister. The Second World War drove the Arraus to the United States in 1940–41.

His arduous itinerary, generous programs, and catholic repertoire have long been trademarks. He still plays more than seventy concerts a season. He makes his home in suburban Douglaston, New York, a half hour's drive from Manhattan, but is rarely there. He has a summer house in southern Vermont, four miles outside the village of Weston (population 500), but spares even less time for it. His entourage is surprisingly small. The three Arrau children are Carmen, born in 1938, a legal secretary who lives in Springfield, Massachusetts; Mario, born in 1940, once a bronco rider in his own Vermont rodeo and now a blacksmith in Florida; and Christopher, born in 1959, a student at the University of Vermont. In addition to his wife, Arrau's main companions are William Melton, a pupil who often accompanies him on tours, to concerts, and to the theater, and Friede Rothe, who, as his personal manager since 1941, is his devoted gatekeeper, career counselor, and cheerleader. Miss Rothe oversees Arrau's concert and recording calendars, and plots his additional public exposure. She scrutinizes his health, marvels at his intensity, and frets about his reviews. At concerts, if she is present, she supervises access to his dressing room. When Arrau is in the United States, she telephones him nearly every day. When he is abroad, she calls as often as once a week. Arrau himself rarely telephones anyone.

Two overlapping character types permeate his identity: the man-child and the artist. The first is rooted in his prodigy years and

4

evokes images of the pianist in knee pants, his feet dangling above the pedals. In Chile, escorted by his mother, he played for the President. In Europe, under Krause's supervision, he sat in the laps of duchesses and queens. Early photographs suggest a shy, silent child with soft features and strangely experienced eyes.

The autocratic Krause, with his goatee and twirled mustache, might almost have been one of E. T. A. Hoffmann's Svengali-like music masters. Most of the authority figures from Arrau's early years, however, were maternal, beginning with his hovering mother, who dressed in black for decades after her husband's death, and who lived to be ninety-nine.

Arrau's enduring innocence is partly a legacy of his childhood eminence. He remains the least cynical, least devious of men. He does not drink or smoke. He distrusts machines: he cannot drive a car, boil an egg, or even operate a phonograph. I have seen him struggle for minutes, with mounting exasperation, to disengage the three locks on the front door of his home in Douglaston.

A second portion of his innocence arises from his vocation. He guards the purity of his environment. He shuns parties and loses track of small talk. He spends time alone with music and—especially in Vermont, where he weeds and plants—with nature. In conversation, as at the piano, he discloses emotional strife with startling frankness. He plainly embodies the nineteenth-century model of the artist as solitary, suffering hero.


Arrau's concentrated life style suits his stark concentration of mood. He is not an ironist, and knows no puns. Even at its gentlest, his presence registers with palpable force.

He is a small man—about five and a half feet tall—and when he is tired his outsized head can seem an archaic burden under old, brittle legs. His hands, also large for his frame, are prepossessing. The fingers are individually articulate, the fingertips cushioned and slightly spread. The ranginess of his thumbs, resulting from the peculiar elasticity of the joints, makes them seem longer than they are.

Because every mood consumes his features, he has many faces. His flaring nostrils and prominent cheekbones, dapper mustache and shiny hair at times still connote the dark good looks of a South American cosmopolite. When he is suddenly pensive, his hazel-green eyes cloud over and his gaze wanders. At the piano, his profile is chiseled, the flesh stretched taut and marked with lines of pain. In repose, he is round-faced and cherubic; his eyes crinkle, his cheeks soften and inflate.

His conversation dramatizes the moment—sometimes consciously, sometimes not. Describing another pianist's way with Chopin, he sits forward, pauses to reconsider, then confides in an incredulous whisper, "From an interpretive standpoint, it was absolutely *disgusting.*" Giggling over his inability to light the kitchen stove, he shrinks into his chair, sticks his hands in his pockets, and casts furtive glances to either side. "Probably," he declares, "I would set the house on fire." When a large, friendly dog lumbers into view and will not leave, his face darkens and grows hard. "Go away, dear," he tells the dog. "Go to your mistress." The creature does not budge. Arrau's lips purse, and his eyes, which are enormous, bulge to circles, stranding the pupils. He whips around toward the back of the house. "Ruth! Ruth! Call Rexie. He is bothering us!"

His voice is a gentle baritone, used softly and expressively. The words themselves are often ancillary, for in terms of language Arrau is an effortful speaker. Sometimes, before answering a question, he will draw a breath and look away. His sentences break down when a phrase or name will not come, and the ensuing silences can seem dangerous. Even when the verbal stream is steady, it is usually short: four or five sentences materialize, then the engine runs down.

Especially when music obtrudes, Arrau's words tend to dissipate. In fact, music is so distant from his social self that to play the piano for students or friends would be inconceivable. It is really not farfetched to surmise that for Arrau words and music occupy distinct personal realms, and that the pronounced civility of the first moderates the instinctual abandon of the second. His gentle manners, his fastidious attire (*Time* magazine once likened him to "a fugitive from a Man of Distinction ad"), the artifacts that embellish his work environment—these suggest a striving for order whose musical equivalent is his absolute fidelity to the text, and whose adversary is a substratum of fire and ice.

To witness Arrau performing the Liszt sonata is to know how

thoroughly this substratum can obliterate his normal self-awareness. Even while asleep, the demons cast a trembling glow from
behind his mildest public face. And they penetrate the timbre of
his voice.

Arrau listens to his own recordings with visible discomfort; he
perceives the clothes of civility being stripped away.

The conversations comprising the bulk of the present book took
place between May 1980 and July 1981, in Douglaston and Vermont. Arrau, typically, volunteered few anecdotes or sermons;
for the most part, his remarks were concentrated, short-winded,
and direct. The reader should bear in mind that the emerging
portrait is of an artist late in life; Arrau's manner was once brisker
and more gregarious. Rather than patching together a first-person narrative, or incorporating Arrau's information into a third-
person biography, I have retained the conversational framework
in which his remarks originated. A fabricated first-person narrative would have been misleading. A biography would have for-
feited the advantages of close, flexible interaction in which the
style and temper of a person's speech reveal as much as its content.

The conversations, which were tape-recorded, have been edited for grammar, accuracy, and concision. But I have resisted
glamorizing Arrau's speech; there are no new words or interpo-
lated subtleties of expression. Unavoidably, the edited transcripts
imply a faster pace and greater fluency than we usually managed.
And the reader will have to use some imagination to hear the
kindness of Arrau's voice, which is never aggressive, hard, or flat.

Since I am as garrulous as Arrau is not, my contributions have
been more heavily edited than his. Where possible, I have compressed my questions and comments. But there was no getting
rid of them without having to stitch together Arrau's sentences in
a false or clumsy manner.

The organization of the conversations reflects the book's dual
focus. The second through fifth conversations constitute a sort of
autobiography; the seventh through eleventh are devoted to music. The final two conversations fix Arrau in two recent moments
in time. In places, the music talk grows fairly ambitious. Even if
the reader is defeated by the references or musical examples,

7

however, the aim of Arrau's commentary will be apparent. His discussion of technique may prove revelatory to musical laymen for whom the physical side of piano playing seems mainly to consist of agile fingerwork.

The conversations with Arrau are followed by conversations with four musicians who have worked with him as colleagues or students: Philip Lorenz, Daniel Barenboim, Garrick Ohlsson, and Sir Colin Davis. A 1967 magazine article by Arrau himself, "A Performer Looks at Psychoanalysis," comes next. I have supplied introductions to the various conversations. In some cases, my introductions are lengthy, more ancillary than preparatory; the introduction to Arrau's childhood reminiscences ("Chile: 1903–11"), for instance, is partly an essay on the prodigy phenomenon in music. Since the conversations, too, tend to digress, the reader should not anticipate a linear progression of events or ideas. I have also supplied a conclusion, "Arrau on Records," which is less a critical discography than a summing up of Arrau's artistic evolution, using some of his recordings to illustrate details of technique and interpretation. Here, too, certain recurrent thoughts about the creative act are mulled over once more, with Arrau serving, as elsewhere, as a case in point.

Obviously, the book's core of personal beliefs and experiences precludes objectivity. I have checked dates and other hard facts with Arrau's family and friends, and with newspapers, magazines, and programs. But Arrau's accounts are necessarily partisan.

Arrau's own portrait is by no means scrubbed clean of blemishes. Within limits, he did not resist discussing episodes of self-doubt. Some readers will probably feel our conversations did not go far enough in this direction. Others will feel they went too far—that a cloak of mystery shielding an artist's personal life is no bad thing.

To some degree, the lifting of the cloak is a sign of the times, and inescapable. Certainly Liszt never had to submit to questions about his fears and failures, or talk into a tape recorder. But if one does choose to conduct behind-the-scenes investigations of the performer's gift, Arrau is a prime candidate. This is because, in his case, man and artist are quite simply one and the same— not in the sense that music is Arrau's entire life (it plainly is not), but in the sense that he manages to put his entire life into his music. In what follows, the interpenetration of man and music is an ongoing theme.

# PART II

# Conversations
# with Arrau

# Roots

Arrau's two homes have much in common. Both are concealed. In Douglaston, where the Arrau house is one of many closely spaced along Long Island Sound, the means of concealment are a towering hedge and dense foliage from the narrow yard within. In Vermont, where the Arrau house sits by itself, concealment is provided by some four hundred generously wooded acres. A hand-lettered sign, "ARRAU," points to a winding dirt road densely shaded by trees. The farther one penetrates the road, the more enclosed it becomes. Only with the house in view do the trees give way to a broad expanse of sky. The final approach is lined by a dozen weeping willows. Arrau has also planted weeping birch, weeping crab apple, and weeping beech nearby. (He laughs at this proclivity, but he does adore the trees.) The house, a little farther on, is a sprawling wooden structure, part of which dates from 1806. In the back is a large pond Thoreau would have appreciated.

Inside, both Arrau homes are patiently ordered and well-furnitured, deep-toned and redolent of dusk.

In Douglaston, Arrau's study is a spacious room down a flight of steps off the main entryway. The curtains are kept drawn. The decor, with its dark woods and muted upholsteries, is soothing rather than plush. Of the many paintings, most are non-Occidental or very old: Byzantine icons, Japanese watercolors, a Bassano, a Van Dyck. Of the many artifacts, the most prominent, commanding the mantelpiece, are several dozen ebony figurines from Africa, some over two feet tall. A second, equally large collection is of anthropomorphic pre-Columbian pots. Arrau's prize individual pieces, on a corner table, are wooden sculptures from Egypt (Twelfth Dynasty), New Guinea (Sepik River style), and China (Han dynasty). Books, magazines, and scores are shelved and stacked in profusion. The photographs are of Weber, Liszt,

Clara Schumann, Martin Krause, and Karlrobert Kreiten, the last a student of Arrau's who was murdered by the Nazis. A piano dominates one end of the room. Above the keyboard, to either side, are a metronome, a stopwatch, two cups of pens and pencils, and, incongruously, a telephone. The piano lid is kept closed, being covered with candles, bell jars, and a miniature bookcase holding rare volumes of Shakespeare and Lessing. The soft light and extreme orderliness of the room negate its clutter. The rest of the house remains in hiding. The birds outside sound far away.

Arrau's study in Vermont is somewhat cooler and smaller. It, too, is set below the main level of the house, and to the side of the front entryway. The floor, walls, and ceiling are of stained wood. The ceiling is low, and made to seem lower by hanging lanterns and heavy beams. The windows, opening on dense evergreens, shun the sun. Most of the furnishings, including a seventeenth-century straw bench and an elaborate wooing chair, are New England antiques. There are two pianos. One, a nineteenth-century square piano, serves as a table for scholarly magazines. Compared to the study in Douglaston, this is a rustic, more casual space, but painstakingly elegant all the same. Except for some of the light fixtures, a vinyl reclining chair, and a couple of paintings by contemporary Chilean artists, it could be transplanted from another century.

CA / My father's family came originally from Provence, France. The name was "Arrault." Later, in the Middle Ages, they went to Barcelona, and dropped the "lt." The first Arrau who went to Chile was an engineer sent by the king, Charles III. Don Lorenzo de Arrau—that was his name. He got, as a present, a huge piece of land near Chillán, where I was born. There are in my father's family also some Scottish elements. Probably from pirates. [Laughs.] Probably Scottish pirates who went first to Panama, then to Peru and Chile. And that's about all I can tell you about my father's ancestors. He himself was an oculist. He died when I was one year old, in a horseback-riding accident. The horse got scared, my father was thrown; he lived for a few days, and then he died. He was only forty-eight.

Now, my mother. Her maiden name was Ponce de Leon, probably in some way related to Ponce de Leon, the man who discovered Florida. Her family was from a very small town north of Chillán. Their background was Spanish—partly Andalusian and partly Castilian. Probably they came to Chile in the beginning of the eighteenth century—that's what I calculate.

JH / You have no memory of your father?

CA / None at all.

JH / Did your mother talk about him?

CA / She was very restrained when she talked about him. Later, through her sister, I heard that it had been an unhappy marriage. We were told that he couldn't leave women alone. He is supposed to have had many illegitimate children. I knew only one. But that's what they said. And so she suffered horribly.

JH / Did you feel deprived for not having a father?

CA / In a way, and in a way happy. Because he came from a family with severe ideas about what a man should do. His idea was that music was wonderful, but for the girls. So one can imagine what I would have had to go through. On the other hand, except for his machismo, he was a wonderful man. Whenever he knew someone was poor, he would treat them for nothing.

JH / Was it very prestigious in Chillán to be an oculist?

CA / Yes. You could call our family landed gentry. But the land we had owned was being divided all the time. What was left was rather small. And, on top of it, my father left a lot of debts. So my mother had to start immediately teaching piano when he died, to make ends meet. And she had to sell the last piece of land we had.

JH / Do you think she ever considered remarrying?

CA / Probably. But my older brother, Carlos—I was the youngest of three children—was in some ways worse than my father. She once said to me that there was a man she would have liked to marry, but my brother said that if he came near the house again, he would kill him. Remarrying in those days was something dishonorable. Women would mourn the rest of their lives. You know that my mother for about twenty years never wore anything but black.

JH / Your mother lost her husband and never remarried. That must have directed her energy toward her children, especially toward you.

CA / She lived actually only from the moment they discovered my talent. From then on that was her life, to see me make a career. Whenever anything went wrong with my development she was desperate. But she never interfered. She was a very intelligent woman. She was clever enough to know that from the time I began to study with Martin Krause, if there was any problem, she should leave all the decisions to him. And my education she left to Krause. The only time she pushed me, a little, to practice was in Berlin just before we met Krause, at a period when I had lost interest in the piano. That's the only time she pushed me.

JH / What kind of a person was she to others?

CA / It was always said that she had tremendous charm. And that she was witty. She liked to tell them stories from my early childhood. She was intensely attached to me.

JH / Was she a forbidding person?

CA / Not really. She was a little bit a Latin-American matriarch. But she knew her limits.

JH / Did your mother seem to prefer you to your brother and sister?

CA / Unfortunately, yes. My sister suffered under that. She was always very, very sweet to me. My sister was like another mother in those days.

JH / Did your brother suffer too?

CA / I don't think so. He was too much involved with women. He was always out. I liked him very much. But he treated me too much like a child.

JH / All the forces in the family seem to have converged on you. Your father died. Your brother lost interest in the family. Your sister was like a mother.

CA / My Aunt Celina, too, was like a mother. She was my mother's sister. She followed us to Berlin, I think, two years after we left Chile. And then she stayed there many, many years. The world of the mothers.

JH / You once told me that your mother never learned German all the years she was in Berlin.

CA / No. She was educated in a French convent school. She spoke French quite fluently. But never English and never German. German she refused to learn—she said it was too difficult.

JH / I have this image of your mother as someone always hovering in the background, never really conversant socially or even verbally except within her immediate family. And she lived to be ninety-nine.

CA / She died four weeks before her hundredth birthday. It could have been one of those relations where there is too much love, and too much desire for the child. But she was too intelligent for that. She knew about those cases where mothers choke child prodigies.

JH / Yet she does seem to have lived through you.

CA / Yes. She felt it was her mission to make it possible for me to grow into an important artist. But of course at a certain moment I felt it was a little too much. She always wanted to know what I did and where I went. So I started a very healthy rebellion against that, beginning perhaps at the age of fifteen or seventeen. And she accepted it without much fuss.

JH / Did you live with your mother most of your life?

CA / I lived with her until I married, in 1937. Then in 1953 she came to live with Ruth and me in Douglaston. You see, she left Berlin with my sister and my niece to move to Chile in 1938. In Chile, she was spoiled; she was considered the mother of a national hero. When foreign pianists came to Chile, she was always invited, and given a seat in the opera house. She always went. She understood a lot about piano playing. And she would criticize during the recitals. Like so many old people, she thought she was whispering, but actually she was talking quite loudly. I was there several times. "HE HAS A VERY BAD SOUND." And people would turn around and say "Sh!" Oh, it was terrible. "MUCH TOO SLOW." "TOO FAST."

JH / How often would you see her when she was living in Chile?

CA / When I toured in Chile every three years. Of course, my arrival was always a big event for her. But when I left, she suffered. She had such an attachment to me that to live far away was a torment for her. So Ruth and I decided we should take her, for her last years. To our house.

JH / How was it living with your mother those last six years of her life?

CA / She was rather an easy old lady. She wasn't very demanding. Of course, she had a nurse to be with her all the time. I was just thinking how *tough* she was physically. At the age of ninety-five or ninety-six she was still curious. She wanted to know where every door led to. Once when she was left alone for a few minutes, she opened a door into the cellar, and she fell down about fifteen steps. And she didn't break a thing, nothing. She stood up, and with our help she came up the steps again. [Laughs.] You know, her grandmother lived to the age of a hundred and twenty. And they say that she still read the paper. And her sister died at the age of ninety-five.

JH / I understand that you would always translate for her at meals.

CA / I sat next to her, and translated her Spanish into English. Or into German, if the children were not there.

JH / Do you care to recall your mother's death?

CA / It was a terrible shock. I don't know—I thought it would never happen. And I wasn't there. I was on an Italian tour, in Milan. I came in time for the funeral. I think it was the greatest shock in my life, until I adjusted myself to living without her in the background.

JH / Have you ever considered how her death may have changed you, either as an artist or in your daily life?

CA / The thing is, you see, though I worshiped her, I had already made myself so independent—actually from anything, and from anybody. It was a gradual process. And the fact that I never had another teacher after Martin Krause also made me independent.

JH / Independent. I find this striking in you. You don't even seem to have any close colleagues in music.

CA / Yes, it's strange. Yet on the other hand I find it quite a healthy thing, when I see so many musicians asking all the time, "Please, how do you play this?" or, "Do you think this is right?" They all do that. They all live in cliques now, and play for each other. That's something I can't understand at all. It's *dangerous* to yield to the taste of a group of people.

JH / Do you ever play privately for anyone—in order to elicit feedback, I mean?

CA / Yes, but never for musicians. One of the few I used to play for was Erich Kleiber—the Beethoven concertos, and the Schumann concerto, when I was about twenty-five. When he decided to accept a soloist, he would study the concerto as much as he would study a symphony. In the second movement of the Schumann concerto, he taught me to give a meaning to

Nobody had ever told me, and I hadn't noticed, that this is the announcement of the cello theme in the middle section of the movement. Oddly enough, conductors very seldom realize that. Furtwängler also taught me something in the same movement. There is a forte-piano nobody takes [measure 52], and he made a terrific rubato there—moving forward to the forte-piano, and lingering on it a little. It was really beautiful. Things like that— when I found somebody with something beautiful to suggest, I always accepted it. But pianists—I don't think I have ever had such good suggestions from pianists. Another influence in the Schumann concerto that I remember, a bad influence at a certain moment, was Klemperer. The first time I played with him. I was, I think, twenty-three, twenty-four. He was with the Wiesbaden orchestra at that time. Schnabel canceled the Schumann concerto, and they engaged me. Klemperer was so *nasty*. After many, many years, when we played together again and I had become much more self-assured, I said, "Do you remember what you did to me in Wiesbaden?" *"What did I do?"* And I told him. Oh, it was appalling. Just before the concert, he was playing for me, showing how certain things were supposed to be done. It was one of my worst experiences. He couldn't believe it when I told him about it—how much damage it had done to me, at a moment when I was still developing.

JH / Do you think Klemperer's behavior—"correcting" your interpretation the day of the concert—made you fearful of subsequent encounters with musicians in which you might be criticized?

CA / Of course. But fortunately all the famous conductors of that time were very positive. I never again had such an experience. It was so odd because, though I was terrified, I still had to think that the way he was playing, to demonstrate—it was *atrocious*. And he thought it was marvelous.

JH / These are instances, are they not, from a period of some uncertainty, artistically?

CA / Yes. I was in the middle of a transition.

JH / And since that time you seem to have become completely self-reliant.

CA / Well, yes. Not that I began to think everything I did was right. Many times I dropped a work that I didn't understand— for years, sometimes. But self-reliance is a wonderful thing if you are a person who likes to be alone. It can be dangerous for people who do not have enough intuition to take care of themselves. It can be terrifying.

JH / Sometimes you practically conjure up a *Sturm und Drang* image—the wanderer atop a mountain peak, buffeted by the wind, receiving inspiration streaming down from the sky.

CA / Nature mysticism—that I feel very strongly. I sometimes experience a sort of mystical trance. Sometimes I come out of those states, and suddenly I know how to play problematic passages. Also, in dreams, I become obsessed with one passage of a work that is never right. It's quite awful, that obsession. The passage comes back and back and back. But then I wake up and, suddenly, I have the solution.

JH / Do you visualize anything in your dreams, when this happens?

CA / I sometimes actually see written music. And I hear it—up to the point where I get stuck in the dream.

JH / In such dreams, or in trance-like waking states, is there an articulate *voice* in your mind?

CA / No, no, no.

JH / There are no words.

CA / No. In fact, I find that at certain moments—or for days, even—I absolutely cannot talk. In any language. I can't verbalize anything. I live in another language.

JH / Even when you *are* speaking, you're never a glib conversationalist. You're no raconteur.

CA / As a young man, I suffered over that. I thought something was wrong with me. I was afraid of going places where I had to converse. But later on I understood this wasn't an inferiority of any kind. I didn't go to school, of course. That, I think, has something to do with the fact that I can very seldom make light conversation. I only went to school for six months, in Berlin. They took me out because I didn't have enough time to practice. I must have been about eight. Then I became a sort of circus animal. Children of my age either thought I was something amazing, to be able to do such feats with my hands, or they thought I was funny, strange, not a normal person. These two reactions were awful—both of them.

JH / You were made to feel apart, outside.

CA / Yes.

JH / And in some respects you've remained an outsider all your life.

CA / Yes, absolutely. I have tried to overcome this isolation. And shyness. You see, I was very shy until the age of about thirty-five.

That I have overcome to quite an extent. Not completely. It used to not bother me only when I played. Then I could feel this communication with the audience, particularly when I played well. That moment of communication with a collective is very satisfying. It makes me quite happy.

# Chile

## 1903–1911

Chillán, Chile, capital of Nuble province, is located about 250 miles south-southwest of Santiago. A 1970 census gave its population as 80,270. In 1903, when Arrau was born there, Chillán had about 30,000 inhabitants. A dusty seven-hour train ride connected it to Santiago.

The city was founded in the late sixteenth century, but was razed several times by earthquakes. The 1906 earthquake which Arrau witnessed in Chillán damaged the city less than the far-flung 1939 earthquake he witnessed in Santiago. In addition to Arrau, Chillán is the birthplace of two other famous Chileans—Bernardo O'Higgins (1776–1842), a leader in the independence movement, and Ramón Vinay (b. 1914), the distinguished opera singer.

Something of the flavor of the place is conveyed by the voluminous obituary notices Arrau's mother culled from the local papers in 1904 when her husband died. These include full transcripts of six funeral orations, given by a subinspector of police, the chief of the third company of firemen, a representative of the Radical Assembly of Chillán, a representative of the local medical association, the administrator of the local hospital, and a friend of the deceased speaking on behalf of Dr. Arrau's friends. Each of these men proves a florid, highly practiced speechmaker. Sertorio Yañez, the policeman, goes so far as to say: "Gentlemen: when death, implacable and cold, ends the existence of a necessary member of a family, of a man still useful to his country and to his fellowmen, a tear, shed on the coffin—a tear, the most sublime and eloquent manifestation of human sentiment—must signify, in this moment that we share before the open grave, all the sadness of our hearts, so that we may bequeath our eternal farewell to the one whom Mother Earth sadly draws to her fecund bosom." The procession to the cemetery was said to have comprised musicians, half Chillán's policemen, all its firemen, multitudes of townspeople on foot, and "an interminable file of private and official carriages." The only comparable tribute anyone could remember, according to one reporter, was "occasioned by the death of another doctor greatly beloved by the people of Chillán: Dr. Midleton." Though Arrau believes him to have mainly been an oculist, Dr. Don Carlos Arrau, also identified as "vice-president of the assembly and a prestigious member of one of Chillán's most distinguished families," was clearly a prominent local physician, practicing a gamut of medical services. He is further described as decisive, vigorous, youthful, generous, civic-spirited, and a proponent of "principles of the most advanced liberalism."

Arrau vaguely recollects Chillán as the backdrop to a fairy tale. At an age too early for most to discover music, music discovered him. There was never any question that he would devote his life to the piano. His first public performance, in Chillán's municipal theater, seems to have taken place when he was five. Subsequently, the Arraus moved to Santiago so he could study with Bindo Paoli, an established pedagogue. In Santiago, as well, he played for members of the government. The sought-for result was a scholarship to learn abroad. All this was watched over by the indomitable Doña Lucrecia Leon de Arrau, who imbued her son with music and supervised his public exposure.

Arrau's memories of these first years, in the conversation that follows, are necessarily fuzzy. In some details, they slightly conflict with newspaper accounts. Arrau remembers teaching himself to read music. There can be no doubt that he received no formal instruction prior to studying with Paoli. But remarks by his mother in a 1939 newspaper interview suggest she took an active role: "Claudio didn't play with the other children; he stayed at my side and listened to me play the piano or finger the notes. When he was three, instead of scribbling as children will, drawing little houses and stick figures, he sketched out lines, clefs, and notes. Then he'd bring his drawings to me. Since he persisted in this game, I helped him with his writing and later taught him to pick out the notes on the keyboard. . . . In truth, I spent a long time astonished at my son's ability and afraid that people would laugh at me if I spoke about it. One day the little one amazed me by demonstrating his good taste: each time I played Bach, he tugged on my dress and said, 'More!' "

In the interview, Doña Lucrecia says that Claudio's first recital took place in 1908. Arrau believes the program to have included pieces by Mozart, Beethoven, and Schumann. Antonio Orrego Barros, in his 1909 article for *Selecta* (see page xii), reports that Arrau made his debut performing "the music of his favorites, Beethoven, Mozart, and Liszt." A September 22, 1908, notice in the Chillán newspaper *El Comercio,* headed "September 19 Concert at the Municipal Theater," reads as follows: "The five-year-old Claudito Arrau Leon gave a perfect rendition of the *Aire Luis XIII* of L. Streabbog. The ecstatic audience showered him with applause until he returned to play a four-hand piece with his mother, Doña Lucrecia L. de Arrau. This child arouses keen expectations in the music world; he lives by and for music. If his love of the art endures, he is sure to become a musical sensation."

In October 1909, Claudio was again heard in Chillán. A writer for *El Comercio* reported: "First honor of the evening goes to a creature who is just beginning to walk: Claudito Arrau Leon. Lacking the time and space to give a proper assessment of this phenomenal child . . . let me say simply that he more than did justice to his remarkable reputation, enrapturing the distinguished and sizable audience with his masterful interpretation of such difficult pieces as Haydn's *Gypsy Rondo,* the piano solo *Für Elise* by Beethoven, Schüller's *Friedrich Seitz* Concerto—accompanied on the violin by Mr. Heriberto Urrutia, whose handling of the instrument was a portrait in perfection—and Grieg's lovely suite *Le Matin,* with the affectionate accompaniment of his mother, Doña Lucrecia Leon de Arrau." A second Chillán paper, *La Discusión de Chillán,* called Claudio "the hero of the evening" and continued: "His performance was incredible; it was clearly the work of an artistic genius, of one who is destined to see his name crowned in glory."

Arrau, in what follows, remembers playing for the members of the Chilean legislature, who consequently voted to send him abroad with a scholarship. Newspaper stories suggest that the Chilean President, Pedro Montt, was instrumental in securing the scholarship. He invited Arrau to play for him shortly before the second Chillán concert. The child was rewarded with a book, *Les Nationalistes musicales,* bearing the inscription "To Claudio

Arrau, in remembrance of the fond admiration with which I heard him play the piano at the age of six years. Santiago, September 30, 1909. Pedro Montt." Sometime afterward, according to an account in *La Discusión de Chillán*, a further encounter with the President took place: "One day the boy was invited to a reception attended by ambassadors and artists, ministers and writers. They asked him to play the piano, but he was in an uneasy and temperamental sort of mood, so they had to ask many times. After a while the guests became rather tired; finally Don Pedro said to him: 'Very well, Claudio . . . if you don't want to play . . . there will be no trip to Europe.' No sooner had the President finished speaking than the sly child raced to the piano and set the ivories ashimmer with a cascade of lovely sounds."

Shortly before leaving for Germany in 1911, the Arraus visited Valparaiso, where Claudio was again found temperamental. The magazine *Sucesos* reported:

> An exceedingly well-groomed, thin, elegant boy—the child of a wealthy family, it would appear—walks gravely through the offices of *Sucesos* with two women trailing behind.
>
> Claudio Arrau, the child musician who has aroused so much interest in the musical world, has kept his promise to pay us a visit. He is on summer vacation in Valparaiso and will soon be leaving for Berlin. We exchange greetings. Looking rather bored, the boy takes in the room with his eyes, which finally rest on the caricatures of Wiedner scattered along the wall.
>
> We'd like to talk with him, but he remains moodily silent. His companions tell us, as he sits gazing absent-mindedly, that he's seven [*sic*] years old and has been interested in music since he was four. He picked up theory and practice with astonishing ease, and learned to read and write on his own.
>
> "Would you like to give us an autograph, Claudio?"
>
> "I'm so tired!" He makes a weary gesture.
>
> "Oh, come now, lad. . . ."
>
> And the boy calmly and confidently scribbles out, "Warmest greetings to *Sucesos*."

One surviving witness to Arrau's prodigy feats is his sister, Mrs. Lucrecia van den Daele. Born in 1897, she is an implausibly vigorous, well-preserved woman whose devotion to her younger brother remains intense. As a youngster, she was herself a pianist. She began taking lessons from her mother when she was nine. In Berlin, where her studies continued, she played two-piano works by Mozart and Arensky with Claudio. But audiences unnerved her, and she discontinued lessons before the age of twenty.

Speaking in German, Mrs. van den Daele remembers her infant brother devouring her lessons with his ears and eyes. "My mother taught me the piano. He stood and looked on, and when I played inaccurately he would start laughing. Mother said, 'If you laugh you have to leave the room.' And then Mother played something—the Mendelssohn *Rondo capriccioso,* which she played wonderfully. And he said, 'I love it so much I want to copy it.' So he stretched out flat on the floor with the music and copied the notes, and he kept this copy in his room. The neighbors would come and ask to see him play, and Mother would call him. He already played little things by ear—Mozart and so on. When I had a lesson from Mother, he would sit and listen. Then, later, he would go to the piano and play what Mother had taught. He still couldn't read and he couldn't write.

"I was never jealous. I was like a second mother to him. He was such a good child—so loving, and never angry. He had an unusually small body, but an unusually large head; whenever he fell down, he landed on it. He loved flowers. Every morning he put on a white apron and went into the garden to pick his favorite flowers—violets, carnations—and put one in the pocket of his apron. He would stand in the garden smelling the flowers, inhaling the scent."

When Claudio, dressed entirely in white, gave his first recital, his sister led him onto the stage, picked him up, and placed him on the piano stool. "Then we realized that he was still wearing his white gloves, and we had to take them off quickly so he could begin to play. He was not nervous or anxious at all. The audience applauded his playing so much that Mother went on stage, and I think they played four-hand—I think they did but I'm not sure. This was in the municipal theater, when it was new. It's still in use today."

Then Claudio's mother told a sister, Clarisa, about her son. "She wrote to my aunt, 'I'm afraid this child is not normal.' And my aunt wrote back that she thought my mother was exaggerating, and that she would visit Chillán and see for herself. Then when she came and saw, she said right away, 'Pack everything up! Sell everything! Go to Santiago! This child must study! This child must meet the President! This child is a phenomenon!' So we all moved to Santiago."

Even if Arrau's early gifts were tucked away on an unlikely continent, their emergence followed an established pattern. The classic example of extreme musical precocity is Mozart, who toured Europe at the age of seven. He, too, had an older sister who played the piano, and was hoveringly supervised by a parent whose own musical abilities were substantial. "When you sat at the clavier or were otherwise intent on music," the father once reminisced in a letter (February 16, 1778) to the son, "no one dared to have the slightest jest with you." In the same letter, Leopold Mozart recalled Wolfgang's "ever grave and thoughtful little face." The young Arrau was equally devoted to his instrument, and photographs of him show a face as prematurely grave as Mozart's. And, like the young Mozart, the young Arrau supported his family—an obligation that, far from going to his head, redoubled his sense of filial duty.

Innumerable prodigies fail to outgrow the innocence and self-absorption of their early years, and their careers vanish accordingly. (I know of only one modern instance—the pianist Shura Cherkassky—in which the unbridled innocence of the child-prodigy musician sustains the adult, unmolested by self-awareness.) Arrau, by comparison, evolved and survived. Yet the prodigy imprint has by no means been erased. Artistically, he retains the thoroughness of one who is never distracted. In certain mundane affairs, he retains the respectfulness of one who looks for approval and does what he is told. I have heard him explain with a mixture of perplexed resignation and arbitrary resolve what things others have said he must do: that he must, for instance, rerecord the Beethoven concertos in digital sound to insure that his recordings will remain competitive. One area in which he wholly resigns authority is money. His memories of the calamitous inflationary cycle he lived through in Germany are, by his own admission, unaccountably fuzzy. "Of course, I remember that it happened to many people—that in one day their money was worth less than the day before. But I don't remember anything about our own situation. Sometimes I would buy a book, and then we couldn't eat for three days. That kind of thing would happen." When he got married, Arrau put his wife in charge of his finances.

Even as an adult, Mozart, in Alfred Einstein's view, "was not worldly-wise in any way."* Though an articulate and frequently acute observer of human behavior, he was, according to his father, easily deceived. And according to Friedrich Schlichtegroll's celebrated necrology of 1792, "For sensible management of money, he had no feeling. He always needed a guiding hand, a guardian, to take care of domestic affairs for him."†

Today's children are too worldly and, in a certain sense, too privileged to perpetuate the classic prodigy syndrome. So much willful authority and selfless dedication among parents and teachers has grown unfashionable. Anyway, technology discourages protective seclusion and healthy innocence; movies and television foster more unsupervised "traveling" than the itinerant Mozart ever did.

A little over half a century ago, Yehudi Menuhin re-enacted the venerable prodigy script. Steeped in Old World values, his parents minutely guarded and supervised his regime. Louis Persinger, his violin teacher, gave him up to five lessons a week, and accompanied him on tours. At home, where his parents were never absent, he studied with private tutors. He knew no other children except for his two sisters, both of whom (like Arrau's sister and Mozart's) played the piano. His father clipped articles from the newspapers for him to read; uncensored, the papers were forbidden. On a guided tour of Los Angeles in 1926, nine-year-old Yehudi and his mother were shown the home of Douglas Fairbanks and Mary Pickford; neither name was known to them.

Menuhin made his formal debut at the age of seven. His orchestral debut, with the San Francisco Symphony, took place a year later. He was ten when he played Lalo and Tchaikovsky under Paul Paray in Paris. At eleven, he performed the Beethoven Violin Concerto under Fritz Busch at Carnegie Hall. He began touring at twelve, appearing with Beecham, Enesco, Koussevitzky, Monteux, Toscanini, Walter. He performed and

---

*Alfred Einstein, *Mozart: His Character, His Work* (New York: Oxford University Press, 1945), p. 27.
†Quoted in Einstein, p. 29.

recorded the Elgar Violin Concerto under the composer's baton. Nothing comparable to the young Menuhin has been seen since.

JH / What is your earliest memory?

CA / We went through a horrible earthquake when I was three years old. It was at the same time as the famous earthquake in San Francisco—the whole Pacific coast was affected. I was almost buried by it. I can still remember the scene; I'll never forget it. The Spanish colonial houses, you know, had many courtyards, and I was in the third or fourth from the street, with my nurse. Suddenly, all the houses started caving in, and of course the connections between the courtyards were closing. Luckily, my nurse was strong, and very enterprising. She took me in her arms and waited for the next quiet moment. Then she ran through to the next courtyard, and waited again. Finally she managed to get me out. My mother thought I was dead—she was standing in the street weeping like mad. But this wonderful woman managed to carry me out in her arms.

JH / Do you remember experiencing fear?

CA / Oh yes. And also the power of the elements, which is a feeling I have kept.

JH / I don't think I've ever known anyone else whose first memory is of a natural disaster.

CA / Yes, it made a tremendous impression. And you know, later, when our two older children were babies, we were in a hotel in Santiago and experienced another horrible earthquake. It was in 1939. I ran into the room where the children were sleeping, and took one child under one arm, and one under the other, and ran down the stairs into the street. I still don't know how I did it. I acted instinctively, to save the children and myself. I felt as if someone else had done it.

JH / After the earthquake of 1906, what is your next earliest childhood memory?

CA / The next thing I remember is hearing my mother play. I must have, again, been three. One thing I remember her playing—and I remember very little—is the Mendelssohn *Rondo capriccioso*. She played very well, but never in public.

JH / Many times musical prodigies are conversant musically before they're conversant verbally. Was your musical aptitude more developed than your verbal aptitude?

CA / It must have been, because before I could read words I could read music. I can't explain it to you, but I guess from hearing my mother play and then later looking at the music I gradually got to a point where I could read the notes.

JH / No one ever taught you?

CA / No. My mother thought it was too early for me, that it would do me some physical harm. She didn't want to give me any lessons. But one day I could read music. How it happened I can't explain.

JH / Did you ever have the feeling that music, in a sense, originated with your mother?

CA / I think they must have belonged together in my subconscious—music and Mother.

JH / What were the first things you played?

CA / I remember the little C-major Sonata by Mozart [K. 545], and the Schumann *Kinderszenen*. I got the music somehow, and started deciphering it. They left me completely alone, you see, because my mother was shocked to have a child with such gifts. She decided not to push me. It was a wonderful attitude—she would never impose anything on me.

JH / You gave your first recital when you were five. What was on the program?

CA / The Mozart C-major Sonata, and the Beethoven Variations on "Nel cor più non mi sento." I think it also included a Chopin etude—the one in F minor from the *Nouvelles Etudes*.

JH / It's difficult to envision a five-year-old child playing such music. Obviously you couldn't even stretch an octave.

CA / I had to break the octaves. And I couldn't reach the pedals, so I had a wooden box with two sticks which somebody had made for me, and I was able to pedal using the sticks. I remember that the concert was in a theater with no electricity—there were candles all over. I played an upright piano that had candleholders built into it. I remember being afraid the piano might burn down. And my sister stood behind me so that I wouldn't fall off the chair; she could catch me if I leaned too far to the side. I remember also that the concert started rather late, because I started falling asleep before it began; they had to keep me awake by telling me stories.

JH / Did you enjoy the concert?

CA / I think I did. I was not nervous at all.

JH / Do you remember anything about the audience?

CA / There must have been hundreds of people. We had arrived in a coach. And afterward people from the audience insisted on pulling the coach, instead of the horses. The ladies from the audience pulled it back to our house.

JH / How did you react to such adulation?

CA / As something natural, in the beginning. The psychological complications came only later, after I had left Chile.

JH / So the Chilean experience was pervaded by innocence.

CA / Yes, by a safe feeling. I was only a little conscious that there was something special about me. I wasn't conceited as a child. *As a child.* [Laughs.]

JH / Everyone must have known about you in Chillán.

CA / In fact, it was in the papers all over the country. Eventually there was a proposal to give me a scholarship to go to Europe, and it had to be approved by the Congress. My mother was instrumental in that effort, along with several relatives. They decided it was the only way for me to get to study abroad. So my mother and I went to visit, one by one, all the senators and deputies, and I played for them. After that, they voted almost unanimously in my favor. And I was given a marvelous scholarship to study music abroad.

JH / Did you enjoy playing for all the congressmen?

CA / Yes. I was getting a little cocky. I remember watching their reactions.

JH / When Mozart was being shown off, he would identify chords on the piano from another room. Would you perform tricks like that?

CA / Yes, they did that with me, too. Someone would play bunches of notes, almost like modern music, and I could name every note from another room. And I would transpose preludes by Bach.

JH / A striking characteristic of the young Mozart was his complete immersion in music. I brought along a description by Andreas Schachtner, the court trumpeter at Salzburg. Schachtner wrote of Mozart: "No sooner had he begun to busy himself with music than his interest in every other occupation was as dead, and even children's games had to have a musical accompaniment if they were to interest him; if we, he and I, were carrying his playthings from one room to another, the one of us who went empty-handed always had to sing or fiddle a march the while."* Were you that single-minded as a child?

CA / I think so. All I wanted was music. I was even fed at the piano. Otherwise, it seems, I wouldn't eat. I used to play with my mouth open, and my mother used to put food in it. I was so preoccupied with the music I hardly noticed. Whenever food was put in my mouth, I chewed it so I could get rid of it.

JH / What sort of piano did you have at home?

CA / An upright. It must have been very bad. I always felt it was a part of me, like another limb to my body.

JH / Was your mother able to use it as well?

CA / She taught a lot. Whenever she was teaching, I was on the floor, listening, in the same room. That's what first awakened my musical gifts.

JH / Schlichtegroll's necrology says of Mozart that "in general he was full of enthusiasm and was very easily attracted to any

*Letter to Marie Anne von Berchtold zu Sonnenburg, April 24, 1792. Quoted in Otto Erich Deutsch, *Mozart: A Documentary Biography* (Stanford: Stanford University Press, 1965), p. 451.

subject."* There are these stories, you know, of Mozart being taught arithmetic, and making his calculations all over the floors and walls, writing numbers everyplace. Every activity he undertook consumed him. Were you like that?

CA / I concentrated on what I was doing. Still today, whatever it is, even something very unimportant, I am totally there.

JH / Schlichtegroll says that Mozart was "a thoroughly obedient child."† Were you?

CA / Oh yes. I shouted at my mother at the age of fifteen or so. Just one time, then never again. As I remember, she asked where I had been. And I felt she was interfering. Then she cried, and I asked forgiveness. It was the only time. I was a very obedient child. Too obedient—it's not healthy, psychologically.

JH / And yet your equanimity must have had something to do with your "divine innocence," if one could call it that—being totally devoted to the task at hand, and immune to the things around you.

CA / Of course. I didn't even have the influence of school to distract me. Naturally, I had tutors. But, as I have said, school was something I never had to go through. For years I thought it was something valuable I had missed. Now I don't feel that way at all. I think many of my good qualities result from the fact that I was never made to conform in a school. I can see, watching my own children, that they do things at a certain age because they are expected to. I didn't have this struggle. I didn't have to take anything for granted, as schoolchildren do.

JH / A final question about the prodigy experience. Are there artistic aptitudes early in life that are in some sense superior to the aptitudes of an adult?

CA / There are advantages and disadvantages. I must say that I remember Yehudi Menuhin playing a fabulous concert of Bach, Beethoven, and Brahms concertos with Bruno Walter when he was twelve. It was one of the greatest listening experiences I've ever had. But then I heard him many years later at the Buch-

*Einstein, p. 25.
†Einstein, p. 26.

arest Festival playing works for solo violin, and it was as marvelous as the concertos in Berlin. He must have been forty or forty-five. The playing was more involved, more thoughtful. It was a synthesis of that, and this spontaneity of childhood.

JH / When you heard Menuhin play with Walter, did he seem to personify the artistic advantages of childhood innocence?

CA / Only the advantages, I would say. The music just *flowed* out of him.

JH / That's what one hears on his first recordings—as if his conscious mind weren't intervening at all. This is very difficult to recapture later on in life.

CA / Yes. It wouldn't be right even to *try* to recapture it.

JH / You have to develop a new understanding of yourself.

CA / Exactly.

# Studies with Krause
## 1913–1918

In 1911, following his departure from Chillán, Arrau gave recitals in Santiago and—en route to Europe—Buenos Aires, where he was also feted in wealthy homes. He was accompanied to Germany by his mother, brother, and sister. One of his mother's sisters, Celina, joined the family in Berlin several years later. His studies with Krause commenced in 1913, and continued until Krause's death on February 18, 1918.

Martin Krause was born in 1853. A pianist, he studied at the Königliche Conservatory in Leipzig, and with Franz Liszt. In 1885, he founded the Liszt Society in Leipzig. He appears to have first played for Liszt in 1883, and thereafter became Liszt's pupil and constant companion. By 1900, when he left Leipzig to teach at the Dresden Conservatory, he was known as one of Germany's foremost pedagogues and critics. From the Dresden Conservatory he moved on to Munich in 1901, and to the Stern Conservatory in Berlin in 1904.

Krause arranged for Arrau to enroll at the Stern Conservatory although Arrau was underage. Arrau's lessons, however, took place at Krause's home. Here he came to be regarded as an ex officio member of the Krause family, which also included many daughters and a single son ("a tenor with no career," according to Arrau), all older than Arrau. Krause and his wife were divorced.

Photographs of Krause show a stocky man with narrow eyes and a trim mustache and goatee. Arrau remembers his "concentrated physical power," his coarse Saxon accent, his sense of humor, and his vehement temper.

Krause inculcated a reverence for music, and for music as a calling. He accepted no payment from the Arraus (an example Arrau has followed in later life—he teaches without fee). Mindful

34

of his own venerated teachers, Liszt and Carl Reinecke, he taught as one bequeathing a tradition; his students comprised a sort of guild apprenticeship.

A letter of recommendation, signed by Krause and dated December 28, 1914, reads as follows:

Claudio Arrau, a highly endowed Chilean youth, has under my direction made the most astounding advances in piano playing. There is no question that he will attain the highest peak of virtuosity. Since he now performs under my direct supervision, I can see how easily he grasps what others attain only with the greatest struggle. He is engrossed with his whole soul and enthusiasm in his art, and that is the most important factor for one of his age.

Not only outwardly, but inwardly, this boy is thoroughly endowed for the highest artistic endeavor, which always is and always was the origin of great deeds.

CA / In 1911, just after I was given my scholarship by the Chilean Congress, my mother, my sister, my brother, and I took a ship to Hamburg. It was half cargo and half passenger, and it was called the *Titania*—that just occurred to me now. The trip took quite long—almost four weeks. I was terribly excited, and terribly afraid, because nobody in our family spoke a word of any language but Spanish except for my mother, who spoke French. But she couldn't speak German. My mother had never been outside Chile before. She had tremendous courage.

There were people to receive us in Hamburg, and then we went to Berlin. There a Chilean lady who was very domineering decided that my teacher should be Waldemar Lütschg. He had a certain name as a pianist, but he was the most boring teacher you could imagine, and he slept through the lessons. He was the one who wanted me to forget everything I knew and begin again—he made me play nothing but five-finger exercises. Yet this lady insisted that I continue with him—for about a year, I think. Then my mother must have put her foot down.

I met then my second teacher, a very nice man, very intelligent and full of ideas, but a little crazy. Paul Schramm, who was also a rather well-known pianist. I liked him and I did learn a lot.

But it wasn't systematic. With him I think I stayed about another year. I felt I wasn't advancing fast enough.

Then I met Rosita Renard, a pianist from Chile. At one time, in New York, people said she would be the second Guiomar Novaes; they were about the same age. Anyway, in Berlin Rosita Renard was studying with Martin Krause, and we met her. My mother told her I didn't have any enthusiasm anymore for playing, that I wasn't practicing well, and that we probably would go back to Chile and renounce the scholarship. But she said, "You must try Martin Krause." So she took me to Martin Krause. I adored him immediately. But I was also afraid of him. He was terribly severe. And he asked so much of me—almost too much, I think. Some of my later difficulties were probably due to Krause. At the age of eleven I was studying the Liszt *Transcendental* Etudes. Of course, according to him I was not living up to what I promised. By constant demand, he made me achieve things as fast as possible. He said I should always remember that after twenty years of age you don't acquire any more technique. I don't think it's true, actually.

JH / Do you remember your first meeting with Krause?

CA / Yes, of course. I went with my mother. I had an inferiority complex—I thought I was still too undeveloped to play for such a famous man. But he was so nice. He was a mixture of kindness and severity. I don't think I said a word, I was too shy. But he was very enthusiastic. He said to my mother, "This child shall be my masterpiece."

JH / Can you imagine what it must have been like for Krause to be presented with a ten-year-old child from Chile?

CA / As a matter of fact, he had never liked to teach child prodigies. But somehow he thought he could do something with me. And shortly after, you know, I saw a postcard that he wrote to Herrmann Scholtz in Leipzig, who was the editor of the German Chopin editions. He had written to Scholtz—I'm not saying this myself; please don't think I am conceited!—he had written to Scholtz that in his opinion I was the greatest piano talent since Liszt.

JH / Did Krause have the reputation of being a terrifying person?

CA / All his pupils were afraid of him. I remember when girls came to play for him who were not great talents, he would say, *"Heiraten Sie, meine Liebe, heiraten Sie!"* "Get married, my dear." And if you had stage fright, he would just say, "Pull yourself together!" I can still hear him say it. *"Nimm dich zusammen! Nimm dich zusammen!"* He never praised very much. He only praised you in front of other people.

One experience made a tremendous impression on me. He assigned three of Liszt's *Transcendental* Etudes—I think they were *Mazeppa, Eroica,* and *Feux follets.* I had one week to learn them. And of course I wasn't ready. He gave me a lecture—you should do much better, this is not up to expectations, and so on. I ran away to his daughters, and started crying like mad. I actually had six or seven mothers at Krause's house. All his daughters were much older than I was, you see. And they were all unmarried.

JH / You must have spent a great deal of time at Krause's house.

CA / Oh yes. We lived two houses away. I would go to Krause's house at nine or ten every morning. In one of the back rooms they had an upright piano. I actually practiced there, seven to eight hours a day. And he could come once, twice, three times to listen to my practicing. Then in the evening, after he had finished with all his other pupils, I got a lesson from him. Every day, an hour and a half at least. I would also have meals there—even four or five a day, because Krause felt I was not strong enough. He also decided what I would eat. And we would take walks together, nearly every day, for half an hour, an hour.

JH / Did Krause have any special teaching methods?

CA / He believed in practicing difficult passages at different speeds, and in different rhythms, and in different keys. And then staccato, leggiero, martellato—all sorts of combinations. In fact, he always told us that you shouldn't perform a work in public unless you were able to play it *ten* times as fast and *ten* times as loud as it would have to be in performance—that you only gave the feeling of mastery to an audience if you had tremendous reserves of technique, so that it seemed you could play much faster if you wished, or much louder. For years, the first thing I played in the morning was the fugue of the *Hammerklavier* Sonata, five or six times in a row. Faster and faster and faster, successively. Also certain of the more difficult preludes by Chopin—faster than written, and louder. And whenever there were skips, always with the eyes closed. When I see pianists today playing the second movement of the Schumann Fantasy and rearranging the skips—I don't understand!

JH / What about hand position and arm weight?

CA / There he left me alone to a great extent. You see, I moved on the piano like a cat. I played by nature—very relaxed. So he didn't tell me about special motions of the hands and arms. All that I found by myself, somehow. Sometimes he told me not to be stiff, that all the joints must be relaxed. But I don't think he ever told me very much about using my arms. I have noticed that a number of his pupils never lifted their arms very much.

JH / Did Krause ever demonstrate at the piano?

CA / No. I never heard him play. He no longer gave concerts. I don't think he ever played very much. He had all these other activities. He founded the Liszt Society in Leipzig. And then he was for years and years the first music critic in Germany. Everybody went to Leipzig to be reviewed by Krause. This was before he went to Berlin.

JH / When you began working with Krause, his most famous pupil was Edwin Fischer. Yet Fischer's attitude toward textual fidelity was much different from yours. And he wasn't as polished a technician. Krause must not have stamped his students from a mold.

CA / He encouraged them to develop their own approach. One thing I remember about him is that he hated people who just played, senselessly. *"Klimpern"* [tinkling], he called it. And he always said that one should have a general cultural base.

JH / Would he often discuss interpretation with you?

CA / All the time. I never disagreed with him. Everything he said was inspiring, and I could work from there. He had heard Brahms, Clara Schumann, Carreño, Busoni, Sophie Menter. And of course Liszt. He would speak of Liszt's way of breaking chords, and of trilling. He taught us several ways to break a chord: to start slowly, and then accelerate toward the highest note; or to make a crescendo to the highest note; or to make a diminuendo; or to do it freely, with rubato. But always so that broken chords would have a meaning coming from what went before.

JH / And the trills?

CA / The speed of a trill is one thing nobody knows about anymore. The speed of a trill has to be in relation to the *Stimmung*— to the atmosphere. Once, when I was playing the five Beethoven piano concertos in London with Klemperer, we came to this little trill in the second movement of the *Emperor* [measure 25]. Klemperer said, "What are you *doing* there?" "Just playing a trill the way I think it should be." "*A trill is a trill!*" He thought all trills should be fast. Which is amazing, because he was a great artist.

JH / I've also heard you speak of Krause teaching Liszt's type of finger vibrato.

CA / He taught us to use the bebung effect.* It was something all the Liszt pupils did. I use this in the *Petrarch Sonnets* and the *Dante* Sonata. There were all sorts of things Krause taught. Pedaling. That at the beginning of Beethoven's G-major Concerto, for instance, never to strike the chord and then put down the pedal, but to have the pedal down already, and then strike the first chord. This is terribly important, because the sound is different. And then for the long pedals in Beethoven—in the D-minor Sonata, for instance—to use a very fast vibrato pedal. I do this also in the slow movement to the C-minor Concerto, and in the coda to the first movement of the G-major Concerto.

JH / You have said that Krause had you play all the preludes and fugues from *The Well-Tempered Clavier* in different keys.

CA / Yes, in front of all the pupils in the conservatory, he would test whether one could play in another key—usually one very far away, not just one tone or one half-tone. He also insisted on having us memorize single voices. Bach in general was one of the bases of his teaching. In those days, of course, there was no doubt it was correct to play Bach on the piano. It was the only way. Landowska hadn't appeared yet.

---

*On the modern piano, a trembling effect produced by redepressing the key without letting it come all the way up.

JH / What was considered the correct way to play Bach on the piano? Was there a consensus, for instance, on how much pedal to use?

CA / Very little pedal. Almost without pedal. Krause wanted the preludes and fugues very clean, and in slow tempos. The fugues were mostly metronomic. But he insisted upon phrasing them dynamically—bringing out certain voices, and so on.

JH / Yet Fischer would play Bach with a good deal of pedal. Was that his own idea?

CA / Yes. And also Furtwängler. When he played the piano in the Fifth *Brandenburg*, he would employ every means of modern piano playing. It was very beautiful. And Busoni's Bach was completely different again. Krause admired Busoni tremendously, you know. I have this marvelous photo of Busoni with a dedication to Martin Krause. He thanks Krause for awakening young talents.

JH / Studying so much Bach must have enhanced your ability to hear polyphonically, which is a striking aspect of your playing.

CA / Definitely. What they call now "inner voices." [Laughs.] You know, Hofmann and his pupil Shura Cherkassky, and others—at a certain moment they *discovered* inner voices. As if nobody had ever noticed them before.

JH / Isn't there a difference between Hofmann or Cherkassky bringing out an inner voice momentarily in order to produce a textural effect, and being able to hear inner voices continuously?

CA / Continuously, yes. I always got so angry when I heard Hofmann, or Shura, bringing out so-called inner voices that didn't have much importance. I thought, Why are they doing it? Just to amaze. Just to attract attention.

JH / What about other repertoire with Krause? Did he think certain pieces were important at certain stages of development?

CA / He believed in a planned development. Starting with Mendelssohn, for instance; one of the first pieces I learned with him was the Mendelssohn G-minor Concerto. He was against beginners playing Mozart concertos. And he thought one shouldn't play Schumann very early. He taught the Henselt concerto as a preparation for the Chopin concertos. Then of course Beethoven was important. But he also believed, *before* playing Beethoven, in playing Hummel, and Moscheles. I remember that the first concerto I did with orchestra was the A-minor Hummel.

JH / Which Beethoven sonatas did you study with Krause?

CA / He was opposed to playing the late Beethoven sonatas too early. He never let me play Opus 111. I studied with him Opus 101 and Opus 109, but he wouldn't permit me to play them in public. He thought young people should play, for instance, middle Beethoven—the *Waldstein*, the *Appassionata*. That he didn't consider difficult. And this idea that I have that Schubert is the very last problem in interpretation—that he also had.

JH / What about Brahms?

CA / He wouldn't let me study the concertos. But the *Paganini* Variations was one of the early things he gave me. I remember playing it at the conservatory. He wanted the pupils to see, because they were all complaining they couldn't do it.

JH / Did the *Paganini* Variations seem forbidding?

CA / No. I wasn't scared of it.

JH / Were there any pieces that did seem intimidating at that time?

CA / *Mazeppa*, as a result of Krause not being happy when I first played it for him. It happened many times in my life that I was scared of *Mazeppa*. As a matter of fact, I had certain difficulties recording it that I wouldn't have had otherwise. I had to do some psychological work. [Laughs.]

JH / Krause also guided your general education, didn't he?

CA / Oh yes, he chose my tutors when it was decided that I shouldn't go to school. I had a French tutor, an English tutor. . . . I don't think they neglected my general education. I was very bad in mathematics. But very good in history. Krause would also take me to museums. And he decided what operas I should hear.

JH / To what extent was he a father to you?

CA / He was *the* father figure in my psychological development—in a good and bad sense, as father figures are. But it didn't do me too much harm. It could have.

JH / You mean, because he was so domineering?

CA / Yes. The authority was always there. He made me tremble.

JH / What did you call him?

CA / "Herr Professor." Always. All his daughters suffered from his tremendous authority. One was an actress, a few were musicians, but none of them really made a career.

JH / How do you imagine Krause perceived you? What were you to him?

CA / He was quite tired already. I'm sure he must have wanted to stop teaching. But then he must have thought, This material is so pliable; something can really be made out of this material.

# Struggling for a Career
## 1918–1927

Under Krause's tutelage, Arrau enjoyed a remarkable career as a prodigy. He made his formal Berlin debut in 1914. In 1915, he was presented the Gustav Hollander Award for young artists and won the Ibach competition, in which he remembers being the only child contestant.

Arrau's earliest German reviews are informative. His name was known. He played for large audiences. His technical command was thought astonishing and his interpretive gift auspicious. He was said to have been born in 1904, reducing his age by a year.

He first appeared before the Berlin public in joint student recitals organized by Krause. In 1914, for instance, Krause's students performed the complete *Well-Tempered Clavier* in four concerts. Arrau was singled out for praise in the press. Wrote the critic of the *Allgemeine Musik-Zeitung:* "In particular, one should mention the ten-year-old Claudio Arrau, a wonderful youngster who played the preludes and fugues assigned to him with amazing self-assurance and independence. One must marvel at the knowledge and skill of this d'Albert of the future. How finely he articulates! The individual pieces were played in a clear, distinct, limpid manner. This was not the result of practice, but rather imbibed from nature in her fullness."

Arrau's debut recital, on December 10, 1914, in the Künstlerhaus, consisted of the Preludes and Fugues in F major, F-sharp major, and G minor from the second book of *The Well-Tempered,* Beethoven's Variations on a Russian Dance (WoO 71), Heller's B-flat minor Sonata (Op. 143), Henselt's B-flat minor Romance (Op. 10) and Etude in F sharp (Op. 2, no. 6), Friedrich Gernsheim's Preludes in C-sharp minor and B-flat minor (Op. 2) and *Legend* (Op. 44), Chopin's Waltz in A flat (Op. 42), and

Liszt's *Hungarian Rhapsody* No. 11. "The little fellow's skill is as fresh and wholesome as his looks," reported Paul Geyer in *Der Reichsbote*. "He does not simulate precocity, but only plays pieces which he has mastered both inwardly and outwardly. This is what makes his playing so congenial. . . . Claudio Arrau will be talked about." Other reviewers likewise coupled reports of digital prowess with praise for Arrau's "modesty" and "musical purity." The critic for the *Allgemeine Musik-Zeitung* wrote: "The young artist, who can already with good reason lay claim to this honorable title, mastered his task with remarkable self-assurance. If the amazingly difficult octave passages and dense chordal sequences of the Heller sonata astonished the listeners, then the Bach compositions from *The Well-Tempered Clavier* notably displayed the spiritual maturity of this young pianist. . . . And what is most gratifying: that he, at the same time, appears to be such a fresh and wholesome youngster."

Arrau followed his debut with a second recital two months later. The Künstlerhaus was sold out; an overflow had to be turned away at the box office. This time, the program consisted of a Handel suite in D minor, Mozart's Sonata in D (K. 576), Weber's *Rondo brillante* in E flat (Op. 62), the C-sharp minor of Schubert's *Moments musicaux*, Mendelssohn's Capriccio [Fantasy] in E minor (Op. 16, no. 2), four pieces by Giovanni Sgambati (Op. 18, nos. 2, 3, and 4; Op. 20, no. 1), and Liszt's *Paganini* Etude No. 5 and *La leggierezza*.

Commented the critic of the *Allgemeine Musik-Zeitung*:

It is truly heart-warming to hear this eleven-year-old boy play. There is here absolutely no trace of hothouse cultivation. Healthily and naturally, musically practical and straightforward, as one expects from a child, but at the same time with all the infallible signs of an extraordinary talent, this good-looking boy played his Mozart, Weber, Schubert, and Mendelssohn. Professor Martin Krause, for whose pedagogic acumen we have to be thankful, is concerned that this boy play only those things which he can encompass in his youthful state of mind and understanding. Therefore, no *Appassionata* and no Chopin B-minor Sonata! It appears to me that this fresh, Germanically impregnated boy must become a distinguished artist.

The *Vorsische Zeitung* wrote:

The cleanliness of his technique, his fine sense of tonal shadings, his basic musical execution are astounding. With all this, he does not exhibit the fatal precocity which is unbearable in the playing of most child prodigies: although his playing is phenomenal, it is always youthful, naïve, and uncontrived. . . . Everything was well played; some pieces—for instance, the Mendelssohn—could hardly be played better. The admiration of the delighted audience manifested itself not with the usual laurel wreaths and bouquets of flowers, but with boxes of candy which were brought to the stage by loving hands.

A November 3, 1916, Arrau program, given at the Beethovensaal, shows him graduating to a more demanding repertoire—in addition to selections by Bach, Haydn, Mozart, and Gernsheim, he tackled Beethoven's *Les Adieux* Sonata, Schumann's *ABEGG* Variations, and Liszt's *Spanish Rhapsody*. Critics reported that the "twelve-year-old" artist, variously described as "the born genius of the piano," "the little piano titan," and "this miracle man [*Wundermann*]," was "besieged with requests for encores."

Two Berlin concerts from early 1918 are of particular interest. On March 14, Arrau took part in an "Elite Concert" at which he received equal billing—not as accompanist, but for two sets of solos—with Joseph Schwarz and Elena Gerhardt, among the leading German singers of the day. On March 11, he gave a Beethovensaal recital for which the program included two *Well-Tempered* preludes and fugues, Beethoven's *Eroica* Variations, three Schubert impromptus, the Strauss-Tausig *Nachtfalter* (Waltz-Caprice No. 1), Liszt's *Mazeppa*, and Variations and Fugue on an Original Theme (Op. 64) by Georg Schumann (1866–1952). Leopold Schmidt, reviewing the latter concert in the Berlin *Tageblatt und Handels-Zeitung*, offered a description of Arrau's sound that could have as accurately been applied fifty years later: "He has a singular technical gift for the piano. He exhibits a healthy timbre which does not conform to the present preference for coquettish and rustling effects, and which in forte is capable of the greatest dynamic intensification with absolute clarity and assurance." Arrau is identified as "among the most promising of the rising generation of pianists," and commended, beyond his pianistic gifts, for "a winning, almost childlike modesty." The review concludes: "He already has a public following which rejoices in his playing and he is in no danger of losing its appreciation. He appears to be destined for a great career."

But Krause had died just three weeks before. Notwithstanding his acclaim, Arrau was cut adrift. For the most part, he increasingly found himself performing less in Germany than in Scandinavia and Eastern Europe—when he was performing at all. And as his career declined, so did his self-confidence.

His mother, sister, and aunt, fortunately, continued to furnish an inviolable pocket of security. Also, in addition to his talent, his evident innocence must have attracted real and would-be benefactors. Photographs of Arrau from the early 1920s evoke a young artist of unusual sweetness and shyness, of a provocative guilelessness.

Arrau describes one of Krause's daughters, Jennie, as a tactfully constructive influence on his musical development after her father's death. His main support outside the family, however, was Dr. Leo Barcynski, a physician turned opera singer, remembered by Arrau and his sister for his wisdom and warmth. Barcynski believed in Arrau. He shared his intellectual interests—it was he who introduced Arrau to primitive art—and offered guidance when Arrau played for him in private.

Gradually the shock of Krause's death receded and Arrau's name recirculated in Germany. One consequence was his first United States tour, in 1923–24. This, sadly, proved a setback: he and his mother wound up penniless in a New York boarding house. Upon returning to Berlin—the fare was paid by the Baldwin Piano Company—Arrau decided to try psychoanalysis. In 1924 this was a step undertaken less casually than today. But Arrau's dilemma bears stressing. His piano career, which had begun so glamorously, progressing virtually by itself, seemed embarrassingly precarious. Withdrawn and unworldly, he was ill-equipped to regain the social and professional contacts he had acquired through Krause. His scholarship, which the Chileans had periodically renewed during and after the war, unequivocably expired in 1921. Nineteen twenty-three, moreover, was the year of the wheelbarrow, when the mark plunged to a rate of 1 trillion to a dollar. Hunger was commonplace. Mores collapsed.

The French occupied the Ruhr. Hitler was mobilizing storm troopers in Munich. It was to this Germany that Arrau, twenty-one years old, returned from America. Expected to support his mother, sister, and aunt, he scavenged for private students with money to pay. At one point—he does not remember the year—the family was reduced to pawning the necklaces and bracelets with which he had been showered by royalty during his glory days with Krause.

Enter Dr. Hubert Abrahamsohn, a Düsseldorf psychoanalyst, who in the course of a friendship lasting nearly half a century became, in Arrau's words, "part guru, part father, and part older brother." Acquaintances of Abrahamsohn remember him as a heavy-set man with soft hands, deliberate in manner, Buddha-like in appearance. Arrau refers to the "wonderful serenity" of his face. In his paternal guise, Abrahamsohn, childless and Arrau's senior by thirteen years, could also be severe. Like Barcynski, Abrahamsohn believed in Arrau the artist; he knew music, attended Arrau's concerts, and was quick to comment constructively. Like Krause, who said, "This child shall be my masterpiece," Abrahamsohn was professionally fulfilled through Arrau's musical fulfillment: if for Krause Arrau was the prize pupil, for Abrahamsohn he became the prize patient. When the Second World War broke out, Arrau secured a Chilean visa for Abrahamsohn, who subsequently moved to Santiago, then New York City, then back to Germany. Even after the war, Arrau maintained contact with him as a sometime analysand. Abrahamsohn died in 1973.

For Arrau, psychoanalysis, like music, has meant rechanneling, not pacifying, emotional unrest. His boldest artistic ventures sometimes ignite crippling bouts of anxiety. When worst comes to worst, he calls off concerts. Behind the scenes, the cancellation drama can be arduous. To cite an extreme example: in 1955 Arrau was to play four concerts at New York's Town Hall for the Mozart Bicentennial, to encompass all the piano sonatas, four fantasies, two rondos, and nine "variations and other works." Mozart or not, much of this repertoire is relatively obscure: of the sonatas, Arrau had performed fewer than half since a Berlin Mozart cycle in the 1930s. At home in Douglaston, he drilled and redrilled, practicing with weighted hammers to make his fingers articulate with maximum clarity. His student Philip Lorenz, who heard dry runs of several programs, remembers: "You wouldn't have thought fingers could work so actively. It was a kind of playing I had never seen him do before, with the fingers pulled far back before striking. And he used a kind of flying staccato that was simply dazzling—he would *throw* his arms and hands at the keys, as if he were shaking water from the fingertips. The ornaments, too, were unbelievable—so fast and at the same time so correct." Then, not long before the series was to begin, Arrau's memory began to slip: the early sonatas were running into one another. A month before the first concert, Arrau announced he would omit twelve pieces from the four-concert total; each program would still run over three hours. Then the first recital was postponed. Then, in a third announcement, the entire series was canceled.

Around the same time, the Mozart concertos, always fragile, caused their share of trouble. In 1953 Arrau balked at going through with a performance of the B-flat Concerto (K. 595) with Howard Mitchell and the National Symphony. Abrahamsohn urged that the performance take place. Arrau told Abrahamsohn he would play the concerto if Abrahamsohn accompanied him to Washington. With Abrahamsohn standing backstage, Arrau performed the B-flat Concerto without mishap. But a scheduled 1956 Mozart concerto cycle never took place, and a 1958 performance of the C-minor Concerto with Josef Krips in Edinburgh left a bad taste—the orchestra handled some of the ornaments differently than did Arrau. He continued to include five Mozart concertos (K. 466, K. 467, K. 488, K. 491, and K. 595) in his list of orchestral repertoire, but only "with two or three rehearsals." His last Mozart concerto performances were in 1964, when he played the Concertos in B flat (K. 450) and D (K. 451) with Erich Leinsdorf and the Boston Symphony at Tanglewood, and K. 450 at the Casals Festival in Puerto Rico.


CA / Krause's death was awful for me. I thought the world had ended. I had the feeling of being abandoned. I felt I couldn't go on playing. And then I had to fight all those ladies who wanted me to go to Schnabel, or I don't know whom, because I was too young to not have a teacher. They thought it was impossible for a young man of fifteen to develop by himself. But I refused. I felt strongly about it out of loyalty to Krause. It was a little childish, this loyalty. But I was afraid that with another teacher I might get confused. I had also the feeling that anything a teacher could teach he had given me, and that I had to digest everything and continue further by myself. It would have been much more comfortable, of course, to have found another father figure.

JH / Did you grieve a long time for Krause?

CA / Oh yes, I was desperate. That was also the worst time in my career. Everybody had prejudices about prodigies. And you know how the Germans are—once they have ideas they never get rid of them. The struggle I went through with audiences—people always said that I hadn't fulfilled what I had promised.

JH / Did you consider giving up your career?

CA / At a certain moment—at the time of the difficult transition from the intuitive way of playing toward a conscious understanding—I thought of giving up my career. But only for a very short time. Maybe three or four years after Krause's death.

JH / To what degree had you begun a career while Krause was alive?

CA / I had a terrific career as a child prodigy. Krause didn't let me play more than fifteen to twenty concerts a season. But I played everywhere.

JH / Were any of your concerts of that period particularly memorable?

CA / I played with Nikisch in Dresden, the Liszt First Concerto. I think I was twelve. It was quite an experience because Nikisch didn't like prodigies. But after the first rehearsal he was very nice. I also played, under Krause, in many European courts. I played for the King of Saxony, the King of Württemberg, the Royal Family of Bavaria, the Queen of Rumania, the King and Queen of Norway. And in all sorts of smaller courts in Germany.

JH / After Krause died, was there a drop in the number of engagements?

CA / Yes. He got me most of the concerts, through his connections. After he died, Germany was almost completely closed to me. So I was offered concerts in smaller countries—Norway, Finland, Bulgaria, Yugoslavia. I was paid very little. But I played, and everywhere I had a tremendous success. So I said to myself there must be something to me that is worthwhile. I also played in Rumania—Rumania was one of my best countries. In Germany I was afraid to play. I would have liked to have been engaged, to be asked for. But it didn't happen.

JH / And you didn't want to push it.

CA / Well, I was never a pusher. I wouldn't have known how.

JH / You made your Berlin Philharmonic debut under Muck in 1920, playing the Liszt-Schubert *Wanderer* Fantasy. How did that come about?

CA / I really don't remember. It went quite well, but it was a bad choice to make my debut with the *Wanderer* Fantasy in the Liszt transcription. People had such prejudices against transcriptions. But I didn't have any choice. It was either that or nothing.

JH / There were other concerts from that period that must have been important. You made your London debut in 1920 with the *Goldberg* Variations. And a few weeks later you played at Albert Hall on the same program with Nellie Melba.

CA / Yes, that was a big success. Melba objected that I had so many bows after Liszt's *Spanish Rhapsody*. She went up to me backstage and said, "That's enough, young man." And she wouldn't let me go on anymore. The *Goldberg* Variations was at the Aeolian Hall. It was quite an unusual program—some Scarlatti sonatas and the *Goldberg* Variations.

JH / And you won the Liszt Prize in 1919 and 1920. Did that help?

CA / That helped a little bit. Also a prize that was famous in those days—the Schulhoff Prize.

JH / Did you need engagements partly for the income, as well as for the career?

CA / Definitely. Also the first recordings I made. Sometimes, you know, they made me shorten a piece, which was horrible. But I needed the money. It was either doing it or starving.

JH / One event which seems to have been a turning point, in the negative sense, was your first American tour. You were twenty years old.

CA / That was in 1923–24. By that time I was already having a little success. The manager Wolfsohn—he was one of the big American managers—came to Berlin to hear and engage Claire Dux, the singer. She was very famous in Germany. And he heard me also, in a concert. He was very impressed, so he signed me for twenty concerts. [Laughs.] When I arrived here, I had two recitals, one in Carnegie Hall and one in Aeolian Hall. Wolfsohn had rented the halls, but on my account. I had to pay for everything. And I had one concert in *Hackensack*. Then I had two big engagements, with the Boston Symphony and the Chicago Symphony. Wolfsohn expected enormous write-ups, and the write-ups I got were good, but not sensational, as he had expected. So he dropped me, and I was stuck here with my mother. The Baldwin company, they were marvelous. Even though I had so few concerts, they decided to give me a monthly stipend. The *things* that *happened* in those days. I went back to Berlin and met with the man who had negotiated with Wolfsohn—Norbert Salter, another famous manager. "How was it?" he said. "A fiasco. If it hadn't been for Baldwin, I would not have been able to come back." And then he got *furious* and said I would have to pay his commissions for the concerts I hadn't given. And I said, "I'm terribly sorry. Put me in jail, because I don't have anything." "I'm going to think it over," he said. Then he called me and said, "O.K. You will give my daughter lessons until this debt is paid." For *years* I had to give her lessons. And she was a disgusting woman.

JH / How did the concerts go in New York, Boston, and Chicago?

CA / I really played my best. And I played tremendous programs. The program at Carnegie I finished with the *Don Giovanni* Fantasy by Liszt. And it went very well, as far as I can remember. I did the Chopin F-minor Concerto with Monteux in Boston. And in Chicago I did the Mendelssohn G minor and the Liszt *Spanish Rhapsody* in the Busoni transcription for piano and orchestra.

JH / I've brought along the reviews of your first two New York concerts.

CA / Oh, fantastic!

JH / I'll read them to you. They're very short. The first one says "Claudio Arrau Heard."

Crouched low before a grand piano, Claudio Arrau, a pianist, educated both in his native Santiago, Chile [*sic*], and since 1911 in Berlin, challenged recent comparisons at Carnegie Hall yesterday in the ordeal of a North American debut. The young artist has played widely in Europe and has given Bach recitals in Berlin. He introduced himself on the present occasion in Beethoven's Sonata Op. 31, no. 3; groups of Chopin and Debussy, and the *Don Juan* Fantasy of Liszt, with a Chopin waltz and Liszt rhapsody for encores.

Mr. Arrau is a musician of some mannerisms, though these serve the purpose of an individual style. His bent is for clarity and lightness, as shown in a Beethoven that never thundered, and for melodic grace, as in his Chopin, the Nocturne, Op. 48, no. 1, gaining in delicate tone tints what it missed of ruggedness and contrast. Most effective were Debussy's *Reflets dans l'eau, Feux d'artifice,* and *Minstrels,* marking the player in all modesty as one who, given the music of his own modern age, has something to say and both the technical and temperamental means to say it.

That's the whole review. Now here's the second one, "Claudio Arrau Gives Recital."

Claudio Arrau, the Chilean pianist, gave his second recital in Aeolian Hall yesterday afternoon, playing three Bach fugues, Beethoven's Sonata of *Adieux, absence et retour,* and groups of Chopin and Debussy. To follow these with Liszt's *Spanish Rhapsody* and Busoni's Fantasy on *Carmen* was a dual gesture toward the player's heritage and his Berlin training. Chilean culture of old looked to Central Europe as surely as the Brazil of Novaes turned to Paris. Mr. Arrau individually is a player of sensitive mood, subtly dynamic, a tone painter, who can charm with a Chopin nocturne or Debussy's *Gardens in Rain,* as he naturally does with congenial rhythms of Spain.

It's curious that both of these reviews suggest that your playing stressed clarity and lightness. Which is not what one would say today.

CA / Maybe I had still a kind of emotional block. Many people said that I was cold, or something like that. But on the other hand I remember that the *Don Giovanni* Fantasy was really very brilliant as I played it in those days. And I remember Borovsky, the pianist, came backstage at Carnegie Hall after the *Don Giovanni* Fantasy and said one *can't* play better, technically! And several other pianists. Nyiregyházi—he also came backstage and was very enthusiastic. I think it was mainly a lack of success with the critics.

JH / You must have been very upset when you read the reviews.

CA / I couldn't *believe* it. I remember thinking, About whom are they *talking?* There must be some *mistake.* Of course it was explained to me that there hadn't been any publicity at all. That nobody knew that I had already had quite a good success in Europe. That I wasn't a beginner.

JH / Was it at this time that you decided to go into analysis?

CA / Yes. I had already been thinking about it. And then I met this marvelous man, Dr. Hubert Abrahamsohn. He was very interested in music. He lived in Düsseldorf. I don't know from where I got the money. I think I borrowed it. But in 1924 I went to Düsseldorf for maybe two or three months. I believe he saw me every day, or every other day. And he never asked for a cent. The case interested him.

JH / Oh, of course. The famous child prodigy.

CA / In those days it was an unusual thing to do, to go to a psychiatrist. One hid it—it wasn't spoken of. But I had for quite some time the feeling that I wasn't playing according to the gifts I had by nature. I felt that something was in the way. And so many times, you know, I would miss passages that I could play with my eyes closed. There was something in me that worked against having to perform and to be in the public eye.

JH / And what was Dr. Abrahamsohn's response?

CA / Well, we analyzed my childhood, of course. You know, for a child to go out and play for two thousand people—it's actually against nature. And many children, because they don't feel at ease, escape into failure. I remember that the older I got, the more preoccupied I was with being the center of attention. It seems that performing is something that has to be really worked on, psychologically. One must *really want* to perform—not one hundred percent, because that doesn't exist, but let's say ninety percent. Less than ninety percent becomes sometimes fatal.

JH / Was this the key—to know with greater certainty that you wanted to play in public?

CA / That was part of it. On the other hand, I never doubted that I was born to perform. Such things have always two sides. I think also the fact that I wasn't living a normal social life must have influenced all these psychological difficulties. I was sort of an outcast.

JH / You used to visit with Krause's daughters. Did you continue to see them after he died?

CA / Oh yes. Very wonderful friends. They were all, of course, older. I grew up with I don't know how many ladies. My mother, my sister, my aunt. And then next door the Krause daughters. Sometimes I think, How did I ever become a *man*? And how did I become an independent artist? Sometimes I think it must have been a miracle of some kind.

JH / At the time you began therapy with Dr. Abrahamsohn, did you know anyone your own age?

CA / *Very* few who were really friends.

JH / You often talk about the transition from intuitive to conscious understanding. Was this a concept Abrahamsohn introduced you to, as a goal to work toward?

CA / Exactly. I knew that I had to do tremendous work on myself psychologically. I never left everything to the analyst, as so many people do.

JH / Did your relationship to music change at this time?

CA / Yes. I realized, from analysis, that the troubles that kept me from giving everything I had had to do with vanity. I wanted to please. And I was afraid not to please. Abrahamsohn worked continuously on that idea. How right he was. The less vain you become, the more creative you are. One gets to the point where one is courageous enough to *dis*please, if it's called for by the composer. There are certain places in Beethoven, for example, where he is almost brutal.

JH / The word "vanity" usually suggests arrogance, or excessive self-confidence. But I think you're talking about a type of shyness—vanity in the sense of worrying what others will think of you, and therefore not expressing yourself in a way that might antagonize or confuse.

CA / I don't mean vanity in the sense of being conceited, but of wanting to please. And that is of course due to insecurity.

JH / Would you say that, as a result of conquering this impulse to please, your piano sound changed?

CA / It became richer, more assertive. Everything had more meaning. People who had heard me before asked what was happening.

JH / It's perfectly understandable. I mean, all your life people had been observing you, commenting behind your back, "Isn't this a marvelous creature who can play Liszt at the age of twelve!" You must have always been aware of people watching, judging.

CA / Of being in the spotlight, and being judged. And I sometimes wasn't quite sure—because I was alone—what they thought.

JH / When you're very young, you're aware of being watched, but it doesn't matter. But when you get older, you begin to wonder what people think.

CA / Yes. Do they like it? Do they not like it?

JH / One of the things you've mentioned in writing about this period is learning to interpret your dreams.

CA / Oh yes. I kept a notebook. And I trained myself, when I had an important dream, to wake up and write it down. I developed this capacity to wake up when I felt my subconscious wanted to tell me something.

JH / And what did you find in your subconscious?

CA / I found out that anxiety is unavoidable. To be a human being is to be anxious. And to act as if one is not anxious is ridiculous—

to act as if one doesn't feel scared before going on stage. I had to learn to live with my anxieties.

JH / You must have remembered your years as a child when you didn't experience stage fright, and thought that that was how you were supposed to feel as an adult.

CA / Yes. But of course it's almost impossible. Some people think they can get rid of anxiety by making a tremendous effort not to accept it. But the anxiety is always there. If you feel too cocky or secure, then something's wrong.

JH / In your playing I find a remarkable capacity to penetrate levels of anxiety another interpreter might never notice. Your recording of the fourth of the Opus 10 Brahms Ballades, for instance, suggests a sort of harrowing night-music. Whereas a lot of people think of this as a lighter piece, with rippling Schumannesque figurations. Does it ever occur to you that one of the uses of anxiety is to locate anxiety as an aspect of interpretation?

CA / But I think that the capacity to feel anxiety—the anxiety of humanity—makes one capable of putting oneself into *any* kind of emotion, into anything human. The capacity for empathy is one of the most important qualities in an interpreter.

JH / I was going to get to that—that anxiety is not merely conducive to uncovering anxiety in the notes, but, as a nervously alert emotional state, to entering into all kinds of emotions. In fact, I was going to suggest to you that in experiencing anxiety in music, you're able, in a sense, to expel it and move to a higher, more exalted state. To take an obvious example, in the Liszt B-minor Ballade you begin with tremendous anxiety and work toward an apotheosis at the end. What I sense is a working out of the anxiety. Perhaps you could even call it an act of therapy.

CA / A working out of anxiety, absolutely. *Using* anxiety. I don't think one should say too much about therapeutic value. Therapy is something entirely different—the goal is simply to liberate people from handicaps.

JH / But what about the purely negative impact of anxiety, when it leads to memory lapses and wrong notes? What determines whether anxiety has a positive or a negative impact—whether you use it creatively or destructively?

CA / I don't know how it happens, exactly. Thirty years ago, anxiety would often get in the way of performance. But with time, I understood that one should try to simply let things happen, and not worry so much about pleasing or succeeding. Then anxiety becomes less of a handicap, and more a part of the creative stream.

JH / You often talk about, say, memory lapses in terms of "self-destructive tendencies." As if there were a part of your subconscious that wanted you to fail.

CA / Almost every performer has to fight against escaping into failure, as Schnabel did in his last years. Once, when Schnabel had a memory lapse in Town Hall during a Schubert cycle, he said, "Sorry, but there was such a draft that I couldn't continue playing." So all the ushers went around looking for open windows, and of course there weren't any.

JH / How do you feel when you're playing and something goes wrong?

CA / I used to think it was the end of the world. It sometimes took *months* for me to recover. I wanted to be perfect, divine— beyond any flaw or memory mistake. But that always produces the opposite effect. Now I don't get so upset. You say to yourself, "It's ridiculous to be so bothered. I'm not infallible."

JH / I used to listen to music with an expectation of perfection. If something went wrong, it would scar the rest of the performance. This was a terribly tense way of listening—waiting for a wrong note or a sloppy entrance.

CA / You know what would happen in my very early years if something went wrong? I gave up. I kept playing but I gave up. As if the rest didn't count.

JH / Something I think we should mention here, because it's well known, is that you cancel quite a few concerts. How do you account for that?

CA / Sometimes I am really indisposed, physically. But most of the cancellations are because of anxiety of the wrong kind. Because of not having played a work for a long time—that's the main reason.

JH / Does the anxiety sometimes lead to physical complaints?

CA / Well, of course, we all know about that.

JH / Your stiffness the other day, when you canceled a concert in Connecticut—did you feel that was the result of nervousness?

CA / Well, you could say it was. Because I was going to play the next day the Chopin E-minor Concerto, which I hadn't played for at least five years. But there was a physical reason also. On the plane, flying back from Chicago, one of the air-conditioning vents couldn't be closed, and it was right on top of me. The same evening I was tired and stiff. And I had been having trouble with my neck for quite some time. You never know exactly how much is psychosomatic, or purely physical.

JH / When you feel you can't go on the stage, is there usually a physical symptom? I mean, is there something in your muscles that complains?

CA / No. It's not technical. Usually it's worrying about memory.

JH / Do you ever go on stage when you feel as if you certainly should not? Do you ever feel that you're really too anxious to play, and play anyway?

CA / Not really. When I feel I can't play, I just cancel. Without any consideration for anybody else.

JH / Does that make you feel guilty?

CA / Guilty and depressed.

JH / For me, you represent a certain artistic personality type, which might be called "Romantic"—solitary, suffering, striving. Do you think that's the basic personality type among artists?

CA / Oh no. Jung's division of introvert and extravert—that you find a lot. The extravert has a much easier career, particularly at the beginning—he is so sure of himself. But most of the time he misses out on the last stage of development. Whereas the introvert, if he has the *endurance* to face all his difficulties—I think he reaches higher.

# Success

# 1927 and After

With Abrahamsohn's help, Arrau put his prodigy years completely behind him. One index to his growing maturity was social: by 1930, the unworldly outsider had become a devotee of Berlin's famous night life, which he sampled with tireless curiosity.

His marriage in 1937 was an anchoring event. Ruth Schneider, daughter of a wealthy business executive, was a fledgling mezzo-soprano. According to Arrau, she was also known as "the prettiest girl in Frankfurt," a verdict photographs of the newlyweds do nothing to refute.

Mrs. Arrau first encountered her husband-to-be in Frankfurt, where Arrau performed in the Saalbau. "When I heard him play, it was the first time in my life that I was enthusiastic about the piano," she remembers. "His sound was so warm, so intense. Since I had wanted to learn to play the piano better myself, I went to him for some lessons. And we would meet here and there. Then he wrote a letter to me in Frankfurt, suggesting that I call him so we could get together socially. And I did. He suggested that we go dancing. I had known all musicians to be terribly bad dancers, but I couldn't get out of it. And he turned out to be a wonderful dancer. After that, we began seeing each other regularly."

Mrs. Arrau decided to abandon her singing career not long after the marriage. "If you were not a golden-haired 'German' type, belonging to the right organizations, the Nazis made problems. I was told that I stressed everything in my personality that made me a non-Aryan type, and that if I did not change my attitude I would find that I was no longer wanted to appear on a German stage. I asked, 'Do you mean that you expect me to dye my hair golden blond?' Their answer was 'This would be just a beginning.' " And she also felt that Arrau's career deserved her full support. As she is a steady, unpretentious woman, more hardheaded and skeptical than her husband, her indispensable background role is easy to imagine.

Meanwhile, Arrau pursued his keyboard regime with unrelenting diligence. He remembers one period, in 1934, during which he practiced at least fourteen hours a day for at least two weeks. He had been asked to play the Prokofiev Third Piano Concerto and the Stravinsky Concerto for Piano and Wind Instruments under Carlos Chávez and Ernest Ansermet in Mexico City. Neither work was in his repertoire—both, indeed, were quite new— but he felt he could not afford to pass up the engagements. ("In those days, I risked anything. I was convinced I could do it, and that I had to do it for my career.") It was in Mexico City, also, that in 1933–34 he performed fifteen recitals in thirteen weeks. (See Appendix A.)

But the greatest test of memory and endurance came in Berlin, where Arrau fervently sought a larger audience. This was his twelve-concert Bach cycle of 1935–36, intended to encompass all the solo keyboard works except those for organ. (See Appendix A.) In subsequent seasons in Berlin, he gave cycles of the Mozart and Weber sonatas, plus a Schubert cycle.

By 1940, according to his own reckoning, Arrau's artistic reputation was at last satisfactorily established in Germany. But so, by that time, was Hitler: Arrau's hunger for German acclaim had delayed his departure. Once he left Germany, in 1940, this same hunger for approval powered a second courtship of American fame. This time, success came swiftly. "Claudio Arrau, the Chilean pianist, enthralled the audience at his recital last night in Carnegie Hall with a series of performances that could hardly be excelled for imaginative detail, wealth of exquisite color effects, and technical virtuosity," wrote Noel Strauss in the *New York Times* on February 20, 1941. The review continued:

> Mr. Arrau is a romanticist primarily, and it was after he had finished the Bach *Italian* Concerto and Beethoven's Sonata, Op. 31, no. 3, and arrived at the Schumann *Carnaval* that his real eminence as a master of the keyboard first made itself completely patent.

In the numbers by Chopin, Liszt, Ravel, and Debussy that rounded out the program after the Schumann, Mr. Arrau remained on the superlative plane reached in the *Carnaval* and in all of them he was the poetically inspired interpreter as well as the purveyor of tonal tinting rarely equaled among pianists of the time.

In the Bach concerto, which opened the list, Mr. Arrau in his attempt to arrive at orchestral sonorities in a work which will not bear them, had an edgy, dry touch that disappeared entirely with the succeeding Beethoven sonata and never re-appeared during the evening. It is true that Bach in this concerto was attempting to convey the idea of the typical concertos of his day by a transference of their orchestral passages to the keyboard, but Mr. Arrau exaggerated the music dynamically without arriving at the goal intended. And in the Andante he resorted to a halting before accented tones, to lend the latter prominence, that interfered with the proper flow of the melodic line.

But the artist's exceptional imaginative powers first came to light in the Beethoven sonata, especially in the Allegretto movement, where the staccato passages were handled with unusually charming application of nuances.

This reviewer never has heard a more absolutely satisfying or more finely unified performance of the Schumann *Carnaval*, next on the schedule. Mr. Arrau was in his element here, and his presentation of each of the many components of the work could not easily be surpassed in play of light and shade, fertility of fancy, or beauty of tone. The whole composition, moreover, was led to a climax of richly resounding forcefulness at the pompously delivered concluding *March of the Davidsbündler*. It was all sincere, sensitive and individual without a trace of exaggeration or eccentricity.

As captivatingly played and as remarkable for bravura were the Chopin Scherzo in E and the Liszt Concert Study in D flat. Yet for sheer enchantment of sound nothing on the program quite touched the uncannily limpid unfoldment of Ravel's *Jeux d'eau*, a phenomenal feat of pianism, matched in its digital dexterity and captivating hues by Debussy's *Feux d'artifice*, with which the recital was brought to a breath-taking conclusion.

Robert Lawrence's review of the same concert, in the *New York Herald Tribune,* is so cogently informative that it, too, is worth citing in full. The prior Arrau recital he refers to took place three weeks earlier at Town Hall.

The finest performance of Schumann's *Carnaval* that I have ever heard—and the hazard of such a generalization is fully realized—was given at Carnegie Hall last night by Claudio Arrau, Chilean pianist, who appeared here with a large degree of success earlier in the season. Even the enthusiastic reports which followed this first concert had not prepared the writer for the quality of playing achieved by Mr. Arrau. Within certain limits that may best be defined on the basis of future recitals, he is a great pianist.

For those who love music of the romantic period interpreted with alternate sensitivity and glitter, as called for by the composer—with an unlimited tonal palette that never once, in agile passages, loses its glossy coloration—Mr. Arrau provided a completely satisfying evening. He has resurrected the glamour and aristocratic sentiment of the nineteenth century so little known to us except in the playing of pianistic titans who are survivors of yesterday. He is able to apply the final touch of filigree to a performance of Schumann, Chopin or Liszt already resplendent in the sparkle of its ornamentation. He has mastered the secret of "romantic" pedalling, so that in the arabesques of Chopin, as well as in the impressionist cascades of Debussy and Ravel, he can achieve a prismatic play of color dazzling to hear.

In the hands of a lesser pianist than Mr. Arrau, Schumann's *Carnaval* might possibly emerge as long and rhetorical. But when played with the full beauty of last night's performance, it holds the listener through its combined fantasy and unified structure. I have heard any number of times the little pieces which comprise this work. I have studied them. Yet never, within a fairly extended range of concertgoing, has this entire composition assumed such significance as under the guiding powers of Mr. Arrau. The peculiar aura that is Schumann's, the spurts of whimsicality, defiance, caprice which mark this music, were all ineluctably present.

Mr. Arrau carried over a ravishing tonal quality from the

*Carnaval* to the Chopin E-major scherzo and the Liszt D-flat major Concert Etude. Here the perfection of his rhythms, the luminous sweep of his phrasing, evoked a type of romantic pianism which one often longs to hear but rarely does. The *Jeux d'eau* of Ravel, played with the objectivity demanded by the composer but also with the sparkle inherent in his music, and the *Feux d'artifice* of Debussy brought the recital to a triumphant close. As performed by most contemporary pianists, the passagework in the Debussy is arid and conducive only to technical display; but caught up by Mr. Arrau's magnificent use of the pedal, all of the strands of this piece formed the unified impression of which Debussy must have dreamed.

I spoke before of certain limitations. These were to be noted chiefly in the chordal structure of *Carnaval*, which was not nearly so secure as the pianist's more agile technique. Occasional false tones marked the massed groupings of notes. Nor was Mr. Arrau's performance of the Bach *Italian* Concerto, with which the evening began, entirely convincing. At this point his tone had not yet gained the freedom and flexibility that marked it later on. The reading of Beethoven's E-flat major Sonata, Op. 31, no. 3, which followed, was more persuasive, yet Mr. Arrau lingered too lovingly on the opening theme, attractive enough in itself without having to be underlined.

These caprices of style in music which was not romantic gave rise to reservations which may indeed be dissipated at Mr. Arrau's next recital. In the meantime any pianist who can achieve such beautiful performances as were revealed last night must be called a master.

Arrau gave another Carnegie Hall recital on November 14, 1941, and was again well received. The repercussions were recorded by *Time* magazine on March 23, 1942, in an article titled "Arrau Makes Hay."

When pianist Claudio Arrau wound up his third U.S. tour and boarded a Pan American Clipper for Puerto Rico last week, he had made plenty of hay in a shining sun.

For a long time the weather had been against him. When

the dapper Chilean pianist arrived in the U.S. last fall, he was just another paid hand in the crowded concert field. A brilliant Carnegie Hall recital last November turned the trick. He was snapped up for concert dates; nine-tenths of them were sellouts. He went to Boston in January to appear as soloist with Serge Koussevitzky's resplendent orchestra. The Bostonians liked him so well that he was called back for a return engagement the same month—a thing the Boston Symphony never does. A fortnight ago he likewise reappeared, for the second time this season, with Frederick Stock's Chicago Symphony. Concert-goers could not remember when, if ever, a musician had gotten return engagements within the same season by two major U.S. orchestras.

A small, trim-mustached man who looks like a blend of Adolphe Menjou and Anthony Eden, Claudio Arrau at 38 [sic] is an old hand in the concert field. As a lad of 20 he made a short U.S. tour in 1924 [sic], but failed to go over, and left with a poor opinion of U.S. musical taste. Europe promptly claimed him. Until the war, pianist Arrau was content to divide his lucrative concert time between Europe and South America, playing 125 concerts a year.

Arrau's well-tailored brown suits, his irrepressible love for jewelry are deceiving. Far from a superficial show-off, he has the elements of true greatness. Though he has a prodigious technique, he does not slug the piano; he approaches his art with sober modesty, plays with fire but no unnecessary sparks.

Equally characteristic is Arrau's thoroughness. He probably holds a world's record for cycle performances; once he performed all Bach's clavier works in twelve recitals; he has also given complete Mozart, Beethoven, and Schubert cycles. To preserve his vitality, he keeps to the Hay diet (separating starches and proteins), eats fruit like a jungle dweller, does Yoga exercises, sleeps ten hours a night.* Says he, "A musician owes it to his audiences not to have off days."

*Newsweek* reported "Arrau's Arrival" on January 18, 1943:

Claudio Arrau looks like a Latin American edition of Anthony Eden—shorter, more ornate of dress, more volatile of

---

*Arrau followed this regime for about two years.

temperament. But Arrau is not a diplomat; he is a Chilean pianist—remarkable at the moment because he is making the largest single concert tour of the current season. His record-breaking 67 dates include 21 appearances with the New York Philharmonic, San Francisco, St. Louis, Cleveland, Chicago, Kansas City, Minneapolis and Cincinnati symphonies. Yet Arrau was virtually unknown in this country a short three seasons ago and was booked on his first tour only last year. . . .

Three years after his "second" New York debut in 1941, Arrau had reputedly accumulated 197 North American engagements, including eleven with the Philadelphia Orchestra, nine with the Chicago Symphony, six with the Boston Symphony, and six with the New York Philharmonic. By the fifties, his worldwide bookings totaled as many as 130 per year (see Appendix B), and his individual tours were sometimes whirlwind affairs; in 1960, for example, he performed seventeen concerts in South America in twenty-two days.

Before the war, Arrau had concertized busily in Europe, South America, and Mexico, and these to some extent remained the arenas of his greatest acclaim. In Chile he had become a national hero. Santiago named a street after him in 1940. In 1959, the street where he was born was similarly renamed. In 1944, in a ceremony broadcast throughout the nation, the Chilean government awarded Arrau a gold medal "in recognition of the honor he has brought to his country." In Buenos Aires in 1946, he played for an outdoor audience of 25,000—at the time, the largest ever to attend a musical event in that city. In Mexico, where he was named an Hijo Predilecto (Favorite Son), he gave a complete Beethoven sonata cycle—his first anywhere—in Mexico City in 1938, followed by cycles in several South American capitals.

Arrau feels he achieved "all-out acceptance" in England earlier than anywhere else except Latin America. "There I didn't have to fight. You know, for years and years, when I had a bad write-up in some other country, I always knew I could look forward to England, to the *loyalty* of the English audiences. And I adore London, as a city. It is not as beautiful as Paris or Vienna. But it has such *distinction*." In London, Arrau gave a complete Beethoven sonata cycle over the BBC in 1952, and a four-concert Beethoven cycle at the Royal Festival Hall in 1959. The latter series elicited a tribute from William Mann in *Record Times* that read in part:

> Concertgoers everywhere have, for the last twelve years, regarded Arrau as one of the greatest of the great pianists who abound in this world of ours at the moment.
>
> Many musicians maintain firmly that he is the greatest of all, because he has everything that we look for in a pianist, whether of technique, of power, or heart, or of mind. There are pianists who rank as outstanding in Bach, Mozart, Beethoven, Chopin, or Liszt. Arrau is the only pianist alive who, at any rate while he is playing, can convince people that he is the outstanding interpreter of *all* these composers and a good many others too. . . .

Arrau has given Beethoven concerto cycles in London both under Klemperer and under Krips. In 1961, he performed nine concertos with Sir Adrian Boult in three gala evenings within a two-week period. In 1973, Neville Cardus of the *Guardian* paid tribute to Arrau on his seventieth birthday as follows:

> Claudio Arrau is one of the most searching of interpreters of music composed for the piano. I deliberately apply to him the term interpreter to mark him off from the virtuoso pianist whose arts more or less begin and end at the keyboard. Arrau's technique is prodigious, but he puts all of his finger skill and his musical understanding to the service of the composer. . . .
>
> Arrau is as objective as [a] great and individual artist well could be. He shares the Schnabel-Klemperer integrity. In fact, he throws back in method and aesthetic to Busoni. Not since Busoni has the *Emperor* Concerto been played with Arrau's grandeur of tone, with the fallings away, the vanishings of tone which were Beethoven's spiritual secret. . . .
>
> His exploration of the Chopin preludes, at an Edinburgh Festival, has become historic. It was Chopin *plus*. The common and superficial view of Chopin as a melodist of refined, perfumed breeding was knocked on the head. Arrau gave us the *whole* of Chopin, the strength as well as the romantic enchantment, strength of harmony and texture. So with each

composer he serves; he seeks out the germ-plasm, finds the style that reveals the man, or gives us his assemblable bulk. . . .

Arrau resumed concertizing in Berlin on March 14, 1954, playing the Brahms B-flat Concerto with the Berlin Philharmonic. He was called back to the stage a dozen times. "Among the pianists who left Germany after 1933 and attained world-wide fame, Claudio Arrau was the last to return," H. H. Stuckenschmidt wrote in the Berlin *Neue Zeitung*.

Berlin knew the Chilean since the 1920s; he lived and studied here. Then, already, his uncommon, seemingly innate technical facility was impressive—the balanced suppleness of all his fingers, right and left; the evenness of his passage-work; the cultivation of his touch. All these qualities have grown in the last twenty years. . . .

The spiritual content of the [Brahms B-flat Concerto] also reveals his great artistic intelligence. When Arrau is at times reproached by American critics for his arbitrariness and subjectivity, one asks oneself what standard they are applying. His Brahms interpretation, with all its freedom of phrasing and dynamics, was faithful to the work. One could not give a more sovereign and musically correct rendering of the playful changes of character in the last movement. A masterly performance, rightfully received with joyful enthusiasm throughout.

Arrau's first postwar Berlin recital came eleven days later. *Der Tagesspiegel* reported:

From time to time one hears the pessimistic opinion that the grand style of musical interpretation belongs only to the past. Claudio Arrau's recital in the Hochschulsaal was evidence that the great works find their proper interpreters again and again. This pianist, a pupil of Martin Krause . . . is today at the age of 50 [*sic*] a peer of the legendary piano geniuses of the past. His playing of Schumann's C-major Fantasy conjures up memories of d'Albert and Ansorge and can only be compared to the performances of Gieseking. Arrau

takes Schumann's marking literally: "to be played throughout with fantasy and feeling [*phantastisch und leidenschaft-
lich*]." He turns the torn passage-work of the first movement
into a demonic shadow play with larger-than-life tonal forms;
he fills every melodic phrase with warm feeling. In a way
that a less passionate player would never permit, he extends
and intensifies the thematic lines until they tear apart. And
yet classical objectivity governs all. . . . One has not in a
long time so forcefully felt, as in Arrau's simultaneously possessed and distanced performance, that this inexhaustible
romantic work . . . occupies a central place in the piano
literature. One can speak with the same enthusiasm about
every selection on the program. . . .

In 1968, he celebrated his sixty-fifth year with two programs with
the Berlin Philharmonic, playing the Schumann concerto, the
Chopin F minor, and the Weber Konzertstück. Kurt Westphal,
in a tribute on behalf of the orchestra, called Arrau the inheritor
of "the throne of Gieseking and Busoni." In 1970, after teaching
a two-week master class in Beethoven at the University of Bonn,
he was awarded the Bundesverdienstkreuz, one of West Germany's highest decorations. In 1978, for his seventy-fifth birthday,
he was awarded the Berlin Philharmonic's Hans von Bülow Medal.

Since settling in New York, Arrau has performed in the United
States more frequently than in any other country. Here, despite
the sudden impact of his 1941 success, widespread recognition as
one of the important pianists of the day has come sluggishly. In
this regard, Arrau's reception recalls resistance Busoni and Furtwängler encountered in America. Such molders of American musical taste as Koussevitzky, Paderewski, and Stokowski were not
among the heroes of prewar Berlin. Harold C. Schonberg, from
1960 to 1980 the influential senior music critic of the *New York
Times*, may be taken as a bellwether. In Schonberg's *The Great
Pianists*,* Edwin Fischer, whom Arrau revered as Martin Krause's
most eminent student, is cited, in parentheses, as "Switzerland's
favorite pianistic son"; Wilhelm Kempff, whom Arrau admires
most among his present colleagues, is mentioned once, in passing, as an exemplar of the "modern German school"; Arrau him-

*Harold C. Schonberg, *The Great Pianists* (New York: Simon & Schuster), pp.
386, 419.

self is accorded a sentence, attesting to "the stupendous extent of his repertoire and the high finish of his pianism."

This dichotomy of tradition clarifies Arrau's derogation, in the two following chapters, of Godowsky, Hofmann, Rachmaninoff, and Toscanini. The interpretive objectivity espoused by Toscanini, and emulated by his followers, puzzles Arrau; he perceives a failure of empathetic commitment. As for the Slavic or Eastern European Romanticism variously espoused by Godowsky, Hofmann, Rachmaninoff, and others—for Arrau, who holds the composer's text sacred, who never plays encores, and who dislikes social gatherings, their rescorings and abridgments, sleight-of-hand encores, and soirées mixing music with anecdotes and food seem oddly cavalier.

To some degree, his disapproval stems from discomfort in the presence of certain rituals of the ego. Once, rehearsing the Schumann concerto with Herbert von Karajan in Edinburgh in 1954, he was so shaken by Karajan's aloofness that he considered bowing out. Neville Cardus, who was present, urged him to persevere. Arrau went through with the concert, but has not appeared with Karajan since. Typically, he cherishes compassion and emotional candor. Following a 1980 performance of the *Emperor* Concerto in San Francisco, Arrau praised Kurt Masur, who conducted, for his "kind face—so warm, so modest. And no airs, no pretensions of any kind."

If such preferences suggest a lingering shyness, they mainly arise from the strength of his humility.

JH / Your social life picked up considerably from the twenties to the thirties. You talk about feeling shy in the twenties. But I have the impression that by the time you got married you had quite a busy night life. Your wife says you had a lot of girlfriends.

CA / Oh yes. But at first I sort of forced myself into this night life. To get rid of my shyness. It was very much in the way.

JH / Is this something Abrahamsohn encouraged you to do—to get out more, to meet people?

CA / Yes. I went out quite a lot just to get loose, to feel less inhibited. I tried to see and experience as much as possible. All my life I have tried to develop in this way. Even if I didn't like it.

JH / Your wife says you were an excellent dancer. Was dancing something you always enjoyed? Or was it something you initially resisted?

CA / I resisted—out of shyness. But I took lessons, to learn all the steps. I remember there were these huge balls. At first I forced myself to go. But then I started to like them. Learning in every field was extremely important to me.

JH / Was there a parallel development of your intellectual interests at about this time?

CA / Yes. That also involved at the start a little bit of forcing. I forced myself, for example, to read the complete *Divina commedia* in old Italian.

JH / Did you read in any other old languages?

CA / Latin and Greek. I happened to meet a professor of classical languages who was crazy about music. We made an arrangement. I played for him, and he taught me Latin and Greek.

JH / In 1926 you were appointed professor at the Stern Conservatory in Berlin, and you also toured England as a co-artist with Richard Tauber. In 1927 you won the grand prize in the Concours International des Pianistes in Geneva. Do any of these events evoke particularly intense memories?

CA / The Geneva competition gave me a *tremendous* push, psychologically. There were something like two hundred pianists, all playing *Islamey*. That was required. You see, I went there because I was told I needed something like that to help my career. I *never* expected to get the first prize. I was amazed that I even made it into round two. Then when it was over, and the audience was expecting the results from the judges, I thought I was seeing things. One of the gentlemen on the committee was fighting his way toward where I was sitting. It seemed he was coming toward me. *I couldn't believe it.* I couldn't believe it. I thought everybody else had played better.

JH / Arthur Rubinstein, in the second volume of his memoirs, mentions this competition. He was on the jury. He says that he and the other judges couldn't understand why you had entered. Because you were an established artist . . .

CA / No.

JH / I'll read to you what he says. Rubinstein had just been in a car accident, and his head was elaborately bandaged. He says: "When I joined my colleagues of the jury at the competition, my spectacular headdress gave me certain privileges. Professor Pembaur was constantly preoccupied with my comfort, looking for the best chair, or trying to get a pillow under my head."

CA / *Pembaur?* How did I ever forget that? He was a famous pianist in Germany—and only in Germany. He was a Liszt specialist. He had all sorts of peculiar ideas about Romantic playing. Actually, I remember a recital that was quite interesting—everything stretched, *tremendous* rubatos. I didn't even recognize a section of the Liszt Sonata! But there were fantastic things in his playing. The *Totentanz,* for instance, I never heard better. And he looked so strange! He looked like a devil. I didn't remember!

JH / "The competition ran for three days because of the large number of participants. It was a dull affair. We heard immature playing and often a complete lack of musical gifts. Then, on the third day, a pianist appeared whose name was already well known in the concert field—Claudio Arrau. It did not take two minutes of his playing before we began nodding to each other, smiling with satisfaction. *'Cela c'est un pianiste,'* said Cortot. He received the prize, which was a Bechstein concert grand. . . ."

CA / No! [Laughs.] *Noooooo!* I don't even remember *what* the prize was. But it was certainly not a piano!

JH / "I had first heard about his talent in Chile, where he had been a child prodigy, so I was wondering why he entered this competition. It was like a race between a thoroughbred and some cart horses. After it was over Schelling gave us a supper in his sumptuous villa on the lake."*

CA / Schelling was on the jury, that I remember. Schelling and Pembauer and Cortot and Vianna da Motta. Well, I have been robbed of a Bechstein piano!

JH / This shows a remarkable gap between the way you saw yourself and the way others saw you. Unbelievable—that the judges, even before the competition began, thought it was a foregone conclusion you would win; and that you were convinced, even after the competition was over, that you would lose.

*Arthur Rubinstein, *My Many Years* (New York: Knopf, 1980), p. 242.

CA / In 1927 that was my psychological situation.

JH / What was the result of the competition? Did you get engagements?

CA / Yes, I got quite a lot of good engagements.

JH / In 1935–36 you performed the complete clavier works of Bach in twelve recitals in Berlin. By this time, were you still worrying about your career, and getting engagements?

CA / Yes.

JH / How did the Bach recitals come about?

CA / There were two aspects. First, I had this eagerness to understand fully the musical language of a composer. That was the first push toward memorizing and playing the complete clavier output of Bach. And then I think there was also a wish to do something outstanding, that would prove what a serious musician I was. Because at that time people were saying that I was a very good technician, but rather the virtuoso type. That was the second aspect—to help my career. But the first idea was to have the *satisfaction* of having in my brain this tremendous amount of great music. People said "Is it a stunt?" A little bit, maybe, it was. But mostly not.

JH / How did the concerts go?

CA / I had a memory slip in one of the partitas; I had practiced so much I was absolutely exhausted. So I decided to reschedule a few of the concerts—I think it was two or three. Anyway, they were a sensation. They took place in the Meistersaal in Berlin, which held about five hundred people, and they were sold out. I had a very clear idea in those days how to transfer Bach's music to the modern piano. Imitation of the harpsichord was out. On the other hand, there are certain things on the piano that are foreign to Bach's time—anything that is sensuous. And no pedaling except for what I call the inaudible pedal.

JH / When did you stop playing Bach in public?

CA / For the most part, very shortly after that. It was partly under the influence of the harpsichord, particularly of Landowska, whom I worshiped. I also had the idea that I should be a *pianist;* that I should only play things that were conceived for the piano, for the piano sound.

JH / You followed the Bach cycle with a Mozart cycle. Was it also successful?

CA / Yes. Not as successful as the Bach, because it wasn't such a feat of memory. Some people resented the amount of sound that I used, and the contrasts, the espressivo. I wanted to really give as much expression as the singers do in his operas.

JH / Up to the point when you left Germany, how well established did you feel you had become?

CA / I was quite well established by then, and not only in Germany.

JH / So when would you say it was that your career anxieties were more or less put aside?

CA / You know, I had always had this *tremendous* frustration with German audiences. Because—silly enough—I thought probably they understood more, and that's why they didn't accept me. Then, when I finally was accepted by the Germans, it coincided with the Nazis. The early thirties. That's why we stayed after they took over—that, and the fact that, like so many people, we couldn't believe the Nazi period could last. I was so eager to enjoy being finally acknowledged. From then on I felt happy about my career. But naturally with still the mountain to be conquered—the United States.

JH / It was about this time that you married.

CA / I married rather late. In 1937, when I was thirty-four. Like so many young men between the world wars, I went from one woman to another, always disappointed. When I met Ruth, I had the feeling this was it. You know, she was starting a career as a singer. She was just studying *Carmen.* It was her decision to stop. She thought a marriage couldn't function with two artists who were always traveling in different places.

JH / This was the first time you lived without your mother.

CA / Yes. Ruth and I bought an apartment. My mother stayed with my sister and her daughter.

JH / Was your mother jealous?

CA / Well, probably. But she never let it be known or noticed. She had been complaining that it was time for me to marry. At first, it was quite difficult to move away.

JH / Was it something that you had been intending to do for a long time?

CA / I had been thinking that I should cut the umbilical cord.

JH / Did you ever consider moving away and living by yourself as a bachelor?

CA / Well, I thought about it but I didn't really have a *reason*, because my mother was so kind and understanding.

JH / When did you all leave Germany?

CA / I left in 1940. My mother left in one ship with my sister's daughter in 1938. Next, my sister left. Then I left because I had concerts in South America. But Ruth had become pregnant for the second time. And because of the way the baby was located, pressing on a nerve, she couldn't leave until early 1941, after Mario was born. The Chilean embassy arranged for her to get a passport. To get it legally she would have had to have lived in Chile for five years. So the passport said she had been born in Valdivia. I must have been in South America about ten months before she arrived with the two babies. I met them in Buenos Aires, and then we found an apartment in Santiago.

JH / Musicians you admired, such as Furtwängler, chose to stay behind in Germany. Were you torn between your allegiance to German culture and . . .

CA / I was torn between the *satisfaction* of being recognized in Germany, and the *horrors* that were happening there. I lived in a *rage*. All the social achievements of the parties of the Left were destroyed. And the culture of the theaters, the opera houses, the concert halls—everything was destroyed in a period of months. The sensitivity of the audiences to a great extent also disappeared.

JH / Do you regret not having left earlier?

CA / Probably I would have been frustrated, not having achieved complete acceptance from German audiences. Even though I probably would have achieved it anyway, after the war—I still would have felt frustrated.

JH / When you left Germany, did you know where you would live?

CA / Absolutely not. We didn't have any plans. We were going to see what happened. And then I came to the United States alone, to try it again. That was another frustration—that I hadn't been successful in America. The first concert was in Town Hall. And the review was just ridiculous, worse than in 1923. You see, nobody knew *at all* who I was, even in 1941. And I gave a very good recital, with a Bach partita and Brahms and the *Pictures at an Exhibition*, which in those days was one of my best things.

JH / The review in the *Times* wasn't really so bad. But it was very short. I'll read it to you. The date is January 26, 1941.

Claudio Arrau, Chilean pianist, who made his debut here seventeen [*sic*] years ago, but who has not played in this country since 1926 [*sic*], returned yesterday to give a recital at the Town Hall. His program was a formidable one. There was not a small work on it, just four major compositions, Bach's C-minor Partita, Beethoven's Sonata in C major, Op. 2, no. 3, Brahms's Variations and Fugue on a Theme of Handel, and Mussorgsky's *Pictures at an Exhibition*.

Mr. Arrau has an individual manner of playing. He places his piano at a slight angle from the listener and sits very close to it, bent far over the keyboard; and while his left elbow is kept close to his side his right one is lifted high. His interpretations also bore the stamp of his individuality, for they were carefully thought out and personal in nature.

Mr. Arrau's program, however, was not one in which he could do himself full justice, for he excels in quick, clear, delicate playing, but he is not able to obtain great sonorities, which meant that the Brahms and the Mussorgsky both went outside his dynamic range. Besides, his concentration is so intense that a succession of three works each a half hour in length became tiring for the listener. . . .

CA / Oh. Tiring for the listener. That's something that had to be considered in those days. They told me that I had *ruined* the early part of my career by playing programs that were *far* too long. And far too heavy. NCAC* told me that.

JH / The review continues:

> The recital would have been more satisfactory if there had been more selections like the Debussy Danse and the Chopin-Liszt *Chanson-polonaise* [*sic*], which he played as encores, for these were played beautifully and Mr. Arrau at his best is a pianist to be reckoned with, for he has something to say and he has a fine sensitivity for both his instrument and his art. R. P.

That's Ross Parmenter.

CA / You know, that was one of the best concerts of my entire career. It was a tremendous success with the audience. Many people still talk to me about this concert.

JH / Then, on February 19, you gave a Carnegie Hall recital. And that was your first big American success.

CA / I think I played one of my best *Carnavals*.

JH / Both Noel Strauss, in the *Times,* and Robert Lawrence, in the *New York Herald Tribune,* described it as the best *Carnaval* they had ever heard. You wound up with an avalanche of engagements.

CA / It must have been more than fifty. I played with the Boston Symphony, the Chicago Symphony . . .

JH / Is this when you decided to move to the United States?

CA / Yes. We moved to the United States right away, so that I could make some money. The move was quite complicated, because the American authorities found out that Ruth was born in Frankfurt, not Valdivia. But the Chileans allowed her to keep her Chilean passport. We went to Peru first, where I had concerts. From there we went to Ecuador, with concerts—the four

---

*National Concert and Artists Corporation, Arrau's American management in the forties.

of us, plus a Chilean nurse. Then Colombia, with concerts. Then Panama, with concerts. Then Guatemala, then Mexico. And then from Mexico by train to New York. At first we lived in hotels. Then we had a house in Forest Hills. We moved here to Douglaston in 1947.

JH / Acclaim in the United States—why was that so important to you? Some artists with great names in Europe—Fischer, Knappertsbusch, Kempff—have been little known in America.

CA / Somehow I had a *tremendous* admiration for this country, and for what it stood. I felt very strongly that it was the future and that Europe was like a museum—which is not at all true; Europe has a great power of renewal. I don't know from where it came. But I was very happy that I could make a living in the United States.

JH / Did you feel it was a reflection on your playing that you had not been successful here before? I mean, did you seek success here as some sort of confirmation of your stature in your own eyes?

CA / That also.

JH / How important was it for you, in the forties, to be famous, acclaimed, celebrated?

CA / Very important.

JH / How do you account for that?

CA / Probably in the first part of one's life performing in public is partly self-confirmation. And then of course the more you become self-centered, in the positive sense, the more it disappears. Although it never disappears completely.

JH / Does striving for self-confirmation ever get in the way of artistic striving?

CA / It is dangerous. But if you are really serious-minded, then you overcome the danger. I have always taken things very seriously. I would have never been satisfied with a success based on playing down to audiences. I would never have forgiven myself.

JH / I want to ask you one final question on the subject of making a career. To what degree, once you moved to the United States, did you feel you were operating in an alien musical culture; that figures like Toscanini, Heifetz, Horowitz, Koussevitzky, Stokowski—who were so celebrated in the United States compared to Furtwängler or Fischer—were outside your musical orbit?

CA / I felt very much like an alien, musically. I remember my reaction when I first came here was that the standards by which people judged musicians were *impossible.* The programs—things like *Kreisleriana* and the *Davidsbündlertänze* you *simply couldn't play.* The managers would warn you. And the Schumann concerto was considered suicide. And the pianists who were famous—Paderewski! You can't imagine how it was.

JH / And some careers were buried here.

CA / Adolf Busch! They *never* recognized him. And you know when Furtwängler came he was torn to pieces.

JH / He was compared unfavorably to Toscanini.

CA / Always. Toscanini was the measure. For a time, I felt completely lost.

JH / Of the Germans, you and Serkin were able to break through. And there was Stock in Chicago.

CA / He was very good. He was a serious musician.

JH / And Schnabel, of course. For some reason he was recognized at an early stage.

CA / It was the political aspect—that he had to leave Germany, and so on. He was almost a refugee.

JH / Toscanini's stature in this country was certainly enhanced by politics—refusing to conduct in Bayreuth and Salzburg, not playing the Fascist anthem in Italy. In order to boost its cultural self-esteem, the United States needed to appropriate such a musician—someone who was both famous and politically correct. The line was "Toscanini's ours, and he's better than anyone else," "the world's greatest conductor," "the greatest conductor in history." He was a symptom of the provincialism of American musical culture. You could graph the posthumous ascent of Furtwängler's American reputation in terms of the decline of the provincialism that made Toscanini into such a god.

CA / Furtwängler's ascent in the last five or ten years—that's a marvelous confirmation of what has happened here.

JH / But still Fischer is not that well known.

CA / I wonder what would have happened if Fischer had conquered his fear of crossing the ocean.

JH / What do you think?

CA / I don't think he would have had a success in those days. Now, yes.

JH / Even in 1950, he would have had no great success in America?

CA / I don't think so.

JH / Kempff, too, is an artist who isn't sufficiently known in the United States.

CA / But many people have his records, no?

JH / In fact, most of his records are out of print here.

CA / Probably if he would come now, and be ten years younger, he would be acclaimed.

JH / Did you ever hear Toscanini in concert?

CA / Yes.

JH / And you didn't like him?

CA / Not *at all.*

JH / Paul Badura-Skoda, who has the same musical orientation you do, once told me that despite his prejudices he had to find Toscanini remarkable when he finally heard him conduct at Carnegie Hall. He thought the sound was extraordinary.

CA / Sound, rhythm, and precision. And a certain transparency. People said, "Oh, here is a melodic line we have never heard before." But when it came to real *interpretation,* it *wasn't there.* He couldn't begin to do what Furtwängler did with the *Great* Schubert C-major Symphony—give you the depth and the anguish along with the musical shape.

JH / What about in Italian opera?

CA / *Neither.* I mean I heard a *Tosca* at La Scala with Claudia Muzio that I didn't like *at all.* It was *too fast.* The singers couldn't *breathe.* That was in the twenties. And *Lucia* I didn't like *at all.*

JH / Did you ever meet Toscanini?

CA / Yes. He came to a rehearsal when I played with Kleiber and the NBC Symphony. Toscanini and Kleiber were sort of friends; Kleiber admired him very much. That was in the forties.

JH / Did you find him charismatic when you met him?

CA / I thought he was very impressive. He was incredibly beautiful. The structure of his face was unbelievable.

JH / He had a great drive, too. A pure fire.

CA / Yes, *Tannhäuser.* The Venusberg music. That was fantastic.

JH / Oh, you liked something he did?

CA / [Laughing.] Yes. It was the only thing that I liked. When you talk about drive, that was really tremendous.

# Remembering Berlin

"Weimar Germany" is a catch phrase for political decay and cultural efflorescence. Dada, Expressionism, and the Bauhaus flourished there. *The Cabinet of Dr. Caligari, The Magic Mountain,* and *The Threepenny Opera* are among its surviving artifacts. Its pantheon of heroes includes Brecht and Mann, Piscator and Reinhardt, Einstein and Köhler, Gropius and Moholy-Nagy, Grosz and Kandinsky.*

Weimar was where the German republic was promulgated in 1919, but Berlin was the hub. "Berlin was a magnet," writes Peter Gay in *Weimar Culture.* "The old Berlin had been impressive, the new Berlin was irresistible. To go to Berlin was the aspiration of the composer, the journalist, the actor; with its superb orchestras, its hundred and twenty newspapers, its forty theatres, Berlin was the place for the ambitious, the energetic, the talented. Wherever they started, it was in Berlin that they became, and Berlin that made them, famous. . . . Berlin was eminently the city in which the outsider could make his home and extend his talents."†

Alfred Kerr, the powerful Berlin drama critic, called the city's culture boom a new Periclean age, according to Bruno Walter in his autobiographical *Theme and Variations.* "What the Berlin theaters accomplished in those days could hardly be surpassed in talent, vitality, loftiness of intention, and variety," Walter continues. "There was a great deal of experimenting. There were oddities, and occasionally even absurdities, but the common denominator, the characteristic sign of those days, was an unparal-

*As exiles, Piscator and Grosz were the two previous occupants of Arrau's present house in Douglaston.
†Peter Gay, *Weimar Culture* (New York: Harper & Row, 1970), pp. 128–131.

81

leled mental alertness. And the alertness of the giving corresponded to the alertness of the receiving. A passionate general concentration upon cultural life prevailed, eloquently expressed by the large space devoted to art by the daily newspapers in spite of the political excitement of the times."*

With its orchestras, opera houses, and conservatories, Berlin devoured music. Ferruccio Busoni (1866–1924), who moved there in 1894, was the musical guru of the early Weimar years—as pianist, composer, and teacher of composition at the Academy of Arts, where his worshipful pupils included Kurt Weill (1900–1950—himself for a time Arrau's composition teacher). When Busoni died, his class at the academy was passed to Arnold Schoenberg (1874–1951). Wilhelm Furtwängler (1886–1954) took over the Berlin Philharmonic in 1922. Artur Schnabel (1882–1951), who moved to Berlin in 1922, was regarded as the leading Beethoven pianist of Furtwängler's generation. His antipode, the reckless Edwin Fischer (1886–1960), took up residence in Berlin in 1904.

Arrau, whose memories of Berlin culture make up the following conversation, first met Fischer when the latter was assisting Martin Krause at the Stern Conservatory. (In the memorial volume *Dank an Edwin Fischer,* Fischer is quoted recounting his astonishment when the Chilean child, whom he misidentifies as a seven-year-old, inquired, "What would you like to hear? I know all of Bach."†) The Busoni Mozart concerto performances that Arrau refers to took place in 1921, when Busoni's Mozart binge was the talk of the city. Arrau also reminisces about two fiery woman pianists from the pre-Weimar period—Sophie Menter (1846–1918), said to have been Liszt's favorite female pupil, and Teresa Carreño (1853–1917), whose teachers included Gottschalk and Anton Rubinstein, and whose four husbands included another great Berlin pianist, Eugène d'Albert (1864–1932).

Carreño was so seminal an inspiration for the young Arrau, and in some respects so recognizable a model, that more must be said of her here. She was Venezuelan but achieved her greatest success in Germany, where she lived for more than thirty years and was known as the *"Walküre* of the piano." In 1913, Walter Nie-

*Bruno Walter, *Theme and Variations* (New York: Knopf, 1946), p. 268.
†*Dank an Edwin Fischer* (Wiesbaden: F. A. Brockhaus, 1962), p. 29.

mann, the well-known author and critic, composed a tribute to Carreño in honor of her sixtieth birthday. Niemann's description of her sound and technical apparatus documents parallels to Arrau's playing and corroborates Arrau's observations of Carreño's physical method in what follows and also in his discussion in "Piano Technique." (See pages 90 and 110.)

I paint two pictures of Carreño's playing. It has never seen its equal in virility and hypnotic power. The first is the Carreño of the 1880's and 1890's, the second the Carreño of today. . . .

The playing of Carreño combines extreme exploitation of force, of masculine sculpting of the tone, with the utmost lightness and elasticity of the entire playing mechanism. Hence her unbelievable endurance and joy in playing, her enormous, inexhaustible strength. Hence her thundering octaves, which she shakes out of her sleeve; her staccato filed to the sharpest point; the sheen, the intensity, and the evenness of her passages; the iron heaviness of her chordal effects (introduction of the B-flat minor Concerto of Tchaikovsky), inspired by the most fiery of temperaments. . . .

Whoever is acquainted with the hard, stinging, and pointed fortes of so many of our younger and young pianists—the concert tone of Liszt misunderstood—breathes afresh when he hears a fortissimo of iron power, yet of absolute beauty and fullness. Royal dignity, aristocratic pride, that is the realm in which this queen of pianists reigns most freely. The great heroic concertos (Beethoven E flat, Liszt E flat, Rubinstein D minor, Tchaikovsky B-flat minor), the polonaises of Chopin and Liszt, the great heroic sonatas from Beethoven to Chopin, Liszt and MacDowell, the "Erlkönig" of Schubert-Liszt, Schubert-Tausig's *Marche militaire,* Chopin's great concert etudes are therefore the blazing highlights of a Carreño evening. . . .

This was characteristic of the Carreño evenings of the eighties or nineties. In them the name of Carreño shone over the whole world. . . .

The Carreño of today has become a different but not a lesser person. D'Albert appears to have signed himself over to pianistic pugilism. . . . How differently, how much more wholly the playing of Carreño has ripened up to the time of golden autumn! Clarified maturity, human as well as artistic, sublimates her playing in a wonderfully appealing and personal way. Today she delights in quiet breadth, still, thoughtful contemplation, loving care for detail, fine technical polish, measure and harmony in everything. . . .

This heavy, golden harvest of autumn shows its fruits in many lights. Such pieces in the grand style as Chopin's Ballade in G minor, or the second movement of Schumann's Fantasy in C major, show, even in respect to temperament, the Carreño of old. Chopin remains the master in whose music Carreño's natural diminution of temperament and fire is compensated for by intensity of inner feeling. It is in Beethoven that her playing shows the most clarification, embodying an objectivity bordering on the classical. . . .

That is the Carreño of today. The Carreño of once upon a time, mistress of the musical alfresco, was the darling of the masses. The Carreño of today, mistress of the landscape, of intimate storytelling, is the darling of connoisseurs and gourmets of the piano. And that is not a step backward, but forward. . . . And so the Carreño of today remains equally to be honored as the Carreño of old, whose volcanic temperament forced the old and new world into the spell of her enchantment. We greet you, maestra and queen of pianists, from the heart!*

CA / Going to Germany was tremendously healthy for me, spiritually. I developed all sorts of abilities I wouldn't have developed if I had gone to France, for instance. The musical world in France is more restrained than in Germany. I would have probably become something like Cortot. Cortot was absolutely marvelous, I adored him. But he couldn't play German music. Maybe Schumann a little bit. But he couldn't play Brahms at all, or Beethoven. His Beethoven was sentimental. I remember how he played the First Concerto. It was not right at all. Much too sweet.

JH / Suppose you had been sent to Vienna at the age of eight.

*Adapted from Marta Milinowski's translation from the German, in Milinowski, *Teresa Carreño* (New Haven: Yale University Press, 1940), pp. 391–4.

CA / Vienna. That would also have been very bad. You know, there has never been a really great Beethoven interpreter in Vienna. Recently, yes, but before the musical world in Vienna was very limited. The people who had success were people like Emil von Sauer. He played Chopin waltzes very nicely.

JH / He played Liszt. He recorded the two concertos. But he must have been very old then.

CA / He was past seventy-five. It's not fair to judge him from that. But I heard him do the two Liszt concertos. In one concert. They lacked heroic quality. And then one of the most successful pianists in Vienna was Alfred Grünfeld. He played elegantly, cutely. And the Viennese went crazy about him.

JH / Mahler was important in Vienna, and he was a musician of stature. But then he didn't get along with the Viennese.

CA / That's why. I remember, all the great German pianists had no success. Edwin Fischer—empty houses. Gieseking—empty houses. But Mr. Grünfeld—sold out.

JH / How about Backhaus?

CA / Backhaus toward the end of his life became popular in Vienna. But not before. *Schnabel* never had an audience in Vienna. And he was Austrian.

JH / Might you have been sent to England to study?

CA / No one went to London to study music in those days. It was either Germany or Vienna. Some went to Italy. Or to France— to learn at the Conservatoire was thought to be fantastic.

JH / Who decided where you went?

CA / It must have been my mother, and the rest of the family. Fortunately, they had good sense.

JH / Why did they choose Germany?

CA / Berlin, from the time we arrived in 1911 until Hitler, was the center of the music world. During the Weimar period, which I remember the best, there was the marvelous Philharmonic Orchestra, with Furtwängler. There were the four opera houses, all on an incredibly high level: Unter den Linden, which had Furtwängler and Kleiber, the Kroll Opera with Klemperer, the

Charlottenburg Opera with Bruno Walter, and the Volksoper with Leo Blech. There was a healthy competition between the four opera houses. Klemperer did many experimental stagings at the Kroll Opera.

JH / How was Klemperer as a conductor in those days?

CA / I found everything too fast. In those days, at least, he was fast. Particularly in Mozart—*Don Giovanni* was over in a *wink*. He said one thing I recall. He said he divided pianists into those who are capable of playing slow sixteenth-notes and those who are not. That was his test for pianists.

JH / We've already mentioned your Berlin Philharmonic debut under Muck in 1920. Who were some of the other conductors you performed with in Berlin?

CA / Who was there? I liked Mengelberg. Him I played with many times. He was crazy. In the Chopin E-minor Concerto, he followed beautifully. All the rubatos. And when I changed something, he was always there.

JH / I've heard you say that the best Chopin accompaniment you ever had was from Furtwängler. Was that also in the E-minor Concerto?

CA / Yes. He was a marvelous pianist himself. Very sensitive.

JH / What set Furtwängler apart?

CA / The intensity, the drive, the freedom, the depth. Furtwängler was as great in Debussy as he was in Bruckner and Brahms and Beethoven and Wagner. He did a wonderful performance of the Schoenberg Five Pieces. All that he touched became gold. Liszt, *Les Préludes*—my God! I was completely swept away by everything he did. *Tristan und Isolde! Otello!*

JH / Busoni was another of your idols. Did you hear him play often?

CA / Quite a few times. Unforgettable, the Mozart piano concertos.

JH / What was his Mozart like?

86

CA / Different from any Mozart you have heard. Always dramatic, driven. He had his own ideas about everything. You could never say to a pupil, "That's the way this concerto should be played." But it was so marvelously done, and so creatively, that you had to accept it. Not as a final interpretation. But it was incredible. I also remember an incomparable Liszt sonata, and an incomparable *Hammerklavier*.

JH / Arthur Rubinstein, in the first volume of his autobiography, says of Busoni:

> Ferruccio Busoni, with his handsome, pale, Christlike face, and his diabolical technical prowess, was by far the most interesting pianist alive. When he played Bach, his uncanny touch could produce at one moment the sonorities of an organ, at another those of a harpsichord, an ideal combination. His temperament and his complete mastery were such that his performances of Liszt's works were unsurpassed, and he managed to make them sound even more important than they actually were. When he played the famous *Campanella*, it became a breathtaking experience, although his Beethoven and Chopin, I must admit, left me entirely cold. To my amazement, he would approach Beethoven's last sonatas in a sarcastic mood, taking great liberties with tempi and rhythm, while his Chopin, always technically brilliant, lacked the warmth and tenderness so important in his works.*

CA / In Chopin, the preludes, as played by Busoni, were incredible. Not the usual Chopin, perfumed. But it was very beautiful. A little shocking, yes, but so exciting and new.

JH / What of this remark of Rubinstein's, that the late Beethoven sonatas—

CA / Excuse me, but that's ridiculous. Great liberties, yes— that's how they should be played, the late sonatas. But sarcastic?

JH / What about Busoni's Bach?

CA / His Bach was orchestral, and sensuous in sound. I didn't like it. And he played mostly his own transcriptions. I found it theatrical. You know, my Italian teacher, Rita Bötticher, was a

*Arthur Rubinstein, *My Young Years* (New York: Knopf, 1973), p. 31.

close friend of Busoni's. She went to one of my Bach recitals in 1935, and didn't like it *at all*. "It's academic!" she said. "Why don't you use your imagination? Why don't you use the pedal?"

JH / The most evocative description I know of Busoni's playing is Edward Dent's. He says of Busoni's performances of the late Beethoven sonatas:

> To hear him play these sonatas was an almost terrifying ex-perience; dynamic and rhythmic relations were treated with such vast breadth and freedom that one seemed taken up to heights of perilous dizziness and made, as it were, to gaze steadily into the depths until one's vision became serene. The last and loftiest plane of serenity was reached in the arietta and variations of the Sonata in C minor. As he was playing it in London, an elderly critic leaned over the shoul-der of a younger colleague and remarked in a stage whisper, "D'you know, I believe the man's drunk!"*

CA / If drunkenness, then drunkenness as Goethe said—drunk-enness without wine. Creative drunkenness. You would get mo-ments like that.

JH / Was Busoni considered the leading musical personality in Berlin?

CA / Yes, I would say. Along with Furtwängler.

JH / Judging from his recordings, Furtwängler, too, could seem drunk with feeling. It's as if his spirit were inhabited by another.

CA / Exactly. It is being possessed.

JH / Do you think this was a more common artistic phenomenon when you lived in Berlin than it is today?

CA / Yes. Also in the theater all the great actors had this ability to the greatest extent possible. You believed they had become the person they were playing.

JH / What happened? What's different now?

CA / Artists are afraid. They are scared of any kind of commit-ment. And the young people are all afraid of emotion.

---

*Edward J. Dent, *Ferruccio Busoni* (London: Eulenburg, 1974), p. 261.

JH / Who were some of the other musicians in Berlin who seemed "possessed" when they performed?

CA / Edwin Fischer, definitely. Very seldom on his records. But he had this divinatory quality. Oh, he had it to an incredible extent. Another was Eduard Erdmann, a pianist nobody knows in this country. He was also possessed when he played, completely in another world. Just before he died, he recorded the last three Schubert sonatas. It's not *at all* like he was in concert. He was said to be terribly nervous in front of the microphone. Still, they are very beautiful recordings. Once I heard Erdmann and Gieseking play a four-hand recital. It was so *funny*—both fellows, you know, were giants, with big hands and long arms. And they both started snorting and making other incredible noises—particularly in Schubert, because they were so excited. It was beautiful playing. But people were actually tittering a little bit.

JH / Did you admire Gieseking?

CA / Sometimes. Unforgettable were *Kreisleriana, Davidsbündlertänze,* the *Bach* Variations by Reger. Those three—unforgettable. You know, he wasn't a man to study much. He left everything to the intuition. Sometimes it worked and sometimes not. But his sound was out of place in Beethoven, I thought. And I didn't appreciate him very much as an interpreter of Debussy— which might sound strange, because he was so well known as a Debussy interpreter. The immaterial pianissimos were fantastic. But he stayed on the level of sound. I admired Erdmann much more as a musician.

JH / Edwin Fischer studied with Martin Krause. Were the two of you students at the same time?

CA / He was just finishing his studies when I started with Krause. I worshiped him from the beginning. I couldn't look at him as a pupil, although he was one. He didn't have very much technique, you know. But you didn't care. There was this group of pianists who considered preoccupation with technique to be superficial. Kempff also believed that. I don't think he ever practiced, or studied exercises. Erdmann neither. Schnabel neither. Elly Ney neither. They all considered it undignified. I remember there was always this argument between Krause and Fischer. Krause said, "Why don't you practice? Do some exercises." But they wanted to make music.

JH / You can see their point.

CA / Yes, it's a marvelous attitude. But it's also a little amateurish.

JH / Let's speak about Schnabel. You once told me that in Berlin he was a much tidier pianist than he later became.

CA / He was flawless. I think the change must have come after his first bad experiences with the Nazis, before he left Germany. It was then that all these technical difficulties started, and all these memory mistakes. And he got this neurotic thing in his playing that was very bad—impulsive rushing. The more difficult the music got technically, the more he rushed, which is a neurotic reaction—to get through faster. Yes, it was terrible afterward. That would *never* happen before. He was flawless, always. And he had a lot of technique. I heard him do the Konzertstück of Weber, *beautifully*. And the First Chopin Concerto—that sounded like Bach, but pianistically it was beautiful.

JH / I know you particularly admired Teresa Carreño.

CA / [whispering] Oh, she was a goddess. She had this unbelievable drive, this power. I don't think I ever heard anyone fill the Berlin Philharmonie, the old hall, with such a sound. And her octaves were *fantastic*. I don't think there's anyone today who can play such octaves. The speed and the power.

JH / What about Horowitz's octaves?

CA / Horowitz never plays octaves for a long stretch—after a while he gets stiff. Carreño would play Liszt's *Hungarian Rhapsody* No. 6 without cuts, and at the end you thought the house would come down, would cave in from the sound. Carreño could be said to be a mixture of Latin feeling and German training. She studied in France first. Later, she changed completely, and learned a lot from her husband Eugène d'Albert. She became a very good Beethoven player. She was a better pianist than d'Albert himself, although he was probably the greater musician. I remember she played once with Nikisch the Third, Fourth and Fifth Beethoven Concertos in one evening. With her you never had the feeling she would get tired, or less intense. And she was a great beauty. I would always sit in the first row at her concerts. She would come on beaming, as if she were very happy to play. She didn't wear any sleeves, and you could see her muscles— how strong and relaxed they were, and how incredibly they functioned, rippling and flowing. After the concerts they would take me to greet her. I remember one time when she said, "Oh, with all the children we have it's so difficult to practice. I have a *loaded gun* on my piano. And I have threatened all my children—if they *open the door,* I shoot."

J H / Busoni and Carreño were the two pianists who influenced you most?

C A / Those two. Carreño more than d'Albert, because he never practiced. He used to have a big technique. Then he started losing interest in piano playing in order to compose. And yet his performance of the Liszt sonata was still marvelous. Full of wrong notes, and missed passages. But the feeling was wonderful— coordinating the whole thing, with each idea coming out of the one before.

J H / In those days wrong notes didn't bother people so much?

C A / No. They thought it was genius.

J H / You mean they actually liked the wrong notes?

C A / Yes. That was the right of the genius.

J H / Who else had that right?

C A / Conrad Ansorge. A wonderful musician. Sometimes he would play nothing but wrong notes. I remember Krause saying, when one played wrong notes, "It's not important. It's not important. Go ahead."

J H / Recordings are certainly one reason that we don't accept wrong notes as readily as before.

C A / Yes, I think it's probably the main factor. And then there's this silly perfectionism that people appreciate too much. The other day a young pianist, a former pupil of mine, went to a concert of somebody, I won't mention the name. And I asked how it was, because I usually don't appreciate the particular pianist he had gone to hear. "It didn't mean anything, but it was perfection. Flawless. Not one wrong note the whole evening." Is that such a great thing?

JH / We're talking about a near revolution over the course of fifty years in the way people play and listen. D'Albert's recordings are astonishingly messy—no one could get away with that today. Cortot's wrong notes would not be acceptable today. Fischer would not be acceptable. The idea of Edwin Fischer making a modern phonograph recording is a contradiction in terms. Can you imagine? The producer would tell him, "Play the exposition again so we can correct the wrong notes." And he wouldn't be able to.

CA / That's true.

JH / And we don't have any Fischers or Cortots today. Nobody plays with that kind of freedom.

CA / Or that kind of nobility. *Ach!* It's the only word I can use for the few times I heard Fischer in complete control. One never had the feeling in performance of hearing a pianist. One heard a poet.

JH / Almost as if the piano were an avocation. Cortot's recordings give me the same feeling. I'm left with the impression here's a great musician who didn't have time to practice.

CA / Oh no, Cortot practiced a lot. D'Albert and Ansorge didn't practice. But Cortot knew exactly how to do everything. He wrote all those exercises. His problems, I think, were more psychological.

JH / What about all the celebrated pianists from Russia and Eastern Europe—Paderewski, Hofmann, Godowsky, Horowitz, Rachmaninoff? Did you hear them in Berlin, too?

CA / Oh yes, of course. One should talk about them, because this worship young people are taught today for these pianists, it's so unhealthy. It has nothing to do with reality. Paderewski was not a great pianist. A very famous one, but not great. Hofmann was another—I heard him many times. Godowsky was one of the greatest technicians, but his playing was boring. He never played very loudly—never above mezzo forte. Horowitz, he's a special case. Tremendous electricity. Him I would call a great pianist. I heard them all. I don't know if I should really be so outspoken.

JH / What about Rachmaninoff?

CA / Rachmaninoff was a really great pianist, but not a great interpreter, because he made everything into Rachmaninoff. He was a sensation in Berlin after the First World War. I heard a few recitals—it must have been in the twenties. Technically, he was phenomenal. But I thought the sound was not very good. And from the standpoint of interpretation, it was appalling. He didn't seem to care at all what the composer meant. He even added several bars of his own to the end of the *Funeral March* Sonata of Chopin. You know, once I played the Beethoven *Eroica* Variations in Chicago and Rachmaninoff came backstage during the intermission to tell me how beautiful it was. He had never heard of the piece before. He was very friendly, very complimentary. But he wasn't even surprised that he had never heard of it! The *Eroica* Variations!

JH / Horowitz, too, caused a sensation in Berlin. Did you hear his first concerts?

CA / Oh yes. We were both about twenty. I remember he played the four Chopin ballades, and the Liszt sonata, and the *Funeral March* Sonata of Chopin. He also played, very well, the Beethoven Thirty-two Variations. Oh, I was tremendously impressed by him. It was some of the most volcanic playing I've ever heard. I remember I was sitting with my mother in the first row of the Beethovensaal, and I was *amazed* by the things he could do in spite of this incredible stiffness of the arms. The first movement of the *Funeral March* Sonata I'll never forget. The second theme! My mother, who was very musical, and was never pleased with *anybody*—that night she was carried away. On our way home she said, "You better get to the piano and practice, because he plays better than you!" [Laughs.]

JH / Did you meet Horowitz while you were in Berlin?

CA / Never. I was too shy. I didn't know anybody personally.

JH / Were there any other pianists who made an especially potent impression on you in those days?

CA / Saint-Saëns! Leaning back with a big beard, and a huge belly, and playing the piano with *incredible* ease. I heard him play two of his own works with orchestra—the *Africa* Fantasy, and the *Wedding Cake*. The most even scales you can imagine, and great power in the fingers. Ice cold, but amazing. And then there was Sophie Menter, who was a very close friend of Martin Krause's. He took me to visit her once. She lived outside of Munich with fifty cats. She hated human beings, and she hated her daughter. I remember she had a huge garden surrounded by chicken wire, to keep the cats in. Anyway, she was a very impressive lady, still gorgeously beautiful. And still very elegant, with lots of marvelous jewelry. She told us that the jewels were given to her in Russia by royalty—while she was playing, people would rip off their jewels and throw them on the stage, at her feet. Krause asked her, "Please play something so that this boy can hear you." At first she resisted. Then she played excerpts from the A-major Liszt Concerto. She complained, "I don't play anymore, I don't practice." But it was very beautiful. She must have been about seventy.

JH / Are there any other memories of cultural life in Berlin that you care to mention?

CA / I was just thinking that in the twenties there was also a great dance movement that started in Berlin, with Mary Wigman. I think she inspired Martha Graham and the whole American modern movement. Before the war she would go every year to the United States with her company. Dance had a tremendous audience in Berlin. I remember once seeing [Gret] Palucca dancing in the stadium in Berlin, for maybe twenty thousand people. It was a sensation—she developed a special style, with the steps and gestures all bigger.

JH / I once heard Christopher Isherwood talk about audiences in Berlin between the wars. He said he was amazed when he remembered the level of intelligence he encountered even at the movies.

CA / The arguing that went on after the first showing of *The Cabinet of Dr. Caligari*! I don't know if such a thing will ever be repeated. And of course the audiences at concerts were very serious and attentive. As a matter of fact, I used to think that was the only way to listen to music. Later, I went to other countries and couldn't believe what I saw. In those days, mainly in Italy, but also in Spain, people would talk during a performance, or walk out and come back. In Berlin, it was totally different. I'm sure that the twenties in Berlin was one of the great blossomings of culture in history. The city offered so much in every field, and everything had a greater importance than in other places.

JH / Have you any idea why it took place—this cultural efflorescence?

CA / You see, there was a great misery. Many people were starving. There were no jobs. Such times are always fertile. Everything was so difficult that people sought a better life in culture.

JH / And of course you were close to that—the difficulty of daily life in Berlin.

CA / Oh yes. After my scholarship finished, we went through terribly difficult times. We were actually starving. We simply did not have a penny. My mother didn't speak any German. My sister did, but it was difficult even for Germans to get jobs. For foreigners, it was nearly impossible. I was trying to find pupils. I had to walk to their houses, because I didn't have five cents for the underground.

JH / So you really experienced the misery of that period.

CA / And I'm very glad I did.

# Piano Technique

In *Anatomy of an Illness*, an account of his recovery from a supposedly incurable disease, Norman Cousins spends a chapter pondering "Creativity and Longevity." Here he describes in some detail the daily regime of Pablo Casals, whom he visited in Puerto Rico a few weeks before Casals's ninetieth birthday. Upon rising in the morning, Cousins reports, Casals dressed with difficulty. He suffered from emphysema and apparent rheumatoid arthritis. "He was badly stooped. His head was pitched forward and he walked with a shuffle. His hands were swollen and his fingers were clenched." Then, playing Bach on the piano before breakfast, Casals's fingers unlocked, his back straightened, and he seemed to breathe more freely. Next, playing Brahms, "his fingers, now agile and powerful, raced across the keyboard with dazzling speed. His entire body seemed fused with the music; it was no longer stiff and shrunken but supple and graceful and completely freed of its arthritic coils." Having finished at the keyboard, Casals stood up, straighter and taller than before. "He walked to breakfast with no trace of a shuffle, ate heartily, talked animatedly, finished the meal, then went for a walk on the beach."*

For some years, Arrau has suffered from a stiffening of the neck that can make him look tired and unsteady onstage. But the piano anchors and recharges him. Sometimes, in the throes of protective concentration, his eyes harden and his head pushes forward and down. But the music, once it takes hold, is a visible relaxant. An hour later, he is sitting erect and gazing aloft.

His face, too, is transformed at the keyboard. The features, which can seem haggard and inert from nervous stress, catch fire.

---

*Norman Cousins, *Anatomy of an Illness* (New York: Norton, 1979), pp. 71–9.

Characteristically, they suggest a tragic mask: Arrau's lips droop and harden, and his eyebrows, which are feline, curl upward. At moments of climactic stress, his eyes burst wide and his breathing deepens and accelerates; he heaves the air in and out with audible force. And yet backstage, resplendent in his post-concert cape, his bearing is dapper and his countenance luminous, the anxiety having been burned away.

There are pianists in whom emotional tension mandates physical tension, constricting their hands. The style of others is supple digitally, but emotionally slack. Arrau's strange juxtaposition of clenched feeling with bodily resilience—he does not even perspire—helps explain his continued emotional and technical reserves. His sheer stamina can be exhilarating: following a Beethoven sonata, Schumann's *Symphonic Etudes*, a Debussy set, and Chopin's F-minor Fantasy, he launches Liszt's *Dante* Sonata, shaking out the trills and broken chords, gliding across the interlocking octaves. While the visceral knots are yanked taut, his body disgorges the passage-work with tireless equanimity. Two weeks before his seventy-eighth birthday, he performed the Fourth and Fifth Beethoven Concertos in three consecutive concerts— the equivalent of six concertos in three days—with Gerard Schwarz and his excellent Y Chamber Symphony in New York. Backstage after each concert, Arrau was radiant. Schwarz, forty-six years Arrau's junior, was flushed and wet. Four days later, by which time Arrau had already given two more *Emperors* in Montreal, Schwarz reflected: "I've never felt so tense as I did at those concerts. I never felt it was so difficult to go on stage as I did the first night. When I finished that concert, I had pulled a muscle in my left arm. I have no tension when I conduct—no back pains, nothing. But after that concert my left arm was destroyed. I still don't understand why it was so hard. Except that, to me, it seemed like an incredibly important event."

Arrau's balancing of intensity and repose is no accident: to his students he recommends a book, *Zen in the Art of Archery*, by Eugene Herrigel, exploring this correlation. For the Zen master who tutors Eugene Herrigel in archery, athletic prowess demands training in self-forgetfulness to revive the unmediated reflexes of childhood. Arrau's tortured face and desperate breathing are personal extravagances no Zen master would prescribe. Still, sentence after sentence of Herrigel's book illuminate the art of piano playing as expounded by Arrau:

> You must learn to let . . . your arm and shoulder muscles remain relaxed, as though they looked on impassively. Only when you can do this will you have fulfilled one of the conditions that make the drawing and the shooting "spiritual."

> The master followed my efforts attentively, quietly corrected my strained attitude, praised my enthusiasm, reproved me for wasting my strength, but otherwise let me be. Only, he always touched on a sore spot when, as I was drawing the bow, he called out to me to "Relax! Relax!"

> "Don't think of what you have to do, don't consider how to carry it out!" he exclaimed. "The shot will only go smoothly when it takes the archer himself by surprise."

> [The master said:] "I expect you above all not to let yourself be confused by the presence of spectators, but to go through the ceremony quite unperturbed, as though we were by ourselves."

Also pertinent are Herrigel's observations of Zen swordplay:

> The swordmaster . . . holds himself in reserve . . . without the least desire to show off.

> The reason [for failure] . . . is that the pupil cannot stop watching his opponent and his swordplay; that he is always thinking how he can best come at him, waiting for the moment when he is off his guard. In short, he relies all the time on his art and knowledge. By so doing . . . he loses his "presence of heart." . . . The more he tries to make the brilliance of his swordplay dependent on his own reflection, on the conscious utilization of his skill . . . the more he inhibits the free "working of the heart." How does skill become "spiritual," and how does sovereign control of technique turn into master swordplay? Only, so we are informed, by the pupils becoming purposeless and egoless.*

*Eugen Herrigel, *Zen in the Art of Archery* (New York: Vintage, 1971).

Arrau preaches against reliance on will. Uninstructed, the physical impulse is fluent and self-sufficient; not merely competent, but *creative*.

As a young man, Arrau relied on intuition; he moved on the piano, he says, "like a cat." Later, partly for his own purposes, partly as a teaching aid, he set up a mirror and even used film to study his own technique. His central observation was that pianists' bodies should be relaxed; that tense arms and shoulders, or—except where musically essential—steely fingers, impede self-expression. And his basic means of avoiding such tension, he observed, was reliance on natural body weight; rather than pressing down on the keys, he let gravity do the work for him.

In fact, closely observed, Arrau at the piano can resemble nothing so much as a dangling marionette. And he capitalizes on his mechanical freedom and versatility. Unlike many players, who favor a relatively fixed hand position, he sets his fingers, wrists, elbows, and shoulders at various angles and heights, and readjusts the levers and joints as needed. According to their volume, speed, and ease of access, he approaches trills, for instance, with his wrist high or low, stationary or rotating. Frequently his arm takes part in the trill as well: the entire cylinder, from fingers to shoulder, limp and limber as a rag doll's, turns on its axis. Sometimes he flattens his hand and depresses the keys with gentle strokes toward the body. Then, for a sudden accent, he makes the digits pistons, striking perpendicularly from a height. For additional volume, he tugs his hands down from the wrists. The doubled blow jars his shoulders and jerks his head back.

His fingerings, which are often idiosyncratic, document the flexibility of his joints. In the opening of Beethoven's *Pastoral* Sonata, the awkward connections binding the right-hand voices are secured without help from the pedal as follows:

In the first movement of the *Emperor* Concerto, he forces himself to articulate turns in thirds that are almost invariably smudged, adopting a laborious fingering few pianists would bother to think of or wish to risk:

His movements to and from the keys are never hectic. At a quick tempo with many notes at stake, his supple, economical address implies a slower speed: the preparations remain fluid and steadily paced. Characteristically, his lifted hand becomes a wedge, folded tightly at the knuckles and weighted at the finger-tips. As the hand falls, it unfurls—as a parachute might, or a fluttering handkerchief—until, open, it settles on the keyboard.

Beyond agility, stamina, and emotional freedom, Arrau's tech-nique confers a distinctive sound. The ten agile, individually weighted fingers, attached to rotating wrists that insure demo-cratic access, promote clarity and polyphony. The general reli-ance on body weight promotes tonal depth without stridence or roughness.

JH / Is there a certain type of piano sound that you seek to produce?

CA / The sound one produces without *hitting* the piano. Without hammering, which is ugly. This means the body must be relaxed, and one must use the weight of the entire upper part of the body. One of the first things I teach students is to drop the full weight of the arm. This means lifting the arm completely—not just from the elbow. You have to develop a feeling for the arm as a unity, not divided into hand, wrist, forearm, elbow. The arm should become a sort of snake. It is important, for instance, never to think of the action of the fingers as independent from the arm. That shouldn't exist.

JH / Does this make you feel more intimately bound to the key-board?

CA / Exactly. The idea is to become one with the instrument. Not to have the piano as a dead thing in front of you, to be *attacked*. Of course, sometimes you need power, and you must make the instrument produce it. But one must not brutalize the piano.

JH / What about the legato playing as an aspect of cultivating a nonpercussive sound?

CA / There are schools that say there is no legato on the piano. That's nonsense. What produces legato is of course not lifting the finger from the key until the next finger has struck the next key. The legato sound is something Martin Krause was keen to teach. He made his students practice without pedal. Legato technique is less practiced today, I think. Many times I have heard someone playing and thought, This is beautiful, but it sounds like Prokofiev, and it is supposed to be Beethoven.

JH / You have a passion for legato fingerings. When you play legato octaves, you not only connect the outer notes, but also the inner notes by crawling around with your thumb.

CA / I think this must be my own concept, because I have never even heard it mentioned by anyone else. I use a rotational movement with the thumb. [Demonstrating, Arrau makes his rubber-jointed right thumb crawl like a caterpillar from a white key to a black; the top joint ascends first while the bottom joint maintains contact with the white key.]

JH / Beyond connective fingerings, are there any particular principles you apply to legato passages?

CA / Never play two notes at the same dynamic. That's the only way you can imitate the human voice. For this, moving up and down with the arms, and to the sides, is very important. It is a question of discipline, of remembering that you have to sing. The notes must move in *waves*.

JH / Do you actually think in terms of hearing a singer, or being a singer?

CA / Krause did this. Particularly if somebody couldn't produce a cantabile, he would make them sing, and then copy on the piano what they had sung. I do this myself, when I study something and there is a section I don't quite understand. I sing to myself, again and again, until suddenly I can make it work on the piano. Singing has always interested me—not only the phrasing, but also the physical gestures of good operatic actors. When I was very young, we even had a little opera group, including Krause's daughters. I remember a performance we did of *Il trovatore*. I sang the baritone—the Count di Luna. We actually sang all the music except the choruses.

JH / When you suggest vocal phrasings at the piano, do you also try to imitate the breath span of a singer?

CA / Actually, in the music of the nineteenth century all the phrasings have to do with the movement of breathing.

JH / I know that you apply such principles not only to slow cantilenas, as in, say, the Chopin nocturnes, but to rapid legato figurations, as in the Chopin concertos, or the lyrical passage-work in the outer movements of the Beethoven G-major Concerto.

CA / To play such passages as rapid melodies is one of the things I always try to teach, and to do myself. The dynamic shadings are what give meaning to very fast passages; the notes cannot be played at an even dynamic. That is why I sometimes think it is wrong that for a hundred years people have tried to play scales as evenly as possible, as an ideal. Takatakataka—the typewriter approach. That's what they are all after.

JH / Is phrasing fast passages mainly a matter of finger strength?

CA / Also the position of the hand. You see, people used to never lift the wrist, and many young people still play that way. But the moment you are allowed to raise the wrist, along with the entire arm, the phrasing develops naturally; it takes care of itself. Really one should try to shade all passages, to do what the Germans call *"beseelen"*—to put your soul into it. The first movement of the Beethoven G-major Concerto, which you mentioned, is a very good example. You have to create meaning and atmosphere even in the left-hand arpeggios.

JH / You make a point of shaping passages in Chopin that are normally treated as filigree. I find this especially noticeable in your recordings of the G-minor Ballade.*

*E.g., in the scherzand section beginning at measure 138. By slowing down so emphatically in measure 141, and stressing the last of the six high G's in the right hand (measure 144), Arrau turns the usual filigree into a writhing melody that accumulates tension through reiteration.

CA / I don't think I've ever heard a decent performance of that ballade. The other ballades, I don't know why, are generally played better than the G minor. Pianists always divide it into lyrical sections, and those where suddenly they can run.

JH / Another example that occurs to me is the way you articulate the left-hand arpeggiated passages in the opening pages of the Liszt sonata; in many performances, they're just a blur.

CA / This also has to do with thinking polyphonically. And there are passages in those pages with completely different dynamics and articulation in the two hands. Sometimes one has to follow different dynamic lines even in one hand. When you are relaxed, it's much easier than with a stiff hand—you can simply lean to one side of the hand or the other.

JH / Pursuing the subject of polyphony, you have a way of playing chords so that the textures are full-bodied and active. Many pianists will bring out a middle voice in a chordal progression, but in such a way that there isn't very much else to listen to. You, in a sense, seem to voice everything.

CA / Exactly. Chords should never be filled octaves. Every note should be important.

JH / To what degree are you able to follow with your ear when you play a chordal progression? Is it necessary to hear every voice? I'm thinking, for instance, of your recording of the slow movement of Beethoven's *Funeral March* Sonata, in which the voicing is exceptionally rich.

CA / I would say it is necessary to follow every voice with the ear, providing that every voice is supposed to be heard. I mean, in Debussy many things are just to be hinted at. In the *Funeral March* Sonata, the slow movement is an ensemble. The voices are equivalent, but different, and the dynamic of one can go up and down, independent of the others. The middle voices in that movement are generally more important than the octaves; the octaves are more like a frame. Incidentally, were you surprised by my tempo in the last movement? It's played by many people like a Cramer etude. For me, the idea of the entire last movement is *das Keimen der jungen Natur* [the germination of young nature]—that after death there is a restarting of the flow of life. It should be kept in as slow a tempo as possible. Then the relationship between the Funeral March and the finale makes sense.

JH / One of the distinctive features of your playing, visually, is the way you will sometimes lift the entire upper half of your body before landing on a fortissimo chord—almost as if your arms and shoulders had been pulled up from above, and then released.

CA / Actually, I have three ways of striking such chords. One, which is the one you mentioned, is to begin with the fingers hanging just above the keys, then lifting the entire arm and dropping. The second is to begin touching the keys, and *yank* the arm weight down by suddenly pulling the elbows in. The third is to again begin with the fingers already touching the keys, and then pushing away, and up with the wrists.

JH / I have noticed that you will use the first method for a climactic chord at the end of a piece.

CA / Yes, because the tension is then over—that method produces less tension, and a fuller sound. In the first two cases, the higher you start, the more weight you have, and the more volume.

JH / These are all methods to get power without punching the keys.

CA / Yes, exactly.

JH / And also, in a sense, to interpret with the body.

CA / Yes. You reach a stage of development where these things are done automatically by the body. When the music has become part of you, when you have digested it, then these movements don't have to be thought about. At times, I feel very much like a dancer.

JH / Another one of your characteristic movements is to rotate the entire arm, as for a trill, rather than just the hand.

CA / Rotating the arm is very important for trills and broken octaves. There are also circular movements of the wrist, and vibrations of the arm. Sometimes, as in the arpeggios at the very end of the first movement of the Brahms D-minor Concerto, you have to use every possible means of making the piano come through the orchestra.

Analyzing it, there are three movements. One is to circle out with the arm and then come down on the tip of the thumb. And then, for the last two notes [A and D], rotation of the arm. And also, throughout, vibrating the arm. All these movements must be done with tremendous weight.

JH / Nobody seems to play the octave glissandos in the finale of the *Waldstein* Sonata as smoothly as you do. How do you make them sound so easy?

CA / It has to do first with the stretch—octave glissandos are comfortable for my hand. And of course it depends on the action of the piano. You know, the *Waldstein* was written for a piano with the old Viennese action, which made octave glissandos very easy. Sometimes I get to a hall where I am scheduled to play the *Waldstein*, and I find a piano on which the octave glissandos are impossible. Then I change the program. I won't play the *Waldstein* unless the piano responds.

JH / You mentioned the size of your stretch. Is there an ideal hand size for playing the piano?

CA / I think my hands are exceptionally good for the piano. I stretch eleven notes. From the index finger to the thumb, I can stretch an octave, easily. That makes skips much simpler. I can also stretch an octave, two to five. As far as I can judge from watching other people play, when the hands are bigger than mine they don't seem to have a sure feeling for the size of an octave. And some people have very thick fingers. Brahms is supposed to have had thick fingers—that's why he played so many wrong notes.

JH / Do you have any sense of your hands being a privileged part of your body?

CA / I do a lot of things that actually are dangerous for my hands— weeding with a sickle, for instance. I'm not fussy at all. It's important—otherwise you become self-conscious about the action of the hands.

JH / What about the size of your body. You're very compact. Do you think that's important?

CA / Yes. I think some people are better built for the piano than other people. On the other hand, the power of the spirit is sometimes so strong that it overcomes such difficulties. Many fine pianists have had a bad hand. The most incredible case is Alicia de Larrocha. Her hands are tiny; she hardly can stretch an octave.

JH / Do you maintain any type of physical regime to keep in shape as a pianist?

CA / Today, almost nothing. In former days, I did a lot of exercising. I even had a trainer in Berlin. We met several times a week in the stadium. One of the things we did a lot was to throw the medicine ball. Swimming I never liked. I did a lot of rowing. Even here [Douglaston], we had a boat from 1947 to 1950.

JH / When did you stop doing so much exercise?

CA / I was still using the medicine ball fifteen years ago, usually with pupils. We threw it down by the water. And in Vermont. I always wore boxing gloves with it. Otherwise the fingers are endangered. You can throw it many ways—above your head, from the side, turning around . . .

JH / It keeps you limber and loose.

CA / Exactly. And at the same time you're pushing quite a weight.

JH / One aspect of technique we haven't touched upon is stamina. How do you build up endurance so that the hands don't grow tired?

CA / Actually, the hands should never get tired. I don't know what it means, getting tired.

JH / You never experience cramps or stiffness?

CA / *Never.* To cramp is due either to psychological problems, or something in the way one plays, physically.

JH / How many hours at a time can you practice?

CA / I used to go up to fourteen hours. That was, for instance, practicing *Mazeppa*. Even my aunt, who loved music, came in after the thirteenth hour and said, "Darling, *please stop*. I'm going mad!" And I couldn't have cared less. That's when I was eighteen, nineteen. Another time I got a bill from a neighbor who had to go to a nerve sanatorium for six months. That must have been in the late 1920s. Today I usually practice two to three hours. Sometimes, when I am relearning something, or studying something I have never played, five to six. But that's very seldom.

JH / Don't you get tired practicing, say, the Liszt sonata? Even if your hands don't tire, doesn't it become emotionally exhausting?

CA / When I practice, I play almost without emotion. It's like being in a workshop.

JH / When you do play with emotion, in concert, is it more difficult to remain relaxed physically?

CA / That's one of the main problems in playing the piano—being able to stay physically relaxed in moments of great emotional tension. I have seen many cases where pianists, even famous ones, get completely stiff and cramped. Busoni had this strange theory that the less involved you were, the more it stirred the audience. I never understood that. Because I have always observed that when somebody seems perfectly balanced, emotionally, he gives the impression of being cold. And he is cold. I don't like that sort of dissociation.

JH / Another person might find it hard to understand how you can be so involved and relaxed at the same time.

CA / You see, that is becoming one with the music. You even become one with the audience. You can't *divide* things like that. Controlling the emotions—I don't think that's helpful.

JH / Do you ever feel emotionally exhausted after playing a concert?

CA / No.

JH / And you never feel physically exhausted afterward?

CA / Absolutely not. Sometimes, in fact, if I feel unwell or depressed beforehand, and think how on earth will I go through with this concert, the moment I get on stage I am another person.

JH / How do you go about warming up before a concert? You mentioned testing the octave glissandos in the *Waldstein*. Are there other passages in your repertoire that you always try out beforehand?

CA / No. Except for the octave glissandos, I never test pianos before a concert. That, too, was part of Krause's training. He said people who have to warm up before concerts have a technical problem—they are not relaxed. He always said if someone wakes you up at four o'clock in the morning and tells you you have to play a recital, then you must be able to do it—without warming up.

JH / Did Krause feel it was psychologically harmful to warm up before a recital?

CA / Yes, that it would make you nervous. I can't understand these people who practice until the very last minute. And it ruins something really marvelous about the experience—the spiritual energy you start out with.

JH / What precisely do you do before a concert?

CA / First of all, I always sleep—usually two hours. Rest is very important before a concert. And through sleep you get to the core of your creative subconscious. Then I like to get to the hall an hour before starting. And I wake up an hour before that—two hours before going on stage. Backstage, at the hall, I look at the music. I go through at least half the recital, mentally. Then at intermission I look at the rest. That way, when I go on stage, I have a feeling of elation—that something wonderful is going to happen to me.

JH / Does that mean there are times when you play an instrument you have never touched?

CA / Very often. Sometimes I prefer it. You see, the average piano, both in Europe and America, has improved tremendously. Also, through my fame—is that right to say?—people are much more considerate. Many times, I am either provided with a piano which I know, or a technician I trust is sent to work on the piano beforehand. So I can go to a concert now with the assurance that the piano will be of a certain quality. And then, I believe one should be able to adjust on stage, *instantaneously.* From the first chord, you should know immediately what kind of piano you are playing.

JH / One final question on technique. You've indicated that, while Krause always told you to relax, most of the specific technical principles you espouse were not acquired from Krause. When and how did you work these things out?

CA / It all became conscious long after Krause died. At first I played without thinking about technique, because I had this natural gift. Much later, I decided it was better to be conscious of how I played. I put a mirror next to my piano—it must have been when I was eighteen or nineteen. Then I began to notice the rotation, the vibration, the use of arm weight, and so on.

JH / Isn't there a considerable awareness, today, of the importance of natural body weight as an element of piano technique?

CA / Yes, but the fact is that today I don't know of *anybody* who plays using natural weight. Anybody, except in our group.* One of the first people to write about it was Rudolf Breithaupt, who taught at the Stern Conservatory in Berlin. I remember he once asked me to play for him, and while I was playing he began saying, "Yes, yes, yes! Exactly right!" [Laughs.] His books were widely read for at least twenty years. But nobody seems to remember them anymore. There was one fundamental problem in his teaching—he only taught arm weight. His pupils didn't develop their finger technique at all. Not Carreño, of course—she knew better. But the playing of the others was always messy. Breithaupt neglected absolutely the development of the finger muscles.

JH / When you say you don't see anybody playing with natural weight today, are you thinking of pianists from an earlier period who did?

---

*Arrau is referring to his students, his students' students, and students of Rafael de Silva, Olga Barabini, and others who have taught according to his principles.

CA / There was always Carreño. She played in an ideally natural way. She studied with Breithaupt when she was, I think, about forty-five. Before that she had been playing in the French way—with *jeu perlé,* and a stiff hand. She didn't have any power. Then she changed completely. I remember Carreño as a perfect example of natural weight technique.

# Interpretation

Arrau's South American tours of the late thirties and early forties were accorded newspaper tributes worthy of a returning favorite son, including excited interviews with the artist unlike anything likely to be found in the German daily press. Read back to back, these furnish a colorful sketch of Arrau's public persona in the early years of his marriage, by which time his career had rebounded from the traumatic post-Krause period.

His manner is called youthful, energetic, unpretentious; one 1939 account, in the Santiago newspaper *Ercilla*, ascribes to him "the air of the serene adolescent." A full-page 1939 interview in *Frente Popular*, a Santiago tabloid, includes these observations: "Claudio Arrau totally confounds those who look for something exotic in every artist. . . . Arrau appears to be a sportive type, buoyant and smiling, as he energetically gives us his hand. He has a good sense of humor and his conversation is vivacious, embellished with eloquent and sudden gestures. He is a man of today, modern, whose genius doesn't require—either in him or in his artistry—extravagance in order to make itself manifest."

An elaborate two-page interview appeared in 1941 in the Bogotá tabloid *La Razón*. In his hotel room, the newspaper reported, "Claudio Arrau is a good friend of everybody. Of the reporter, the photographer, the bellboy, of as many people as wish to talk to him, of as many spontaneous friends as wish to shake his hand. He exudes a striking natural gentility. He doesn't talk without accompanying his words with a gracious and amiable gesture, and each of his phrases has a cordial sentiment, a tone of friendship and simplicity."

The most informative feature of these two particular articles, however, is Arrau's own accounting of his artistic philosophy. Asked by the *Frente Popular* "How do you conceive of interpretation?" he answered: "There is arising in all art forms a new type of interpreter, a type that is the negation of the arbitrary artist, of the sensationalism that is such a product of the nineteenth century. I think that this phenomenon can be ascribed to a search today for a more sincere and just mode of interpretation. A work of art should not be a pretext for the artist to expel his feelings, let's say. Neither should one try to use the work to show oneself off; really, the interpreter has the sacred duty to render intact the thinking of the composer whose work he interprets."

And to *La Razón*, Arrau said: "I believe there exists a fundamental difference between the performers of today and those of the earlier artistic school, the generation that preceded ours. Before, the interpreters, the performers, had a concept of authorship that made them interpret in a way that was arbitrary and many times false, where the vanity of the performers came to loom larger than the goal of a faithful interpretation. . . . This seems to me to be very poisonous to art."

This version of Arrau's artistic credo, with its distinction between modern objectivity and the personal aggrandizement of an earlier period, suggests the historical setting for the interpretive principles he espouses in the conversation that follows. It should be remembered that, notwithstanding a popular stereotype that equates Weimar culture with Dr. Caligari and glitzy cabarets, Expressionism was already on the wane in interwar Berlin. A new, cooler aesthetic preferred practicality and self-discipline to passionate subjectivity. This was the *"Neue Sachlichkeit,"* usually translated "new objectivity" and connoting, as John Willett comments in his excellent *Art and Politics in the Weimar Period,* a network of ideals including "a neutral, sober, matter-of-fact approach, thus coming to embrace functionalism, utility, absence of decorative frills." In music, the representative *Neue Sachlichkeit* composer was probably Paul Hindemith. Among performing musicians, Willett plausibly nominates Otto Klemperer as the "most radical and most objective" of Weimar-period conductors.*

Arrau found Klemperer's pre–World War II performances too fast and insufficiently inward. Even after the war, as his anecdote about trills in the *Emperor* Concerto (see page 39) reflects, he

---

*John Willett, *Art and Politics in the Weimar Period* (New York: Pantheon, 1978), pp. 112, 161.

and Klemperer could disagree over whether an ornament was fussy or expressive. And yet Arrau consistently honored Klemperer for his integrity, and Klemperer would most likely have endorsed Arrau's statements in the South American press avowing objective fidelity to the composer's text.

In this regard, it is worth adding that, of the musicians Arrau most respected, Schnabel, if less austere than Klemperer, was also a pioneering objectivist in his day. Paying tribute to Schnabel in 1952—the year after his death—Arrau went so far as to write as follows for *Musical America:*

> Long before the war, Schnabel was already considered in Berlin to be the supreme intellectual authority on Beethoven, Schubert, and Brahms—hence, also, dry. Schnabel's younger contemporary Edwin Fischer, on the other hand, was known as a volcanic, eruptive Beethoven player. But whereas Fischer often became *selbstherrlich* in performance and was not above putting in things that were not in the score, Schnabel was the first to insist on faithful adherence to the written page. In this field he was the first celebrated performer to illustrate the concept—strangely enough, a new one in his time—of the interpreter as the servant of music rather than the exploiter of it.*

In fact, Arrau practices textual fidelity with a rigor surpassing Schnabel's model. As much as Schnabel, he adheres to every authorial indication of phrasing and dynamics. More than Schnabel, he stresses the importance of rendering every note accurately and significantly. In awkward or densely scored passages, his fingerings are clean rather than expedient, and he refuses to slight subsidiary notes. Where there are disparities between editions, he consults manuscripts and other scholarly aids in an effort to negate personal whim. Where there are ambiguities in notation, he attempts to infer a systematic understanding—in Mozart and Beethoven, he always begins his trills on the upper note; in Chopin, he always plays grace notes on the beat.

The relatively brisk tempos and exceptionally clean lines of

*Claudio Arrau, "Artur Schnabel: Servant of the Music," *Musical America*, February 1952.

Arrau's earliest recordings (discussed in my conclusion, "Arrau on Records") document the impact of *Neue Sachlichkeit*. Over time, however, his offsetting allegiance to such Dionysian activists as Furtwängler and Fischer apparently took deeper hold. The result was a balancing of abandon and control that shifted according to the music at hand, and as intellect and emotion became better fused. To again use Arrau's recordings as a guide: by the sixties, the subjective thrust of his interpretations was sometimes so extreme that his rules of fidelity were made to seem a safeguard against obliterating waves of temperament. In any case, a dialectic was established in which fidelity to the text channeled profound subjective immersion.

As much as anything, this combination of pronounced correctness and pronounced entanglement—half "modern," half Romantic—constitutes Arrau's mature interpretive signature. It mirrors Arrau the man, in whom interior disquiet—so much more discernible today than when the South American press found him a "sportive type"—is sheathed by decorous habits of dress and address. A further component of his pianistic signature, again arising from a judicious modesty, is his abhorrence of technical display. I have only heard him italicize a technical feat inadvertently, as in the final pages of the *Waldstein*, where his octave glissandos draw gasps. (He plays these octave scales as glissandos, rather than from the wrist, because Beethoven wanted them that way; that he plays them with surprising ease is incidental.) He uses his superb equipment to liberate expression, so that fingers, hands, and arms are themselves creative, not mechanical adjuncts to creativity. It is no semantic accident that "gravity" and "weightiness" apply equally to the methodology and temper of his playing. In the music of Brahms, particularly, his reliance on emphatic finger and arm weight creates an undertow both physical and visceral—to see him is to hear him.

A final aspect of Arrau's approach to interpretation is the much-remarked diversity of his repertoire. He feels the two are related—that "the wider the ground an interpreter stands on, the deeper his roots." He is identified with Beethoven, Brahms, Chopin, Liszt, Schumann. It is sometimes forgotten that at one time his catholicity was all the more pronounced. The programs he played under Krause already reflect not only a broad range of affinities, but a habit of inspecting new scores. A review from

1915 comments: "To the teacher's credit, the program was made up not only of well-known composers and oft-played works but also of seldom-heard pieces." The second half of the Arrau recital in question, in the Beethovensaal, consisted of a Rigaudon (Op. 204, no. 3) and Gavotte (Op. 125) by Joachim Raff, Hans von Bülow's A-minor Tarantelle (Op. 19), and five *Tonbilder* on Stifter's *Studien* (Op. 2) by Felix Weingartner. In December 1918, Arrau played an entire program of works with orchestra consisting of the B-flat Concerto of Hermann Goetz (1840–1876), Chopin's Variations on "Là ci darem," Richard Strauss's *Burleske*, and Liszt's First Concerto. Commented one critic: "The diligence with which the young pianist searches for worthwhile lesser-known works puts to shame many of his piano colleagues, even some of those of well-known name and rank."

In later years, Arrau made the first American recording of the Strauss *Burleske* and gave the Mexican premiere of Carlos Chávez's complex, substantial Piano Concerto. Of Stravinsky, he performed the Concerto for Piano and Wind Instruments, the *Piano-Rag Music*, Three Movements from *Petrushka*, and the Serenade in A, the last of which he studied with the composer. While he was never heard in much nontonal music, he did perform, of Schoenberg, the Piano Concerto, the Sechs kleine Klavierstücke (Op. 19), and, frequently, the Expressionistic Drei Klavierstücke (Op. 11).

Arrau's combination of Latin birth and German training perhaps partly accounts for his breadth. He admits to being an exceptional sight reader and, at one point, an extremely rapid memorizer. Career building also played a role: though he regards Rachmaninoff as a shallow composer, between the wars he performed the Third Concerto frequently, and occasionally the Second. I have also heard him express distaste for the Ginastera Piano Sonata and the Brahms First Piano Sonata. Usually, however, he has only nice things to say about music, and this explains his omnivorous musicality as much as anything does. Rather than denigrate, his impulse is to appreciate. His favorite word is "marvelous," and he uses it with conviction.

This is the psychological setting for Arrau's grueling cycles of Bach, Beethoven, and Mozart. He has also performed all or nearly all the solo keyboard works of Brahms, Chopin, Debussy, Ravel, Schumann, and Weber. In the thirties, when he was part of a trio bearing his name (the other members were the violinist Hermann Hubl and the cellist Hans Münch-Holland), he covered the mainstream literature for piano trio, piano quartet, and piano quintet. His cycle of the Beethoven Violin Sonatas with Joseph Szigeti at the Library of Congress in 1944 is available on record. His chamber music performances since World War II, while infrequent, include notable festival appearances in the Brahms Piano Quintet with the Amadeus Quartet, and the *Liebeslieder* Waltzes with Benjamin Britten, both at Aldeburgh, and the Brahms C-major Trio with Isaac Stern and Pablo Casals, at the Casals Festival in Puerto Rico.

The fifteen recital programs he played in Mexico City in 1933 and 1934 (see Appendix A) indicate the scope of the Arrau solo canon at its peak. There are no single-time additions among the works listed—the Bartók *Allegro barbaro*, the excerpts from *Goyescas*, the Prokofiev Toccata, Poulenc's *Napoli*, Ravel's *Jeux d'eau* all turn up repeatedly on Arrau programs from the thirties and forties.

Of works contained neither in the Mexico City programs nor in Arrau's discography (see Appendix C), the following list suggests what nooks and crannies he has combed. The orchestral compositions he has performed include concertos by Henselt, Hummel, and Heinrich Knoedt, Debussy's Fantasy, Fauré's Ballade, Honegger's Concertino, and Tchaikovsky's Concert Fantasy. He gave the New York premiere of Satie's *Sports et divertissements*. In Paris, he gave the first performance of Nicolas Nabokov's Piano Sonata. He has played South American works by Juan José Castro, Juan Lecuna, Domingo Santa Cruz, and Villa-Lobos. He championed Liszt's Variations on *Weinen, Klagen, Sorgen, Zagen* and the Schubert Drei Klavierstücke (Op. Post., D. 946) when both were considerably more obscure than they seem today. As late as 1950, he revived the *Hexaméron*, an outgrowth of the legendary Liszt-Thalberg rivalry consisting of six bravura variations on the March from *I puritani*, composed by Chopin, Czerny, Henri Herz, Liszt, Johann Peter Pixis, and Thalberg. When late in life Busoni complained to Isidore Philipp that he was running out of repertoire, Philipp suggested Scriabin and Alkan. Arrau admires both composers—of Scriabin, he has played the Fourth and Fifth Sonatas; of Alkan, part of the Symphony for Piano. And he adores Busoni's own music, of which he has performed the

Konzertstück, *Indian Fantasy,* and *Romanza e scherzoso,* as well as various solo works, including the *Fantasia contrappuntistica* and the Toccata.

Some of this surface variety is misleading. The Mexico City series opened with a Haydn work—the F-minor Variations; Arrau has played little else by Haydn in public. The Prokofiev Toccata, *Visions fugitives,* and Third Piano Concerto seem to be the only Prokofiev he has performed. Outside of the *Allegro barbaro,* he has done Bartók's Opus 14 Suite and the Opus 18 Etudes, but not the sonata, and only the second of the three piano concertos. He has never played the Ravel concertos, or any substantial solo works by Grieg.

His active repertoire, moreover, has steadily shrunk. In the fifties he was still scheduling morsels of Albéniz, Bartók, Debussy, Fauré, Granados, Poulenc, and Ravel. But in the sixties and seventies the morsels fell away or consolidated as the complete *Gaspard de la nuit,* complete books of the Debussy preludes, or the complete Chopin preludes.

The biggest consolidation of all was of Beethoven. Between the wars, Arrau gave complete Beethoven sonata cycles in Mexico and South America. His 1952 Beethoven sonata cycle over the BBC, however, was his first in over a decade. This was followed by a complete cycle at New York's Town Hall (1953–54), plus a flurry of Beethoven recordings for EMI. In the late fifties and through the sixties, his identification with Beethoven increased. While he gave no more complete sonata cycles (he launched five— in Berlin, Hamburg, London, New York, and Zurich—but all were curtailed about halfway through), it became common for Arrau to play two or more Beethoven sonatas per program. Eventually, his active repertoire congealed about a mostly rugged core: the sonatas and concertos of Beethoven and Brahms, the big Schumann cycles, and the concertos and heroic solo works of Chopin.

Arrau's Beethoven phase was encouraged by Friede Rothe, who felt his American career was not progressing as it should have been, and that "something big" was needed to enlarge his name. And Arrau found himself thriving on the struggle-to-triumph scenarios of the music. Then, in the seventies, the pressure to win seemed to relent. Turning away from the likes of Opus 111 and the *Appassionata,* Arrau began recycling phases of the literature that are gentler, more spacious, or more frankly virtuosic. He found himself especially drawn to Debussy, Liszt, and Schubert.

In the recording studio, where memorization is not required, he tackled the Debussy preludes, the Liszt *Transcendental* Etudes, the C-minor and B-flat Sonatas of Schubert. His active repertoire, meanwhile, had by 1979–80 diminished to a single recital program and seven or eight orchestral works per season. Still, the stylistic gamut was sustained. Alongside the Beethoven, Schumann, and Brahms concertos he continued to perform the Chopin F minor, the Liszt A major, the Strauss *Burleske,* and the Weber Konzertstück. Of Debussy, he reacquired *Estampes* and *Images,* Book I. Of Liszt, he returned to the *Dante* Sonata, which he had not played in more than forty years.

Between concerts and recording sessions, Arrau's musical appetite remains avid. He is impressed by Ives's *Concord* Sonata, the Boulez piano sonatas, the Elliott Carter Piano Concerto. He thinks that Bernd Alois Zimmermann's *Die Soldaten* is one of the great twentieth-century operas and adores Tippett's *King Priam.* He cannot peruse his early repertoire without pausing to admire Chabrier's *Idylle,* Juan Lecuna's *Suburbio,* or the Liszt-Busoni *Spanish Rhapsody* for piano and orchestra. "Marvelous!" he will exclaim. "Why don't I *play* that anymore?! I would like to record it."

JH / Since we've already discussed technique, and we're about to discuss interpretation, perhaps we can begin by considering the relationship between technique and interpretation. Is there a risk of becoming too conscious of technique?

CA / A great risk. This has a lot to do with the way one plays, physically. One can do marvelous things, sometimes, even when the arm is stiff. But it means being overoccupied with the technical process. I found out very early that playing in a relaxed way makes one more creative—because it is so natural; because the whole body is involved; because there is a unity of body and psyche.

JH / I brought along a quote from Furtwängler on this subject, from his book *Concerning Music:*

The moment that technical problems are treated as ends in themselves, the "spiritual" unity of the whole is destroyed. In a good performance the technical aspect should not be divorced even for a second from the "spiritual" aspect, not even when it would be "effective" in itself. Granted, it may produce an effect, but it is nevertheless an illegitimate effect since it detracts from what is essential. But of course, the only people who can feel and know this are those who are already familiar with the work from a previous performance commensurate with its true nature. This is the reason why such interpretations of the great living masterpieces of the past, based on technical virtuosity, are so dangerous in practice: they thoroughly corrupt taste.*

CA / Oh, I like that very much. Another thing Furtwängler says in the same book is that he is always amazed that people who play Romantic music beautifully, with terrific emotional involvement, shrink in *awe* when they play Beethoven or Mozart—that they become completely uncreative, and that this is wrong because they should mold the music as much as before. Actually, the better you play Beethoven, the closer you come to the essential meaning, then the better you will play Tchaikovsky.

JH / This raises a point I'd like to pursue at some length. Here is a review of one of your recent New York recitals by Andrew Porter in *The New Yorker* [March 3, 1980] in which he comments that you may be the victim of a prejudice—"a feeling that a pianist whose 'specialties' encompass those of Schnabel, Cortot, Kempff, Rubinstein, and Serkin must be something of a chameleon; that someone who plays so much, day after day, in country after country—here Brahms or Beethoven, there Debussy, next Schumann or Chopin—cannot be fully committed to everything he does." Some people distrust the scope of your repertoire. Even to excel in both Chopin and Beethoven is unusual.

CA / It's an idea they have about interpretation. They think an interpreter can only play well the things that are akin to him.

---

*Wilhelm Furtwängler, *Concerning Music*, trans. L. J. Lawrence (London: Boosey & Hawkes, 1953), p. 53.

And it's exactly the opposite. A real interpreter is somebody who is able to transform himself into something he is not. You know, they used to say in Germany, *"das liegt ihm"* [that suits him]. But that's not interpretation. That's like an actor who plays himself. The best Debussy I have ever heard from an orchestra was conducted by Furtwängler, not by a French conductor. Or was there anybody who conducted the Tchaikovsky *Pathétique* Symphony in a more profound way than Furtwängler? If I knew any outstanding cases, you see, of people who were so-called specialists . . . But generally these people play their particular "specialty" more superficially than those who play everything. The worst Chopin I know is played by so-called Chopin specialists. In Germany, a man named Koczalsky was an idol. He played only Chopin. It was *awful.* Or Brailowsky! The worst Chopin you ever heard. Limiting yourself to two or three composers, or one field, is unhealthy. I must cite the case of Fischer-Dieskau. The other day by chance I heard a record of Fischer-Dieskau singing Verdi. It was simply a revelation. And he is great in Schubert, and Wagner. The Busoni *Goethe* Songs—incredible. *Lear* by Reimann! The *Wozzeck* I heard in Berlin—that I heard a week after hearing him do *Falstaff* in Italian. That, to me, is interpretation. You must have the capacity to submerge yourself in different worlds. Otherwise you are not a real interpreter.

JH / What you seem to suggest is that interpretation at the highest level draws on gifts that every great interpreter has in common, arising from depth of character or emotion. Something that has nothing to do with nationality.

CA / It has also to do with nationality, of course. You can't separate things like that. But the national element is usually the least interesting, and the least important. Particularly in works of genius. In Debussy, for instance, the national element is not as important as in Chabrier.

JH / And yet some of the greatest German artists, including Furtwängler, would speak of themselves as upholders of "German art."

CA / That's an old-fashioned type of thinking. Like saying that only a German can play Beethoven. It's ridiculous. Or the Viennese, when they say only a Viennese can feel Schubert.

JH / When you say this type of thinking is old-fashioned, do you mean to say that it used to be more valid than it is today?

CA / Not more valid. It was a more common way of thinking—during a time of nationalistic tendencies. I remember the amazement in Germany when the Capet String Quartet came to Berlin to play all the Beethoven quartets.

JH / Did you feel discriminated against as a South American in Berlin?

CA / Yes, very long ago. Then I went through something similar to what Carreño went through. I was considered more and more the property of Berlin. Not of Germany, but of Berlin. If someone would say, "You know, he is from South America," he was told, "Oh yes, but his *upbringing* was in Berlin." Fortunately, these things have changed.

JH / What about some of the factors that *are* germane to great interpretation? You're a stickler for absolute textual fidelity. How would you describe the relationship between interpretation and textual fidelity?

CA / Some people think if you apply textual fidelity, you have to be dry. There is this ridiculous either-or. Actually, there isn't any conflict. You should start by respecting the text exactly as it is written. If Beethoven wrote "piano" and you play forte, it's definitely wrong! But that is only the basis for working within these channels with respect to the text. Interpretation is a synthesis of the world of the composer and the world of the interpreter.

JH / You go beyond never altering notes or dynamics. For instance, you never redistribute the notes between the hands, as many pianists do, to facilitate evenness or accuracy.

CA / It's always said that the audience doesn't notice these things. That, of course, is true in a certain sense. But actually one should play for the *ideal* listener. The ideal listener will notice a difference. Take the beginning of the Beethoven Opus 111. People play it with two hands because they don't want to risk dirty octaves. Well, first of all, it sounds different played with one hand, as written. And then technical difficulty has itself an expressive value.

JH / What about the big trill in the main subject of the first movement of the Brahms D-minor Concerto? That makes a much different sound when it's redistributed, doesn't it?

CA / *Completely* different. But of course to do it as Brahms writes you must have tremendous power in the rotational movement. Otherwise the hand gets stiff.

JH / The double chromatic scale at the close of the Chopin B-minor Scherzo—many pianists play it as alternating octaves.

CA / I once saw a review describing how Horowitz played this passage in octaves, and how all the pianists in the hall were *envious* of this incredible achievement. But it's *ten* times easier that way than to play the chromatic scale with the accents as they are written, and the power.

JH / Another aspect of textual fidelity, as you practice it, is that your literalism produces readings that are slightly different from those usually heard. Your phrasing of the theme of the Rondo of the Beethoven C-major Concerto, for instance.

CA / People just don't bother with these things. Czerny confirms that Beethoven felt that the second sixteenth-note should be almost like a grace note. Another example is the last movement of the Beethoven Opus 78 Sonata—the written phrasing is never even attempted.

JH / People probably think it sounds awkward as written.

CA / Yes, because they are not used to it. I was amazed the other day to see Jorge Bolet say in an interview that he considered it "idiotic"—he used this word—to consider every musical detail as it is written. Then you become *pedantic,* he said.

JH / How reliable are metronome markings as an element in interpretation?

CA / It depends. In the case of Schumann, for example, most of the metronome marks are by Clara. And, as we know, she was a little scared of the music of her husband. She always seemed to change the metronome markings—in the fast movements, to make them slower, and in the slow movements, to make them faster. Of course, the famous metronome marking at the beginning of the piano concerto—it's simply impossible. And the andante section of the first movement is also impossibly fast. What happened in the Schumann concerto I don't know. It can't be that our feeling for the music has so completely changed. There's the same problem in Beethoven—the few metronome markings for the piano sonatas. If you play the first movement of the *Hammerklavier* at the metronome tempo, it loses all its majesty. In Beethoven's case, I think probably—I'm just saying probably—that he *hated* this machine. If they asked him for metronome markings, he probably got impatient and said anything.

JH / Have you tried playing the first movement of the *Hammerklavier* at the metronome tempo?

CA / Yes. First of all, it's very difficult technically. Almost impossible.

JH / *Do* you consider it feasible technically?

CA / Yes.

JH / How about Czerny's metronome markings for the Beethoven sonatas?

CA / Those must be considered. They're the only markings from somebody who actually studied with Beethoven and performed under his influence. But they're not too reliable, either. You know, some of the modern composers with whom I have worked haven't known what tempos they actually wanted.

JH / Do you think there is such a thing as a proper tempo for a given piece?

CA / There is a proper range, I think. A rather narrow range.

JH / What are some pieces that you feel are often played at the wrong tempo?

CA / The first movement of the *Waldstein* Sonata—three times too fast. The Brahms D-minor Concerto, first and second movements.

JH / You have a reputation for favoring slow tempos. How do you react when people say that your tempos are too slow?

CA / [Laughing.] There I am *terribly* conceited. I think they are *all* wrong. Only *I* am right.

JH / I've also heard you complain that the tuttis in concertos are often taken too fast.

CA / That's a habit that many conductors have—correcting the tempo of the soloist. They are afraid of boring the audience. I've heard them *say* it—that people will fall asleep.

JH / How about bravura—conspicuous technical display. Is that ever a legitimate way of keeping audiences awake?

CA / It was legitimate at a certain period in the nineteenth century. That was when the pianist emerged as a soloist. There was this cult of personality. Many of the compositions that were played had very little of value, or beauty. They were just chances to show off. That was accepted in those days.

JH / Does this remain a valid approach to certain music today—say, the *Mephisto Waltz*?

CA / I think in the *Mephisto Waltz* every note has so much expressive value, one shouldn't do anything for bravura's sake. I mean, the Liszt *Norma* Fantasy, or the *I puritani* Paraphrase—those were made to show off the capacity of the pianist. At one time this was justified in a sense because concerts were supposed to be a display of skill. Then it was justified. But not now.

JH / Haven't you ever been tempted to choose a faster tempo, or a more drastic dynamic scheme, in order to show off your fingers?

CA / Actually, in my twenties people would complain that I played too·fast. For *years* they complained. I probably did in many cases play too fast, because I was so much in love with the piano, and with my fingers. Maybe I sought a bit more applause. But that I have not done consciously for a long, long time. In a certain sense, I've become indifferent to whether I please an audience or not. Worrying about the audience—that's one thing that can really kill an interpretation.

JH / As a final topic in technique and interpretation, I'd like to discuss how you think your playing has changed over the years.

CA / You know, there are all these people who as soon as they hear about my age begin immediately to speak of the *Verklärung* and the serenity. That's absurd. The expressive intensity is, I feel, much stronger, much more concentrated in my playing than years ago. Of course, this is an ingrained fallacy. People think when a person becomes old, he has to become serene. On the contrary, you love life much more, and your feelings much more. Or they think if you get older you become tired and indifferent. I mean, this idea of people getting weaker when they get older, it may be more the case in general. But if you have been intense all your life, you become more so as you get older.

JH / You said a moment ago that you used to be criticized for playing too fast. Do you find yourself consciously adopting slower tempos in certain music?

CA / The second movement of the Brahms D-minor Concerto I think I play slower than before.

JH / Judging from your recordings, that is certainly the case. Your first recording of the Brahms D minor, the one conducted by Basil Cameron, is faster than the one with Giulini. And the one with Giulini is faster than the most recent one, with Bernard Haitink. Have you listened recently to any of your older recordings?

CA / Only the one of the Chopin E-minor Concerto with Klemperer. I had such a wonderful remembrance of that. I had to almost *teach* Chopin to Klemperer. He had never conducted it. He had never even played any Chopin himself. You know, his teacher was James Kwast, and Kwast's pupils never played Chopin. And, I don't know why, I was a little disappointed by the recording. I had idealized the performance in my memory.

JH / Can you think of instances of gaining new insights into pieces you've played for many years?

CA / In the last movement of the Schubert C-minor Sonata there are passages I used to play in an almost graceful way. Now I feel very strongly that the whole movement is very tragic, very close to the idea of death. Schubert definitely knew he was going to die by the time he wrote it—if he had syphilis, as they say.

JH / What passages in the last movement particularly remind you of impending death?

CA / The descending chromatic scales—in the last movement, and also in the first movement development. The way to perform these sections is as something skeletal, macabre—without any flesh. Really the work of death. This kind of thing is unique, actually, in music. It is authentic. It's not farfetched at all.

JH / I know that you returned to the Schubert B-flat Sonata at about the same time, in order to record both works. Did you find new insights there as well?

CA / The meaning of the last movement, which is so problematic, became very clear to me. I don't know if it's going to be correct on the recording, but what I mainly feel now is the *ambivalence* of the theme. First, amazingly enough, there is the G, sforzato, like a trumpet. Then four bars in C minor, full of growing anxiety. And then, immediately, this sense of giving up and falling back into B flat—this *Todesnähe* [proximity to death], as if there were nothing to be done. And this is repeated again and again. The modulations create tremendous tension within this one theme. Until now I have never heard anyone perform it like that. But my conviction is very, very strong.

JH / How do you feel about the first movement exposition repeat, which most pianists skip?

CA / It *has* to be played. It is omitted because of this ridiculous business about the sonata being too long. That's a bad sign for the quality of the *listener,* not the composer. Length is not a correct criterion *at all.* Schubert needs this long, long breath. People have no patience for him because their concentration doesn't last. To even think of length when one listens to the first movement of the B-flat Sonata already shows that one hasn't been listening deeply enough, openly enough.

JH / What do you make of the first ending of the exposition in the Schubert B flat?

CA / The first ending is like a question—asking if all the sadness and melancholy is necessary.

JH / An attempt to break out.

CA / Yes.

JH / And the repeat itself—what's the point of repeating the exposition at that moment?

CA / It's falling back into this beautifully sad feeling. . . .

JH / A seductive beckoning of death, as in "Der Lindenbaum."

CA / Calling, calling . . .

JH / How would you say your playing has changed technically, mechanically, as a function of age?

CA / Suddenly, one doesn't think about certain technical problems anymore, and the problems disappear. I just leave it to my fingers, to my muscles, so to speak. For instance, one of the *Transcendental* Etudes by Liszt, *Wilde Jagd*, which is really one of the most difficult things in the piano literature—that etude I worked on many times in my life, and I had never been able to reach Liszt's metronome mark. But when I came back to it to record it, I found that suddenly, without much trouble, I could play it up to tempo. You see, when something doesn't come, I don't insist anymore. I let it mature by itself. I let my subconscious solve the problems, rather than using the willpower.

JH / You don't think there's an inevitable physical decline at some point, so that the agility of the hands is diminished?

CA / That I don't believe. Because I've seen pianists like Carreño, whose playing was never more full of life than a few months before her death. Also Busoni. I remember his last concerts. There was not the slightest sign of less fire or power.

JH / Obviously the longevity of your technique is related to the importance that you place on relaxation. We both know many examples of pianists who played with excessive muscle tension, and whose careers were cut short or diminished as a result.

CA / With singers it's the same thing. When they are relaxed, and just let the sound come out, they don't lose their voices until very late. The muscles acquire a wisdom of their own.

JH / Does something comparable happen in the realm of interpretation? Do you find yourself relying more on spontaneous intuition, and less on experimentation with different tempos, dynamics, voicings, and so on?

CA / I never liked to experiment like that. I know that many pianists do. And they ask other pianists, "How do you like this?" or, "Should I do that?" For me, that is unthinkable. If I am in doubt about the way I play something—whether to make a crescendo, whether to make a ritard—I just let it evolve. When you're working on a piece, such things should simply ripen.

JH / This is an important point, I think—both in general and with reference to your playing. Because I hear it confirmed all the time when I compare recordings you've made of the same work. I've compared the Chopin preludes you recorded in 1950–51, for instance, with the version you did in 1973. And I found that virtually every inflection in the 1973 interpretation could be traced back to 1950–51, but that in 1973 the inflections were more fully developed and suggested a deeper level of immersion. In fact, it seems that you very rarely introduce a new idea fully sprung. And I find this absolutely remarkable. There's a certain type of artist, such as Glenn Gould (whom I admire; I don't mean to disparage him), whose approach to interpretation can be ironic. He'll say, "Let's try this passage today at a faster tempo, and with different voicing, and see what happens." And he feels that by hit or miss he'll discover some interesting ideas. Whereas you're a completely different type of artist. I'm wondering—do you even go so far as to try certain passages at different tempos when you're working on a piece at home?

CA / No, no. I never do that. Also to play a repeat piano, or pianissimo, after having played a passage the first time forte— this belongs to the same type of manipulation.

JH / I also can't imagine you sitting down at the keyboard and demonstrating a passage for someone, to show them how it goes.

CA / I never do that. Even when I'm teaching, I never play. There is a danger of imitation.

JH / But I have the sense that's not the only reason you don't play for your students. Playing the piano is not an activity you lightly undertake.

CA / [Laughing.] Well, I'm a very strange fellow.

JH / Do you know of any other pianists with such an aversion to casual playing?

CA / No. When they get together, they play for one another. They literally *push* one another from the piano bench.

JH / I understand that once, when you were about to play at a hall in southern California, you were shown a new piano that had recently arrived. The concert director there wanted you to try it out, because she was very proud of it. And you refused. But she kept badgering you, and so finally you played *one note*. Do you remember that?

CA / [Laughing.] Yes. You see, sometimes I cannot bear to try out pianos even when it's necessary. *I cannot simply play the piano.*

JH / We've already talked about your reluctance to test a piano just before a concert. But surely there have been occasions when you've had to go to Steinway & Sons in order to select an instrument.

CA / Yes, and it was an ordeal.

JH / Would there be other people around?

CA / Maybe a tuner and a secretary.

JH / Would their presence bother you?

CA / Yes.

JH / What would you play?

CA / A few chords.

JH / You mean two or three?

CA / Maybe four. When I hear that Rubinstein used to go to parties after his concerts and play some more, I cannot understand it. For me, everything is like a performance. Probably it's ridiculous to say this, but when I'm rehearsing with an orchestra and the conductor says, "Just play mezza voce—don't waste your energy"—it's simply *impossible*. I stop playing altogether.

JH / To play at half volume would violate your understanding of the music. It would be like an obscene act.

CA / Exactly. *Blasphemy.*

# Liszt

The first person to give a solo piano recital, by most accounts, was one Franz Liszt. This was in London in 1840,* by which time he already was adulated as no pianist had been. Three years later, in Berlin, Liszt in two months gave twenty-one concerts embracing more than eighty works. Women swooned and wept; one salvaged the dregs of his tea as a keepsake, another a cigar butt, which she wore in her bosom. The unpopular Prussian monarch, Frederick William IV, presented Liszt with a purse of diamonds; Liszt contemptuously flung it into the wings. He left town in a coach drawn by six white horses. Thirty carriages and fifty-one horsemen followed in formal procession. Hundreds of private coaches brought up the rear. The streets were thronged with his admirers.

More than a pianist, Liszt was a Promethean embodiment of the Romantic ideal of the artist as solitary, self-sufficient hero. What he did, he did alone, without an orchestra, or a singer or violinist to share the bill. His orchestra was the piano, newly strengthened with metal parts, subtly responsive to every impulse of hand, foot, and brain. Progenitor of all pianists to come, he was not merely the unrivaled magician of the keyboard, but, alternatively, as a pupil of Beethoven's disciple Carl Czerny, an inspired exponent of the *Hammerklavier* Sonata and other summits of the literature. As showman, Liszt made the concert room a theater. As musical penitent, he turned it into a church. "When

---

*Though it was not the first time he dispensed with supporting artists, Liszt's June 9, 1840, solo concert in London's Hanover Square Rooms marked the first time the term "recital" was used and is generally cited as a landmark progenitor of the piano recital format.

Liszt plays anything pathetic, it sounds as if he had been through everything, and opens one's wounds afresh," his American pupil Amy Fay reported. "All that one has suffered comes before one again."

His own music is as notable for its religious strivings as its swashbuckling élan. The same dichotomy split Liszt the man. As his music is too easily condemned for its bombast or sentimentality, he himself is too easily remembered as Casanova or Mephisto. His legendary technique was laboriously acquired. He used his eminence to champion Wagner and Berlioz, and to raise money for flood relief, music schools, and other charities. Notwithstanding his lapses into vulgarity, there remained something unspoiled and benign in his character, rendering him manipulable by domineering women, and justifying the religious impulse that eventually led him to take the four minor orders toward becoming a Catholic priest. "Christ crucified, the 'foolishness' and the elevation of the Cross, this was my true vocation," he wrote at the age of fifty-eight. "I have felt it to the depth of my heart from the age of seventeen, when with tears and supplication I begged to be permitted to enter the seminary in Paris. . . ."

In *Music-Study in Germany in the Nineteenth Century,* Miss Fay offers a celebrated portrait of the "better" Liszt. "Anything like the polish of his manner I never saw," she wrote on first glimpsing him at the theater. "When he got up to leave the box, for instance, after his adieus to the ladies, he laid his hand on his heart and made his final bow—not with affectation, or in mere gallantry, but with a quiet courtliness which made you feel that no other way of bowing to a lady was right or proper." In weeks to come, she further observed his charm ("I can't give you any idea of his persuasiveness, when he chooses. It is enough to decoy you into anything"), his friendliness ("Nothing could exceed Liszt's amiability, or the trouble he gave himself, and instead of frightening me, he inspired me"), his equanimity ("Liszt hasn't the nervous irritability common to artists, but on the contrary his disposition is the most exquisite and tranquil in the world"), his humility ("He never allows anyone to ask him to play. . . . That is the only point in which one sees Liszt's sense of his own greatness; otherwise his manner is remarkably unassuming"), and his kindness ("The *real* basis of his nature is compassion. *The bruised reed he does not break, nor the humble and docile heart despise!").* *

Arrau's relationship to Liszt stems from his relationship to Krause, who esteemed Liszt the composer. Liszt figures prominently in Arrau's early programs and recordings. In 1919 and again in 1920, he was awarded the Liszt Prize. While certain works, including *Les Jeux d'eaux à la Villa d'Este* and the *Mephisto Waltz,* remained conspicuous in his subsequent repertoire, other composers gradually took precedence. Then, in later life, Arrau returned to the B-minor and *Dante* Sonatas and found himself possessed by Liszt as never before.

From Krause, Arrau also inherited an abiding reverence for Liszt as teacher, patron, and man of affairs. He altogether lacks Lisztian irony or ease; still, more than Beethoven, Busoni, or Krause, it is Liszt—or, at any rate, the Liszt Amy Fay knew— whose heroism, elegance, generosity, and unpretentious dignity serve as models for Arrau's manner and ideals. When his solitary presence holds three thousand listeners rapt, the Lisztian legacy is invoked. Once, in Russia, he was carried from the concert hall on the shoulders of young musicians. In Mexico City, police once had to be called to disperse a crowd of disappointed ticket seekers. In Buenos Aires, Caracas, and Santiago, he has needed police escorts to return to his hotel. In Santiago, he was once met at the railroad station by a huge chorus of children singing the national anthem. His post-concert opera cape and Old World jewelry; his grueling programs and lessons without fee; his honorary titles, bestowed by four governments, and the two streets named after him in Chile; the graciousness and real pleasure with which he receives such homage—all are Lisztian attributes. The atmospheric calm of his Douglaston study, with its piano, candles, and black icons, evokes no music so much as Liszt's.

The special susceptibility apparent in Arrau's Liszt performances was made visible when I asked him, in what follows, to describe the sonata and B-minor Ballade. We perused the scores, set on a chair between us, page by page. Arrau applied himself with limitless patience. When words did not come, he would wait silently, his eyes glazed or shut, until the music took hold where

---

*Amy Fay, *Music-Study in Germany in the Nineteenth Century* (New York: Dover, 1965), pp. 205–80.

language cannot. Then, strenuously, he would begin inhaling great shafts of air, as if ingesting the silent pages of notes. Finally, like Tristan after one of his intrepid stupors, he would report what visions he had glimpsed.

JH / What role has Liszt played in your evolution as an artist?

CA / Through Krause, who wanted his students to play Liszt at an early age, it freed me from emotional restraint. I don't know if Krause thought I was somehow blocked inside. But Liszt really made me *ausgehen* [come out of myself]. It wasn't just a question of playing well, or feeling the emotion oneself, but of learning how to *project*.

JH / This question of projection has something to do with the theater, doesn't it? With acting. As opposed to Mozart or Beethoven, in Liszt there is a desirable element of exaggeration.

CA / Desirable at a certain moment. When people in Germany today perform Schiller, I always complain that they seem to be ashamed of the pathos. They think it's old-fashioned. But you can't play Schiller or Liszt with restraint. It becomes unbearable. Schiller's drama and Liszt's music have to be made.

JH / This is one reason people had such a poor opinion of Liszt for decades. They would look at the notes on the page and see nothing there. Even a great piece like the *Vallée d'Obermann* can look like nothing but tremolos and simple chordal textures.

CA / That's not a good example, because that's one piece that is so beautiful that it comes across even without inspired interpretation.

JH / What is a better example of a piece that has to be made?

CA / *Mazeppa* has to be made. *Harmonies du soir* has to be made. Because it's on the edge of kitsch. The arpeggios, for instance, can easily sound trivial.

JH / Tremolos are a big problem in Liszt.

CA / Oh, they're very dangerous. One day, after I had played *Les Jeux d'eaux à la Villa d'Este*, a lady asked me, "Why do you play this *horrible* piece, where one has always the impression the telephone is ringing?" And I had been in ecstasy! Tremolos can have a mystic quality. But the execution is very important. If you play them a little too fast or a little too loud, or a little too clearly, they become vulgar.

JH / The most memorable tremolo I ever heard was from you, at the climax of the Liszt sonata. The big tremolo in the right hand on the next-to-last page. It was a tremolo that always bothered me until I heard you play it. Instead of spewing it out mechanically, you gradually intensified it, and then you retarded at the end, so that the individual notes became more and more distinct as they reached peak intensity.

CA / Everything must take part in the meaning of the moment, no? In the *Dante* Sonata, there are two sections that are absolutely incredible as examples of mystical tremolos.

JH / How about the repeated chords at the apotheosis of the *Vallée d'Obermann*—is that a danger spot?

CA / If you play tatatata—every chord singly. The chords must *tremble*. You must stay close to the keys, without letting them come up all the way.

JH / Getting back to my original question about the role of Liszt in your development—I have the impression that there was a period when you drifted away from him.

CA / Well, that had a practical side. I was advised not to play Liszt so much until I was more established here. I concentrated on Beethoven, Brahms, Schumann.

JH / When did you return to Liszt?

CA / I would say ten or fifteen years ago.

JH / And during the time you weren't playing very much Liszt— and during which time, incidentally, Liszt wasn't being played very much in general—did he come to seem less important to you?

CA / Not really. I always had a great love and *need* for Liszt. I was longing for an opportunity to play Liszt again.

JH / What has it been like, coming back to Liszt? Are there pieces that have changed for you?

CA / Completely. We could start with the *Dante* Sonata. I played that maybe too much when I was still a child. So I thought of it almost as an octave etude. And now I have discovered the depth of it. It is completely new to me now.

JH / You don't play the *Mephisto Waltz* anymore.

CA / I once heard it at a competition in Paris about sixty times. One worse than the other. I just didn't want to hear or see it again.

JH / What about *Funérailles*?

CA / That I always loved. But again what is made out of it is appalling. It also becomes an octave etude.

JH / What about the B-minor Sonata? You recorded it in 1970.

CA / I think that was one of the first times that I played the Liszt sonata after not playing it for at least twenty years.

JH / How did you happen to return to it?

CA / It had always been present in my mind. The love for it never subsided. Again, it was partly advice. Friede [Rothe] thought that since I was now established as an important classical interpreter, it was time to add my other faces.

JH / Was it a great homecoming?

CA / Yes, a homecoming. I enjoyed every note of it. It took me some time. I remember the first public performance was not very good. Then, gradually, every performance was better. I think the fifth performance, in Vienna, it was all there.

JH / When did you first study the Liszt sonata?

CA / I think I was seventeen or eighteen when I first played it in public.

JH / This is such an important piece, and so important to you, that I'd like to talk about it in some detail. Would you call it Liszt's greatest piano work?

CA / Oh yes, definitely.

JH / What sets it apart?

CA / The mastery of construction. In its time such free form in a sonata was completely unknown.

JH / To what extent do you apply a Faustian scenario in working out your interpretation? Do you think in terms of Faust and Gretchen and Mephistopheles?

CA / Definitely. This was something that was taken for granted among Liszt's pupils.

JH / I sense the presence of the Faust legend in the intensity and vision that you bring to the piece—there's obviously an inner life that you identify with. To what extent do you assign different passages to different characters? For instance, the opening theme in octaves.

CA / That is definitely Mephisto. This

is also an aspect of Mephisto. And this

is like a vision of hell—such incredible wailing.

JH / And the big passage in double octaves?

CA / That is the *apparent* triumph of Mephisto. This, of course, is the majesty of the Almighty:

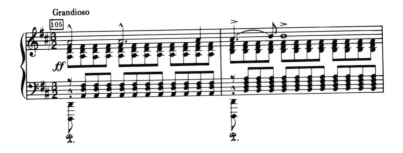

And then out of the Mephisto theme comes Gretchen, with the same melodic line, but a completely different character—sort of pleading to be spared or saved.

JH / Do you see this as the beginning of a confrontation between Gretchen and Mephisto?

CA / Yes. And the diminished seventh chords

I always feel as Mephisto sarcastically aping Faust and Gretchen. Then, on the next page, suddenly, the passionate, sensuous aspect of Faust and Gretchen appears.

This is the first clear appearance of Faust's masculine aspect:

JH / Then Liszt returns to the octaves of the very beginning [measure 286]. Do they have the same meaning as before?

CA / This once again is Mephisto's apparent triumph.

JH / Next comes a page of confrontation.

CA / The important thing here is the staccatissimo.

This is never done—separating the chords. I don't know why. This is not the Almighty, but Mephistopheles. The six-four chord, which always creates tension, here sounds ironic. Whereas next, in the first position, the chords are *drohend*, threatening.

JH / What's happening in between, in the recitativo?

CA / That is the two human beings, begging to be understood and spared.

JH / How is the second recitativo [measure 306] different from the first [measure 301]?

CA / It is more desperate. You see, here Mephistopheles is losing ground. At first, the staccatissimo chords are cynical, sarcastic. The second time, with the chords in the first position, he withdraws a little. And from there he is gradually fading, through the power of this pleading. On the following page, the intensity of the pleading must not decrease, even with the diminuendo. The two last chords before the second movement are like sobs. And the length of the fermata [measure 330] is very important. Then, in the second movement, Gretchen and Faust glorify love. This must really be ecstatic.

JH / What is the significance, in this movement, of the return of the theme that initially signified the Almighty [measure 363]?

CA / One could say that, in spite of everything, the Almighty has accepted these two human beings. As if he could be won over through sheer human pathos.

JH / There is an extraordinary page at the close of the movement, with soft scales in the right hand.

CA / This is always played too fast. It loses all its mystery. I always feel a chill when I play it. The big fugue, which comes next [measure 460], is Mephisto again, just laughing his head off. After that there is the recapitulation, and then the victory of the final pages.

JH / What of the very last page, after the last climax?

CA / There you must be careful not to let the Mephisto theme in the left hand become meaningless.

I apply little rhythmical distortions, even for the last one, pianissimo. And then there's the final Mephistophelian theme, but this time with a D sharp instead of D natural.

It's incredible how all the *meanness* of Mephisto is transformed. Through one note.

JH / What do you make of the very last note of the piece, the low B which you play so suddenly?

CA / The whole vision is wiped out.

JH / Is it like waking from a dream?

CA / Exactly.

JH / To what extent do you envision the characters and events we've been discussing when you play the piece? Do you actually perceive Gretchen while performing?

CA / More the emotional world of Gretchen. The characters are very much present, but as musical emotions. I don't do things just to suggest physical images.

JH / How do you feel afterward?

CA / Well, I stay floating for quite a while. And I've noticed that if I'm with friends, I'm really no good for anything. I am stupid. I cannot speak, except foolishly.

JH / We've talked about this before—loss of speech as an aspect of withdrawing into feeling. While playing, do you remain conscious of the audience?

CA / No, no, no. In the very beginning, yes. But later, if you stopped me, I couldn't tell you where I was.

JH / How has your assessment of the Liszt sonata changed over the years?

CA / I think my admiration has grown. Particularly when I saw the facsimile. When you see how Liszt trimmed away passages that appeared trivial, then you see what a master of construction he was. The original ending, in the facsimile, is a tremendous noise. Just to amaze.

JH / There's one other Liszt composition I'd like to examine with you—the B-minor Ballade. I know you apply the story of Hero

Claudio Arrau in 1908, the year he gave his first recital in Chillán.

With his sister, Lucrecia, and his mother,
Doña Lucrecia Leon de Arrau, 1910.

ABOVE: Arrau in 1919.
LEFT: Martin Krause, Arrau's
imperious teacher from 1913 to 1918.

With his mother, 1917.

Arrau in 1924, the year he returned penniless to Berlin
from his truncated first American tour.

With his wife, Ruth, in Santiago, 1941.

Arrau can easily stretch an octave
from thumb to forefinger.

An octave glissando.

Arrau's hands, December 1981.

In performance in Berkeley, California, December 9, 1977.

1978

and Leander. Not that many people seem to know about this interpretation.

CA / It was well known in Liszt's circle. As far as I can remember, the music follows the original myth. Leander swam the Hellespont to visit Hero every night, and swam back the next morning. In the music you can actually hear that it becomes more difficult each time. The fourth night he drowns. Then the very last pages are a transfiguration.

JH / So the first two pages, with the rising and falling chromatic scale in the left hand, represent the first time Leander swims the Hellespont.

CA / This first time nothing happens, really. It's not a stormy sea—yet. Then you have Hero's theme.

The music for the second night [measure 36] should be played in a stormier way, and the right-hand theme should be more threatening. The third night [measure 70], a terrific storm begins. These of course are big waves; they must not sound like an exercise in broken octaves:

But Leander still manages to reach the other side, gasping for breath. They say Wagner took the love theme here

for *Tristan.*

Anyway, Hero comforts Leander, caressing him, and realizing how close she came to losing him. Then there is the fourth night, and the biggest storm [measure 162]. This is the final struggle:

Leander is absolutely desperate. And this is where he drowns:

144

In this appassionato section

the love theme also represents Hero's anxiety, or sadness—subconsciously she probably senses that Leander is dead. Later, there are funeral bells.

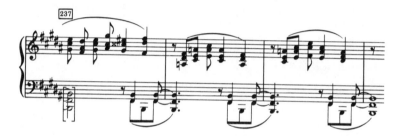

Here Hero's theme must be played in a completely different way—disembodied. Now, perhaps, she consciously realizes what has happened. And then comes the transfiguration—the *Verklärung.*

This has to be really sensuous. But it must also have the quality of remembrance.

JH / It's another one of Liszt's thematic transformations—as dramatic, I would say, as any of the transformations in the sonata. How would you characterize this theme in its first appearance, in the first measures of the piece?

CA / One has to feel a certain struggle with the water. Whereas here, in the *Verklärung*, it is like a vision.

JH / At the end there's a textual problem. There are two versions of the climax, one with chords, the other with scales. You prefer the scales [measure 292].

CA / Yes. Because, first of all, the scales develop more the idea of the water. The chords are too triumphal. And the scales lead much better to the final climax. In terms of interpretation, the scales are a real problem if you don't play them expressively, *lifting* them to the very last note. They must be almost melodic. Otherwise they sound trite.

JH / Then there's the further question of which coda to use.

CA / Oh no, never the first coda. It's the same as with the sonata. At first Liszt finished the piece with tremendous bombast. Then he realized it wasn't right. The revised ending is so beautiful. Here Hero's theme [measure 105] must be played in a completely new way—confronting death. She gives up the struggle and says farewell to Leander.

JH / A lot of people don't care for this piece, you know. They think it's melodramatic.

CA / It isn't. I think it's one of Liszt's masterworks. There is, you see, this problem with program music. Some people think it's unhealthy for a musician to think of anything but the notes. I agree with that for when you finally perform a work. But I've found that sometimes, when you're teaching, if the students cannot enter into the music, the only way is for them to have a program in mind. At least while they're studying it.

JH / We haven't talked at all about the film that you made. Very few people know that you starred in a movie about Liszt.

CA / Mexican pictures were very primitive in those days. I was an improvised actor. I never saw the whole thing—only excerpts.

Actually, I thought some of the love scenes were quite good. [Laughing.] That was where an improvised actor could do best. The worst were the scenes where I had to be angry. That was very difficult for me.

JH / I have a copy of the review from the *New York Times*.

CA / My God! Really? I never knew they reviewed it.

JH / It's dated January 11, 1936, and says:

> Just why it was left to Mexico to turn out a musical film based on the romantic life of Franz Liszt, the great Hungarian pianist and composer, may remain one of the mysteries of the motion picture world. Be that as it may, José Behr, the Argentine actor and director, with the able assistance of Claudio Arrau, the talented Chilean pianist, has produced something worthwhile in *Sueño de Amor* [*Dream of Love*], the current attraction at the Teatro Campoamor.
>
> While it is possible to point out a few technical flaws in this highly entertaining work, they count for little against the excellent acting and playing . . . of Señor Arrau and the generally competent support he enjoys. . . .
>
> From the musical side the high spots are the playing of *Liebesträume, La Chasse* and the *Second Hungarian Rhapsody,* the last by an orchestra. Despite the 'studio' set-up, the atmosphere of Europe of the middle of the last century is fairly realistic. An especially striking scene shows the reception given to Liszt by a band of gypsies when he visits his birthplace after a lapse of many years. It must be admitted that a few more dramatic incidents might have made this offering more popular with the run-of-mine cinema patrons, but that is a matter of taste.

It's signed "H. T. S."*

CA / That's quite a good review. I never read that.

JH / I understand there was one scene in the movie that touched you so much that you wept.

*Harry T. Smith.

CA / Oh yes. The end. Liszt is on a train, as an old man, thinking back. And a beautiful girl is sitting in front of him, and she is laughing at him. I was very moved, and cried.

JH / You have great admiration for Liszt as a man.

CA / He was a wonderful human being, and able to understand and appreciate his contemporaries. Nobody has done as much for other composers as he did.

JH / Some people see him as an actor, a poser.

CA / He was vain, of course. But that's all right. Maybe he was a little bit of a showman, particularly with the ladies. But such a kind and noble character. All the things that the Countess d'Agoult wrote and said against Liszt were of course mostly imagined.

JH / Have you looked at Cosima's diaries?

CA / I think she's appalling. I hate the way she behaved toward her father. I mean, sometimes she didn't even *receive* him in Wahnfried. *She* particularly, not Wagner. Once Siegfried Wagner's daughter Friedelind—a wonderful person; we were friends— once she got angry that I *dared* to praise her great-grandfather as a composer. That's the way the whole Wagner family felt about Liszt the composer. Wagner himself, no. Wagner loved the sonata. But for the family, there was only one composer. Even Beethoven was just a transition to Wagner.

JH / How high do you rank Liszt's output?

CA / The problem with Liszt is that there is so much *Gelegenheitswerke* [occasional music]—a lot of unimportant music that should never have been printed.

JH / But even the great works have frequently been disparaged.

CA / That's the interpreter's fault. Because they've used him to show off their fingers. And there is more in Liszt's music than in Chopin's music or Schumann's music with which to show off one's fingers.

JH / You've been playing Liszt for more than half a century. From your vantage point, can you trace the ups and downs of Liszt's fortunes?

CA / Germany resisted more than other countries. And they *still* resist acknowledging him as a great composer. When they speak in Germany of the "Liszt renaissance," they speak as if it were happening only in other countries. It makes me furious. And in Austria and Italy, and the Spanish- and Portuguese-speaking countries, Liszt is also resisted. But in France the new appreciation of Liszt is really marvelous. There may have been some kind of early Liszt renaissance there, because Debussy and Ravel admired *Les Jeux d'eaux à la Villa d'Este.* In England and the United States, the Liszt renaissance has been going on for at least twenty years, I would say.

JH / In going through your *New York Times* reviews the other day, I came across one from the forties in which Olin Downes called *Les Jeux d'eaux à la Villa d'Este* a "sublimated parlor piece."

CA / That gives you an idea of the way critics and musicians used to speak about him.

JH / But I think he's doing all right now.

CA / Maybe I wouldn't put Liszt as high as Bach, Mozart, Beethoven, or Schubert. But as high as Weber, Chopin, Schumann, and Brahms.

# Brahms, Chopin, Beethoven

In addition to Liszt, the composers with whom Arrau is most associated are probably Beethoven, Brahms, Chopin, and Schumann. Compared to Liszt's, their music lends itself less to analysis via story and metaphor. For the purposes of this book, to have spent as much time talking about a Beethoven sonata or Chopin ballade as about the Liszt sonata and B-minor Ballade would have invited a surfeit of technical detail. My original intention was to discuss Beethoven, Brahms, Chopin, and Schumann somewhat less exhaustively than Liszt, and to combine the four conversations in a single chapter. As it turned out, the Beethoven Fourth Piano Concerto did elicit a "story" from Arrau. In talking about Brahms and Chopin, he stressed certain interpretive guidelines and cited specific applications. Schumann, for whatever reason, proved an unsuccessful conversation topic—Arrau's remarks were scattered and infrequent; I have incorporated one of them in discussing his Schumann recordings in the Conclusion.

Arrau came relatively late to Brahms. Martin Krause felt Brahms's thick piano textures failed to develop the fingers. The only Brahms Arrau remembers studying with Krause was the *Paganini* Variations and Fifty-one Exercises. The Brahms works he has performed most often are the F-sharp minor and F-minor Sonatas, the *Handel* Variations, and the two piano concertos. The later piano pieces (Opuses 76, 79, 116, 117, 118, 119) he has more or less ignored. Krause thought little of them, and Arrau feels they are not much admired in Germany generally. Recently, however, he has discovered more passion in them than he had suspected, and has thought to program a few.

Chopin, according to Arrau, is a composer Krause appreciated but other Germans did not. Except for the chamber works and the little-known First Sonata, he has, as he recalls, played nearly the entire Chopin *corpus,* including—in addition to the many works he has recorded—all the mazurkas and polonaises.

Since the fifties, Arrau has played Beethoven more often than any other composer. His discography, with over eighty Beethoven listings, reflects this emphasis. He has also edited the Beethoven sonatas, in two volumes, for C. F. Peters. (See pages 207–13.)

JH / The Brahms pieces you mainly perform—in particular, the F-sharp minor and F-minor Piano Sonatas, and the D-minor Piano Concerto—are thought of as youthful. Not only literally, in the sense that Brahms was still in his late teens or twenties when he wrote them, but also in the sense of being youthful in spirit. Yet it seems to me that all three works are susceptible to two different types of interpretation. You play the D-minor Concerto expansively, suggesting ripeness and experience. Many pianists play it faster, and with a different kind of passion—more angry, more overt.

CA / It is a mistake to associate *speed* with *passion.* In music that should be played slowly, speed is the opposite of passion. The tension is completely lost. In the D-minor Concerto, I don't think there are two possible interpretations. The first movement is written in six quarter-notes. And it's not even Allegro; it's Maestoso. Where is the majesty if it's played fast? Brahms reached an early maturity, in this concerto particularly. And the way the second movement is played! Conductors usually start it too fast because they have only one note to the beat.

JH / What's the mood of this second movement?

CA / First of all, it's the tragedy of Schumann's madness and death. And it also paints a picture of Clara in her sorrow. And, on top of that, Brahms wrote on one of the manuscript copies, *"Benedictus qui venit in nomine Domini."* All this, and it's played metronomically, this movement! The last movement, with its vitality—there you can have different interpretations. But in the first two movements it is not possible. It is a complete misunderstanding.

JH / Can we talk about the second movement cadenza? I find it one of the high points of your interpretation.

CA / The trills represent a sort of religious ecstasy. I always have to beg conductors—to *beg*, on my knees—not to get any faster after the cadenza. On the contrary, the end of the movement should be still slower. It's like a farewell to Schumann, looking back. The last movement is less problematic. It's an affirmation, an acceptance of life. That's very much the way a young person should feel after such a tragedy.

JH / Do you want to say anything about the opening movement?

CA / It's monumental. It's colossal. There had never been anything like it in music before. Already, in the second measure, Brahms moves from D minor to B-flat major—that alone must have shocked people. To a great extent, it was a terrible failure when Brahms first played it. It took him four years to finish it. And it took, I don't know, half a century for it to become really popular.

JH / Brahms wrote three piano sonatas. You're identified with two of them—the F minor and the F-sharp minor. Did you ever play the Sonata in C?

CA / No. I think it's weak. The slow movement is very beautiful.

JH / You think the F-sharp minor Sonata is a stronger work— even though it was written first?

CA / Yes. The beginning of the F-sharp minor Sonata is so *incredible*, such a challenging of the world. That alone should make people, particularly young people, want to play it. The entire first movement is really magnificent.

JH / Is the coda a technical or interpretive problem? Brahms asks that the whole last page be played fortissimo.

CA / The way it's written is almost impossible—to make the big skips fortissimo. Actually, *without exception* people redistribute the notes. Here, for instance, they take the bottom notes in the right hand—F sharp, C sharp, A, F sharp—with the left hand:

And then, of course, it's very easy. Again, I must say that such facilitation is wrong. Physical difficulty has itself an expressive value. When something sounds easy, its meaning changes completely. Another place in the same sonata that is almost never played as written is the last page of the Scherzo—the lowest notes in the tremolos in the right hand are simply omitted.

JH / This is a sonata that doesn't get played very much.

CA / I think it's because the ending is so strange. Let's say that it doesn't bring down the house. It has to be ecstatic, but pianissimo except for the last three chords. To give a mystical, ecstatic feeling to the scales and trills of the last page is very difficult. I think, compositionally, it isn't absolutely spontaneous.

JH / Would you have preferred a different ending?

CA / [Laughing.] Well, yes. Something more along the lines of the climax just before.

JH / Wouldn't you say that the entire last movement of the F-sharp minor Sonata is problematic?

CA / It's actually less of a problem than the finale of the F-minor Sonata.

JH / But the F-minor Sonata has a more memorable slow movement. Could we talk about that a bit? It's such a peak in—

CA / In all music! For me, it is the most beautiful love music after *Tristan*. And the most erotic—if you really let go, without any embarrassment. And if you play it *slowly* enough.

JH / Are you influenced, in your interpretation, by the passage from Sternau that Brahms quotes at the head of the movement? *"Der Abend dämmert, das Mondlicht scheint/Da sind zwei Herzen in Liebe vereint/Und halten sich selig umfangen."* [Twilight comes, the moonlight shines/Two hearts unite in love/And embrace each other ecstatically.]

CA / Very much so. You know, Sternau was a mediocre, insignificant poet. I don't know from where Brahms dug this quotation up.

JH / I once had a discussion with a well-known New York piano teacher about whether the final section of this movement, which Brahms marks "Andante molto," should be faster or slower than the basic tempo.

CA / It means slower. Brahms didn't know Italian. He thought "andante" meant slow. Particularly in his early works, he was a little confused about the meaning of the Italian tempo marks. "Andante molto"—actually in Italian it would mean rather flowing. There is a question also about the general tempo of the movement. It's written in four beats to the bar, not two.

JH / Then why doesn't Brahms mark it four-eight, rather than two-four?

CA / This two-four you have also in Beethoven many times, and it's taken in four, not in two. Say, in *Les Adieux*, the beginning and the Andante. Did you ever read Rudolf Kolisch's article on tempo marks in Beethoven?* He mentions several such cases. If you count the slow movement of the Brahms F-minor Sonata in two, it becomes *pleasant*. Rather than ecstatic.

*Musical Quarterly*, April and July 1943.

JH / Do you want to say anything about the poco più lento section?

CA / It's a series of groups of two notes. Sometimes they are played as a continuous melody. But it should be a sort of lovers' dialogue. Later

the two voices come together as one.

JH / There's almost nothing else in Brahms like this, is there?

CA / Perhaps, a little bit, the second of the Opus 10 Ballades, which has the same feeling of wide horizons. This ballade reminds me also of a Brahms song—"Feldeinsamkeit." It's about a fellow lying on his back in a field, looking up at the clouds, and just in ecstasy about it.* The Opus 10 Ballades, in general, have something in common with Brahms's lieder. I think in the lieder field he was absolutely inspired—this has to be accepted even by people who usually reject him as pompous.

JH / I find your recording of the Fourth Ballade especially revelatory.

CA / This ballade, too, has a very strong feeling of experiencing nature in a mystical way—first in sunshine and then in sudden

---

*The text of "Feldeinsamkeit," by Hermann Allmers, reads:

> *I lie still in the tall green grass*
> *and gaze a long time upward—*
> *crickets chirping around me ceaselessly,*
> *heaven's blue miraculously woven about me.*
> *The beautiful white clouds drift yonder*
> *through the deep blue, like lovely silent dreams.*
> *It seems to me as though I have long been dead,*
> *and am drifting blissfully with them through the eternal spaces.*

(Translation by Philip L. Miller.)

gloom. The ending is incredible—più lento, then poco a poco ritenuto, then ritenuto, and finally adagio. It's like reaching a point of ecstasy where everything comes to a stop. St. Teresa, the Spanish mystic, wrote about uniting with God at the *peak* of an ecstatic surge; eventually, she can't move anymore. The French have a word, *"hébété."* The Germans say *"erstarrt."* That's what this ending absolutely is.

. . .

JH / You've said that when you performed the Chopin E-minor Piano Concerto with Otto Klemperer in Cologne in 1954, it turned out that he had never conducted Chopin in his life. (See page 125.)

CA / He just didn't know Chopin. In the rehearsal, in the opening tutti, he stopped the orchestra and said, "Gentlemen, this man was really a great composer." As if it were a *revelation.* Many people in Germany, especially before World War Two, didn't consider Chopin a great musician. Even when they admired some of his music, there was condescension. The very fact that he never wrote anything for orchestra, and almost no chamber music, was held against him.

JH / Were any German pianists conspicuous for condescending to Chopin? What about Schnabel?

CA / I think so. I heard him play the E-minor Concerto. It sounded like Bach. It was as if he had decided, I will show people how Chopin should really sound. It was like a Bach invention.

JH / There's a related prejudice about Chopin—the idea that his music is a pretext for display.

CA / Yes, a pretext for personality cults, rather than a music valid for all humanity. Many Germans thought he was a salon composer. They used him for technical display, and for displaying personal *elegance.* There is of course elegance in Chopin's music, and in the most marvelous sense of the word. But it's only one element. This idea people have that his music should be played up to mezzo forte and back, it's absurd. The fact that he was sick, and he didn't have very much physical strength, doesn't mean that others should imitate that. His music is much bigger. People speak about his collection of canes and his beautiful handkerchiefs and cravats, his actual elegance in dressing and in style of living. But I am convinced that composers are very seldom the best interpreters of their own music.

J H / In Germany, did anyone stand out—maybe Busoni—as an advocate of Chopin as a great composer of serious music?

C A / Well, Busoni adored the preludes. But, like Schnabel, he wanted to *rescue* Chopin from the attitudes other pianists had toward him. I never heard him talk about it, but that's what I felt.

J H / Were the attitudes toward Chopin you encountered in the United States any different from what you had experienced in Germany?

C A / The only thing I would say is that in Germany you could be considered a great artist even if you couldn't play Chopin. Whereas in the United States, France, and England, there could be artists who only played Chopin, and they still would be considered great artists.

J H / It was more important for a pianist to play Chopin in the United States than it had been in Germany.

C A / Yes. Definitely.

J H / Did you find that his image was any different?

C A / Well, people were simply *enchanted* with Chopin's music in the United States. They never considered that he might also be profound.

J H / What would you say is the peak of Chopin's output?

C A / I think maybe some of the nocturnes.

J H / That's a heretical view, you know.

C A / It is?

J H / Sure. Most people . . .

C A / What would they say? The ballades.

J H / And the preludes. The nocturnes, I would say, are usually considered more descriptive, less searching.

CA / So many times, you know, people tell me that my Chopin is different. I find it so natural to play it as I do.

JH / To what degree are you conscious of interpreting a piece unconventionally? For instance, I would say that, of your recordings of the nocturnes, the one that challenges the conventional wisdom the most may be the one from Opus 37 in G. One normally hears it played more sedately. You're not conscious of playing this piece in an unusually agitated way?

CA / I don't even know what the conventional wisdom is.

JH / Can you remember having heard another pianist play this G-major Nocturne? Is it possible that you only know it through your own performances?

CA / I can't think of any others I've heard. Let's see, what Chopin have I liked? There was a marvelous performance of the Third Nocturne by d'Albert. That was magic. I liked Horowitz playing the B-flat minor Sonata, in Berlin in the twenties. Of course I heard de Pachmann. The Fourth Scherzo. That was quite beautiful—light, and all the passage-work somehow *beseelen* [soulful] also. Hofmann I didn't know what to do with. The person I liked most in Chopin was probably Cortot. In spite of his breaking of the hands. I remember a marvelous performance of the etudes in London. I heard him also do the preludes.

JH / The preludes. It seems to me that's the body of music by Chopin that most confounds the prejudices against him. Because you couldn't say that the preludes are salon music or a pretext for display. Do you always play them as a cycle?

CA / Yes. As a young man I would play them individually. But I stopped doing that—in the twenties, I think.

JH / Do you have individual favorites among the preludes?

CA / As I say, I never think of them as single pieces. They *answer* one another. When I finish one of them, I *need* to play the next. In a way, they are a survey of Chopin's cosmos. Alternating light and shade.

JH / I recently heard a tape of a performance you gave of the preludes in Los Angeles in 1969. And in some instances you went directly from one prelude to the next, without a break, without any silence in between. This doesn't occur on your recording, because the engineers have inserted bands.

C A / It reminds me a little bit of some of the connections between movements in late Beethoven. One movement *erupts,* in a completely different mood, out of the one before it. In Opus 109, for instance. Or Opus 101.

J H / Which preludes do you usually begin without an intervening silence?

C A / The B-flat minor [No. 16]. Also the D minor [No. 24].

J H / Could we go back to the First Prelude, and talk about some of the preludes individually?

C A / The First Prelude is definitely an introduction. An intensely dramatic introduction. It's over in half a minute or something. And it puts one in a certain tense emotional situation. It has something to do with sexual energy, this prelude. There's something positively orgasmic about it.

J H / The music heaves and heaves toward a climax.

C A / And that would explain the three bars with altered rhythm.

In these three bars, just before the climax, you don't breathe anymore. The A-minor prelude [No. 2] is fantastically desolate. But the next prelude, in G [No. 3], has something to do with a friendly landscape, or with spring.

JH / You make very much of the turn in the right hand [measure 17]—more, I think, than any other pianist I've heard. And you take a big rubato to make room for it.

CA / This is a period in which ornaments become part of the melodic line. Such ornaments should always be treated melodically in Chopin. . . . The E-minor Prelude [No. 4] is again melancholy. I can't think of any other music in which the melody is just two notes, and all the emotional events occur in the harmonic changes, shading the two notes with different colors and moods. And then when the espressivo phrases come in—because of the monotony of the two notes, they make an incredible impact.

JH / In the B-minor Prelude [No. 6] you stress the two-note sighing inflections in the right hand, almost as a countersubject to the melody in the left. Chopin is sometimes stigmatized as a one-handed composer. But I hear in your performances of a number of the preludes an unusual degree of individuality in both hands. In the G-sharp minor Prelude [No. 12] your left hand has such amazing energy and definition that the prelude practically becomes a contest between the hands.

CA / You could say that the G-minor Prelude [No. 22] is a struggle between the hands. The ending is fantastic. The left hand keeps insisting on the same thing, and the right hand, not knowing what to do, ascends to the utmost treble.

JH / I once heard you describe the E-flat minor Prelude [No. 14] as the most "enigmatic" in the cycle.

CA / The tempo is printed as largo in the Oxford edition, rather than allegro. That's why I play it slowly. Chopin wrote it in with pencil or something. You know, it's sometimes interpreted in an impressionistic way. But to me this prelude is full of *Qual*—intense suffering. Exasperation.

JH / The E-flat minor Prelude is often compared to the finale of the B-flat minor Sonata, which is also written as two lines an octave apart.

CA / That finale has of course a lot to do with the Funeral March movement that precedes it. They used to call it "the wind over the grave." The E-flat minor Prelude, especially if you play it at the slower tempo, is more anguished.

JH / Another prelude that's enigmatic or elusive in somewhat the same way—because again there's no melody to speak of—is the F minor [No. 18].

CA / Oh yes. That's *tremendous*. There's a relationship between this and the second movement of the Beethoven G-major Piano Concerto. [See page 168.] It's again two conflicting elements. The upper voice is pleading in an absolutely *desperate* way. And the answering chords are a *furious* denial. The denial grows stronger and stronger. There is a terrific struggle. Here, unlike in the G-major Concerto, there is no solution. The end is a collapse of the pleading voice. The final two chords are a rejection.

JH / Do you want to say anything about the last several preludes as a group—the way Chopin evolves toward a final statement? Is it fated, from the beginning, that the cycle will end so cataclysmically?

CA / No. Only after the B-flat minor Prelude [No. 16], I would say, do you feel that his fundamental approach to life is tragic. The peaceful, positive preludes become like remembrances of the things that make life acceptable. Do you know Chopin's letter to his friend Titus [May 15, 1830] about the second movement of the E-minor Piano Concerto? About spring and the moonlight? The F-major Prelude [No. 23] is very much like that. A bit *Au bord d'une source.*

JH / Do you have trouble integrating the F-major Prelude? Does it ever seem swallowed up by the G minor [No. 22] and D minor [No. 24]?

CA / No, no. It's absolutely necessary—this balancing, always showing the other side of life. If Chopin went directly from the G-minor to the D-minor Prelude, they would kill one another.

JH / And what about the D-minor Prelude [No. 24]?

CA / There is a famous description of it—"blood, voluptuousness, and death." That says everything.

JH / You bring out the left hand very distinctly.

CA / I heard a performance the other day in which the left hand was a complete blur. But it is really a very dramatic element—like a stormy sea. You could say that the *plunge* at the end is like a drowning. Or that it cuts the thread of life—like the Fates in Greek mythology.

JH / What fingering do you use for the three final low D's?

CA / Three-four-five. [Arrau forms a hard wedge with the last three fingers of his left hand.] That's absolutely sure. The possibility of hitting a wrong note doesn't exist, really. And it allows the transmission of the utmost power through the body.

JH / Why is your fingering better than using, say, the thumb, as Cortot recommends?

CA / With the thumb, you have to strike vertically or in a flat position. To strike vertically would be unavoidably hard and ugly. And with the flat position you are less sure of getting the amount of power you need.

JH / Are the preludes the darkest thing in Chopin?

CA / I would probably say yes. The ending is so *definite*. I mean, after this, you cannot find any great enthusiasm for life.*

· · ·

JH / In the cycle of the Beethoven piano sonatas, are there stylistic shifts that dictate a much different approach to, say, the late sonatas as opposed to the early and middle sonatas?

CA / The late sonatas have to be played in a more improvisatory way, and with more rubato. We know that Beethoven himself played very freely. Schindler, for instance, speaks of his changes of tempo.

JH / Can you mark a point in the cycle where the greatest degree of interpretive freedom begins?

CA / Although Opus 81a actually belongs to the late period, there is not much occasion, because the structure is too square. But in Opus 90, definitely.

*While working on the preludes in the winter of 1838–39, Chopin lived with George Sand on Majorca in a decrepit abandoned cloister. Plagued by illness, bad weather, and unfriendly islanders, Chopin worried that he would never leave the place alive. Fourteen weeks after arriving, he was transported back to the mainland in a boat laden with pigs. By the time he reached Barcelona, he was, as Sand later recalled, coughing up blood and phlegm "by the bowlful."

JH / This is made clear in your recordings—the rubatos are much more pronounced in the late sonatas than before. I find your Opus 111 especially distinctive—both in terms of the use of rubato, and of your particular vision of the spiritual journey Beethoven lays out. Perhaps you could trace some of what happens in the second movement.

CA / In the first place, the theme is already hinted at in the coda to the first movement, where all the demonic struggles and collisions that have taken place are found in the left hand, and the right hand leads into the second movement.

JH / When you say the right hand leads into the second movement, do you mean the theme of the second movement—the arietta—is anticipated?

CA / Yes. And it has to be played like that. The first three measures

correspond to the end of the first phrase of the arietta.

And the next two measures, with their wider intervals, correspond to the end of the second phrase of the arietta. A fantastic idea here is that there is no fermata after the final chord, and no rest. It could be negligence, of course. But I think it has a meaning—that the connection must be done in a very conscious way: how long you hold the final chord; when you lift the pedal to breathe—very briefly—before the arietta.

JH / If there were a fermata or rest, it would draw less attention to the silence between the movements.

CA / Exactly. There must be a sort of mystical connection. By the way, there is also a very unusual connection between the first and second movements of Opus 109.

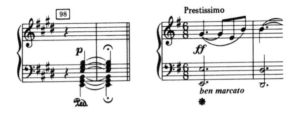

You must take up the pedal a split second before you *bust* into the Prestissimo.

JH / Can we return to the second movement of Opus 111?

CA / Well, there is already a tremendous evolution of the arietta from the first variation to the second, and from the second to the third. Particularly from the second to the third.

JH / The third variation is quite violent. Is it perhaps closer to the struggles of the first movement than to the exaltation of the second?

CA / No, no, no. The type of assertion is completely different. It's like looking back at life before leaving it. It is a joyful assertion of life on earth. I find it wonderful, the way it emerges a last time, this attachment to life. The beginning of the next variation already has nothing to do with one's personal existence. I think of it as the breathing of nature. Or as going down to the mothers—*die Müttern*. Then comes this marvelous ascent to a mystical ecstasy. There is a phrase in Goethe that describes it—"*der Fall nach oben,*" the fall upward:

JH / Another piece I'd like to touch on is the Fourth Piano Concerto, which again seems to me to elicit an especially personal interpretation from you. And I know you've been playing it quite a bit lately.

CA / You know, there is this tradition in Germany that gives the atmosphere for the first and second movements as the legend of Orpheus and Eurydice.

JH / I've only heard that applied to the second movement. How does it fit the first movement?

CA / The first movement is always taken too fast. The "moderato" in Allegro moderato should be written in *red ink.* And also it is usually performed too playfully, with short staccatos. I can't prove it, but I'm certain that this is a sad movement. Which would make it fit in with the legend of Orpheus, Orpheus having lost Eurydice. Then the second movement is Orpheus at the gates of hell, begging the Furies to give Eurydice back. One thing that's very important at the beginning is the way this theme is played.

It's the first time the music goes into a minor key. I've performed this concerto hundreds of times, and the only conductor who did it exactly right—with a really deep melancholy—was Eugen Jochum. We didn't even have to talk about it.

JH / Can we talk about the opening of the development? That's a very special place. In the drama—in the story of the movement—what goes on here?

CA / It's Orpheus pleading for Eurydice. Four times he begs. And then begins his struggle with the powers of the underworld. These passages of arpeggios in the development—you have to make them *speak*. Here the quintuplet in the right hand and the triplet in the left hand must not seem too similar:

JH / That's an important point, because it's characteristic of your Beethoven. There are similar passages in the first movement of the *Appassionata* where you stress rhythmic distinctions in order to make the passage-work more specific, more articulate. Here, for instance, at the climax of the development:

CA / These shouldn't be played as quintuplets. There should be a definite stop on the last note, which is not a sixteenth but an eighth. The more the better—the more drama, the more intensity.

JH / It's not a series of arpeggios in free rhythm.

CA / Absolutely. Particularly in middle Beethoven, rhythmic clarity is so terribly important. And it's much of the time overlooked.

This is another marvelous place, in the first movement of the *Appassionata:*

The sixteenths in the right hand are usually played late. But they must be part of this sixteenth-note motion of the whole movement. One-two-three-one-*two-three-one*-two-three-one-*two-three-one*. The sixteenths in both hands go *exactly* together.

J H / Getting back to the first movement of the G-major Concerto, can we look at the cadenza?

C A / Here, going from

to

makes Orpheus's pleading more intense, more desperate. This idea occurs again in the coda. The end of the coda is of course forceful; this is perhaps Orpheus's resolution—or, at any rate, an emotional preparation for the next movement.

J H / So the first movement, taken as a whole, suggests a failed attempt to achieve the rescue that takes place in the second movement.

C A / Yes. In the second movement, there is this dialogue between the soloist and the orchestra. Gradually, the soloist comes forward. I always tell conductors that the beginning should be played furioso. And not too fast—it's in eighths, not quarters.

The solos should not be too soft. They are of course una corda [soft pedal], but they must really *speak*. The first is marked molto cantabile, and the second molto espressivo, espressivo being *stronger*. Eventually, the orchestra begins to yield. This last chord in the orchestra before the cadenza, after the orchestra has been silent for three measures, is amazing—it's a sign that they have been listening. In the cadenza, it's important not to begin the crescendo too early. I usually start the first trill not too fast. The second I start at the same level, but a little faster. The third is still faster. And *then* starts the crescendo, which represents a sort of rising anxiety. The entrance of the left hand, fortissimo, has to be made in absolute *desperation*.

JH / I think you take more time in this cadenza than any other pianist I've heard. Especially after the trills, where the right hand winds downward toward the cadence.

CA / Although they are written as small notes, I play the sixteenths here the same speed as the sixteenth-notes before the cadenza. And then the eighths and quarters are of course slower. The very last notes, which are marked "portato," must definitely be separated—as if Orpheus has almost no breath left. I mean, this pleading is a tremendous effort—for a human being to face these powers of Hades. You have to give the impression you are *completely* exhausted. The transition to the finale is terribly difficult. You must wait, but not too long. The first statement of the Rondo theme, in the orchestra, must seem tentative. When the piano repeats it, there has been a change in mood, completely. From tragedy to *euphoria*. It is a completely new situation.

JH / You always talk about Beethoven in terms of struggle and transcendence. Even where he is supposedly lighthearted, you caution against "playfulness" or "elegance." You once wrote a program note for the Opus 90 Sonata, in which you said the second movement "is too full of unease to become even a little bit gay and ends abruptly in resignation." Yet many people see this as a cheerful movement.

CA / That I don't understand at all. The melody is lyrical, but not gay. The sonata as a whole has something in common with Opus 111. The first movement is about human struggle. And the second movement has a lot to do with the sadness of farewell.

JH / I've heard you say that you don't think there's any humor in Beethoven. What about something like the interjections in the Scherzo of the *Hammerklavier*—the prestissimo scale, and the tremolo? Most people would say that these are examples of Beethoven's sense of humor.

CA / This I would not call humor, but aggressiveness. In Edwin Fischer's book on the Beethoven sonatas, to my *amazement*, he finds the finale to Opus 10, no. 3, a humorous movement. Actually, I would say it's a little bit similar to the last movement of the Schubert B-flat Sonata: anxiously asking, asking,

and *asking*.

It's so clear. The theme comes from this continuous wailing in the slow movement:

You know, I think that humor has nothing to do with music. Humor has to do with thoughts and words. Only in an artificial sense can one say that music is humorous.

JH / Do you ever find music funny?

CA / No.

JH / There must be something in music you find funny. What about Mozart's *A Musical Joke?*

CA / But the humor is superimposed. It's extramusical.

JH / For the International Beethoven Festival in Bonn, during the Beethoven Bicentennial, you wrote: "For me, Beethoven has always stood for the spirit of man victorious. His message of endless struggle concluding in the victory of renewal and spiritual rebirth speaks to us and to young people today with a force that is particularly relevant to our times. In the sense that his life was an existential fight for survival, Beethoven is our contemporary. In the sense that he mastered both his life and his art to reach the ultimate heights of creation and transfiguration, he will last as long as man's spirit to prevail lasts on earth." I was wondering, with reference to this, how you relate to Beethoven the man. So many of the traits you see in Beethoven—struggle, loneliness, spiritual exaltation—are traits you see in yourself. Do you recognize yourself in Beethoven?

CA / [Hesitantly, then breaking into laughter.] Maybe I shouldn't say this . . . but I don't like Beethoven as a person. I don't like the way he treated his nephew. And I don't like his self-pity, in the Heiligenstadt Testament.

JH / He was sloppy, too. Does that offend you?

CA / That also.

JH / There's the famous story about Beethoven and Goethe meeting the Archduke—that Goethe stepped aside, took off his hat, and bowed, but Beethoven refused to budge.

CA / There I am with Beethoven. Goethe's behavior could be interpreted as a sort of maturity, and Beethoven's as childishness. But I don't think so. Of the two attitudes I take Beethoven's.

JH / How do you like Goethe as a person?

CA / [Laughing.] Also not very much. Although I adore every word he wrote. As a person, he was terribly conceited. And though I shouldn't say it, because the Germans will be furious, he was a little provincial.

JH / Do you know Thomas Mann's description of Goethe in *Lotte in Weimar?*

CA / Yes, and I don't like him there either.

JH / I think Mann rather does. I think Mann excuses Goethe's behavior on the grounds of genius. Do you excuse Beethoven? Or do you hold him responsible for his bad acts?

CA / I hold him responsible. Beethoven's behavior toward his nephew is unforgivable.

JH / So you must admire Liszt as a man more than Beethoven.

CA / Oh yes. Much more.

JH / How do you react to the other great composers as people? Say, Chopin, or Schumann, or Brahms?

CA / Chopin had reactions to people which don't fit the impression one has through his music. His attitude toward Liszt, for example, knowing how Liszt worshiped his music and wanted to be his friend. He was neurotically closed toward Liszt. . . . But I'm talking nonsense. My appreciation of the personalities of the different composers has to do with my early attachment to the image of Liszt.

JH / The people who were nice to Liszt you like, and the people who weren't you don't.

CA / Yes. I always had something against Clara Schumann, for instance, because of that.

JH / How about Robert Schumann?

CA / Schumann I have tremendous admiration for. Brahms, too, was a very nice man. The only thing I mind in Brahms is that he fell asleep when Liszt played his B-minor Sonata for him. Maybe Brahms was tired or something, I don't know. Probably you can't ask great creative personalities to admire other great creative personalities.

JH / I sometimes think the same is true of interpreters. I'm struck by how firm your opinions are when you talk about music, compared to how flexible they are when you talk about anything else. When you talk about the Brahms D-minor Concerto, you become completely single-minded: you believe there's only one possible tempo for the first movement. Which suggests to me that it's really a necessary part of your psychological equipment as an interpreter to believe that you play a given piece the only possible way.

CA / Or maybe one of two possible ways.

JH / But that's not what you say.

CA / I know. But that would make it less disgusting.

JH / In the heat of the moment, you say your way is the only possible way. You become an absolute dogmatist.

CA / My goodness, that's the last thing I want!

JH / Don't you think it could be important to be convinced that your way is the only way?

CA / But when you look into the music, when you look at the *notation*—it's six quarters. You can't play as if they were written as six sixteenths.

JH / You're just confirming my point. It's the same point that you made about creative personalities—that you can't expect them to—

CA / I said *probably*. *Probably* it's very difficult. And I was thinking of composers.

JH / And I changed the subject to interpreters. Doesn't an interpreter have to be armored with the certainty that his interpretation is the correct interpretation?

CA / There are always different possibilities. But there are certain things that are not a question of interpretation. If Beethoven writes "piano" and you play forte, it's *wrong*. It's just wrong.

# Listening to Brahms

Judging from recordings and reviews, Arrau's playing has changed substantially since his Berlin days. The later performances are more notable for depth and intensity. The earlier performances glitter more.

Arrau's own perception of the change is vague. He refuses to dwell on the past. In fact, he will not listen to his early recordings. He hears his recordings once—as test pressings, when they are new. Anything prior, he reasons, "is no longer me." He finds such intimate self-recollection discomfiting. In the act of performing, there is no distance from the music. Hearing the same performance from a listener's chair, he feels "uncovered," "embarrassed."

From the moment I undertook the present book, I envisioned subjecting Arrau to his former self as preserved on disc. The only way I could make him cooperate, he told me, would be to strap him down. Fortunately, Peter Warwick, a New Jersey record buff, supplied what proved the perfect bait: a four-track tape consisting of four Arrau performances of the Brahms D-minor Piano Concerto: with Basil Cameron and the Philharmonia Orchestra, a studio performance from 1947; with Josef Krips and the New York Philharmonic, a broadcast concert performance taped on February 16, 1964; with Rafael Frühbeck de Burgos and the Montreal Symphony, a broadcast concert performance taped on February 10 or 11, 1976; and with Michael Palmer and the Atlanta Symphony, a broadcast concert performance taped on February 4 or 5, 1977.

The Cameron and Frühbeck performances were opposite one another on side one of the tape, facilitating cross reference. Krips and Palmer were opposite one another on side two. The timings alone told part of the story—Cameron: 47 minutes; Krips: 47; Frühbeck: 50; Palmer: 52.

Arrau has performed the Brahms D-minor Concerto for half a century. But he had never listened to tapes of his concert performances, and could not remember hearing the Cameron recording. When I told him about Peter Warwick's tape, he asked to borrow it and promised to listen to it. Months later, it had not been removed from its box. Arrau confessed that he had frequently thought of playing the tape, but had always changed his mind.

Finally, at the start of one of our last sessions, Arrau announced that he had played the tape—or attempted to. He had managed to sit through the first movement of the 1947 performance. And what did he make of it? "It was *awful!* I was going to say, 'Who is *this pianist?*' The truth is that I found it very fast." He paused, grimaced, and rapidly eyed the room. Then he continued in an undertone: "I hated it. Much too fast." I pursued:

JH / Did you recognize yourself in this performance?

CA / Not at all.

JH / Not in any of the details?

CA / Well, in some of the details. In the two solos. Maybe it was Cameron who pushed. When I hear it now, so fast and so straightforward—I just can't understand it. It loses all meaning.

JH / So you were really shocked?

CA / Shocked. Really. I mean, where one expects some lingering, it is metronomic.

JH / How do you feel about listening to the second movement? Would you rather not?

CA / Well, no. I thought we should listen a little bit.

I turned on the machine, and located the tutti that opens the second movement. Arrau sampled two or three measures and declared, "It's too fast. He's rushing already." He squirmed in his chair, then sat forward with his chin in his right hand, looking worried and muttering under his breath, "Oh! . . . Not good! . . ." After ten measures he asked me to run the tape forward to the second movement cadenza, which I did. Now Arrau's expression was stern and pained, and his eyes shifted from side to side. When the cadenza was finished, he remarked: "The trills get too loud too early. But it's acceptable. The parts of the slow movement that we heard were acceptable." He then asked to hear some of the third movement. The moment the music began, he rolled his eyes to the ceiling and cried out, "*Much too fast!*" The tempo slackened suddenly when the second subject arrived in the piano (measure 66). Testing the new tempo, Arrau closed his eyes and began breathing rapidly and heavily. By measure 70 the initial tempo had returned. Exasperated, he opened his eyes, exclaimed "*Ach,*" and asked that the machine be turned off.

JH / I could have predicted this would happen. I mean, all the time that I was badgering you to listen to this tape, it was not an innocent suggestion.

CA / [Laughing.] *No?*

JH / No. Because I knew how you would react.

CA / [Sighing.] Maybe this explains why people once thought my playing was too fast. This was what year?

JH / Nineteen forty-seven.

CA / Well, no. I'm thinking of the time before that, in my twenties. They always said I was too fast.

JH / Perhaps you were even faster in your twenties. Because these tempos are not unusually fast, given the norm for this concerto. They're unusually fast for you today. I must say, personally, that I like your recent recordings better than your older ones. I even like your recordings from 1970 better than your recordings from around 1960.

CA / Maybe I do better not to listen to them. Maybe my instinct is correct.

JH / Let me play you a little bit of the other three performances on this tape. You'll like them very much, I think.

Switching over to the Montreal-Frühbeck track, we found ourselves at measure 55 of the third movement—the rippling transition to the second subject. Arrau's face lit up. To test the second subject at measure 66, he again closed his eyes and, nostrils dilated, began breathing with sharp, sudden intakes. As the theme pursued its craggy ascent, he opened his eyes and slowly exhaled: "Ohhhhhhhhh." He listened to the remainder of the movement with obvious pleasure, then asked to hear excerpts from the two performances on the other side of the tape.

Taken as a whole, the three post-Cameron performances are notable for combining extreme tension with lavish scope, so that the struggle toward victory is noble and prolonged (and, incidentally, more gripping than in the recordings with Giulini and Haitink). The Krips performance is the most volatile; orchestra and soloist press one another toward ever stormier outbursts. The Frühbeck and Palmer performances, coming more than ten years later, are broader and more brooding. In collaboration with Palmer, especially, Arrau fashions an extraordinarily deliberate reading at the same time so steeped in passion that the forward impetus is undeflectable. It is with Palmer, too, that Arrau especially modulates his anguish with intimations of serenity, a striking instance being the second movement cadenza, in which the long double trill, rather than peaking, is unexpectedly pacified prior to its close.

Comparing the Montreal and the Atlanta performances, Arrau expressed satisfaction with various details in each. Especially significant for him was Palmer's "*herzereisend*" [heart-rending] treatment of the first movement's espressivo second subject (measure 26), which he feels loses meaning if taken too fast. Arrau's own handling of the same theme, beginning at measure 123, furnishes an example of the process of unpremeditated interpretive ripening I have already mentioned with reference to his recordings of the Chopin preludes (see page 128): though the left hand is unusually prominent in all four performances, it is particularly in 1976 and 1977 that Arrau's left hand speaks. Similarly, launching the movement's two solos (measures 158 and

382), Arrau invariably stresses the upper left-hand voice, but more individually under Krips, Frühbeck, and Palmer than under Cameron.

With the opening of the finale, as played in New York with Krips, Arrau signaled that he had heard enough. Then he laughed and commented that Krips, while an inspiring musician, was unpredictable and sometimes liked fast tempos.

JH / The point of this exercise, obviously, has been to discuss how your playing has changed. Four months ago, in Vermont, you said you disagreed with people who thought your playing had become more "serene." And then I asked you if you consciously adopted slower tempos than you had in the past. And you said you thought you had slowed down the second movement of the Brahms D-minor Concerto. [See page 125.] Now that you've heard these tapes, you can see that your tempos have actually changed quite considerably in all three movements.

CA / I expected differences, of course.

JH / If this is a fair sampling, one can only say that there seems to have been tremendous growth. Almost to the point where in some instances it's impossible to recognize you in the Cameron performance. Or do you think the Cameron performance was just a fluke?

CA / It's sort of exciting, no? In a way. In a superficial way. But the spiritual values of the D-minor Concerto are almost not there at all. . . . It might have been my fault. I started playing the two Brahms concertos relatively late. I never played them as a child; Martin Krause was against it. I think I must have started working on them only in my twenties.

JH / You were already forty-four, though, when you made the recording with Cameron.

CA / Maybe I was a very late developer. I have many times thought of myself as a late developer.

JH / Does it disturb you to hear the Cameron recording?

CA / Always when I hear a recording of mine, I'm . . . not confused, but . . .

JH / Self-conscious?

CA / No. I enjoy certain things. . . .

JH / Would you rather not talk about these recordings?

CA / Maybe not.

# Taking Stock
# December 1980

In his 1959 appreciation of Arrau for *Record Times*, the critic William Mann wrote:

> Arrau is a seeker, an eternal student of music. He pursues it into the opera house—he will spend hours analyzing and expounding on the greatness of Maria Callas' art—into the music library, the concert hall, and on the gramophone turntable. Last summer I went to spend the evening with mutual friends and found Arrau deep in the score and a recording of Stockhausen's *Zeitmasse*, probing the mysteries of this new sound-world until he perceived how it was put together and what its composer intended. His enthusiasm for other branches of the arts, particularly for painting, is boundless. When he is in London there is so much that he contrives to see and hear and read that I wonder sometimes when he finds time to sleep.

Loretta Goldberg, an Australian pianist now living in New York, and an intermittent student of Arrau's from 1968 to 1973, remembers him whirling through Melbourne in 1968:

"He asked me who were the writers in the vanguard of Australian literature. He had read A. D. Hope, Patrick White, and I think Christina Stead, but he knew there was a lot going on beyond that. So I organized a luncheon with two poets—Christopher Wallace-Crabbe and Vincent Buckley, who were two of the most prominent poets and critics in Australia at that time. During the luncheon, they told him who the main contemporary Australian authors were. He wrote everything down, and we went straight to Cheshire's, the main bookshop in Melbourne.

He spent sixty dollars on poetry, plays, fiction, criticism—in 1968, that counted for a lot more than it does today. The next night I gave a party following his concert, and I invited a Joyce scholar named Samuel Goldberg. I had called Arrau's attention to the books this man had written. Arrau came to the party and engaged Sam in a discussion of the poets—he'd already read the volumes of Chris Wallace-Crabbe and Vincent Buckley he'd bought the day before. He was more familiar with the details of their work, actually, than Sam was, not having read them for many years. He'd also started to read Sam's books, which delighted him, because despite his several readings both of *Ulysses* and *Finnegans Wake* he felt he didn't fully grasp either. I've never met anyone with such an urgent need to know, and to have mental possession of the best that all cultures have to offer."

Goldberg first met Arrau in Melbourne in 1962. The same year, she encountered him at the home of Mrs. Mary Baillieu Adam, widow of the primitive-art scholar Leonhard Adam, and herself a pianist who had studied with Schnabel. Mrs. Adam's daughter Mary Clare and Loretta Goldberg were close friends. Loretta Goldberg recalls:

"Arrau had read Leonhard Adam's book *Primitive Art*. And of course he was fascinated with the idea of looking at Adam's collection. So he visited the house. Mary Baillieu Adam had put up a group of masks in the lobby. They were contemporary European masks that had recently been shown in a Swiss exhibition, but anybody who wasn't well versed in primitive art would say they were primitive—most people guessed that they were South American. And so the first question Mary Clare asked when Arrau walked in the door was 'What do you think of the masks?' He looked at them, and was a little surprised, and said, 'Well, of course, that's not primitive art. These were exhibited in Switzerland,' and he named the year. So he passed the test that the sixteen-year-old had posed. Then he came in and sat down. And beside him was a cabinet full of primitive art from Leonhard Adam's collection. Mary Baillieu Adam had decided that anything she was willing to sell would be on top of the cabinet, and anything that was too valuable to sell, as far as she knew, would be kept inside. But she had forgotten that she'd put out on top two Benin bronzes—just for display, because they were so gorgeous. And of course Arrau saw them the moment he came in. He had a look in the cabinet, but all the time his eyes kept flitting back to the Benin bronzes. Finally he said, 'Well, I'd like to buy them.' And then Mary Baillieu realized her mistake. He reminded her that she had said anything on top of the cabinet was for sale. So it was an emotional moment for Mary Baillieu. She knew their value was around $25,000; she also knew Arrau's playing. And for her the love of music really came before anything else. You could see her weaken. Finally she let him have them both for $1,000. And he lit up like a child that had been given the toy of its dreams."

Arrau's first visit to Australia, in 1947, produced another notable acquisition. "I was crazy about everything—the wildlife, the landscape, the aborigines," he remembers. "And I used to mention in all the interviews that I would love to own a kangaroo as a pet. Even though I was warned that they can be very *aggressive*. And so I came to some small town and the mayor gave me as a present a live kangaroo. Then at the last minute Pan American, which had agreed to transport it in a cage, decided not to. So the poor kangaroo was transported by ship to San Francisco. He died three days before arriving." What was Arrau going to do with a kangaroo? "Well, that was the problem. I couldn't say, 'I won't accept it.' My first idea was to keep it in Douglaston. Maybe I could have given it to the Bronx Zoo."

Today, in his late seventies, Arrau remains a voracious reader. Traveling, he is never bored, even by airports. But he does not sightsee and socialize as he once did. Inwardly, his continued expansion is documented in his art. Outwardly, he has contracted: his range of acquaintances has shrunk and his appetite for company diminished.

Since he still maintains a grueling schedule, his music is relatively more preoccupying than before. His diligence, and the toll it exacts, can hardly be exaggerated. The day of a concert, and the day before, he plays through his entire program—even if he has given the same works fifty times in the preceding fifty weeks. In 1981, Arrau played two Beethoven concertos—the Fourth and Fifth—in each of three consecutive appearances with Gerard Schwarz and the Y Chamber Symphony in New York. The concerts fell on a Friday night, Saturday night, and Sunday afternoon. At home in Douglaston, Arrau played through both concertos Friday afternoon, Saturday after-

noon, and Sunday morning—a total of twelve concerto performances in less than three days. On the road, Arrau normally does
his practicing in a hotel room. He prefers a spinet piano for this
purpose. If he is provided with a larger instrument, he mutes it.
He would no sooner be overheard practicing than appear shabbily
dressed in the lobby.

The following conversation, unlike others in the book, neither
narrates a page from Arrau's life nor concentrates on aspects of
the performer's art. Instead, in addition to exploring the rewards
and tribulations of Arrau's schedule, I tried to touch upon as
many nonmusical subjects as possible without breaking the flow.
Two that did not come up, yet need mentioning, are religion and
politics.

Arrau was raised as a Catholic, but gave it up around the age of
fifteen. "I confessed only once, and thought it was absolutely
ridiculous," he once told me. "And I had one communion. I was
disgusted by the idea of swallowing the person of Christ. I thought
it was actually *cannibalism*. And I found that many of the Catholic
dogmas mainly served the power of the Church. I didn't really
turn against Catholicism. It just lost all actuality." He tried returning to Catholicism in his late teens under the influence of
Jacques Maritain, whom he met in Paris and admired. "I started
getting up at five every morning, attending six o'clock mass,
and going into religious ecstasies. It lasted about six months."
Today he is "not religious in any confessional sense. I think I
have some mystical sensations. But I have no image of God as
a person."

Politically, Arrau describes himself as a "liberal-humanitarian."
In this area, his public profile is low but not indiscernible. In
1977 he was the soloist at a gala Amnesty International benefit
concert, given in Munich and recorded by Deutsche Grammo-
phon. (He played the Beethoven Fourth Piano Concerto.) He has
not appeared in South Africa in many years. Despite lavish finan-
cial enticements and urgings from friends and former students,
he has not visited Chile since the fall of the Allende government,
whose dream of social equality he shared.

He considers himself a "citizen of the world." His detestation
of nationalism derives not only from the Hitler years, but from
the interwar period, when as an outsider in Europe he viewed
competitive patriotic displays with surprise and distaste. He re-

tained his Chilean citizenship, out of gratitude for the government's early sponsorship of his education, until 1979 when, ashamed of the Pinochet regime, he became an American citizen. His admiration of the United States—for its vitality, contemporaneity, diversity—is boundless. He calls it the world's most "international" country. Of recent American political figures, he especially esteemed Adlai Stevenson and John F. Kennedy. He feels the Watergate period, through instigating bouts of rigorous "self-analysis," constituted a certificate of national health. He had planned to vote for Jimmy Carter in 1980—his first opportunity to take part in an American Presidential election—but, entangled in his schedule of traveling and performing, forgot to register.

JH / I thought we could start today by talking about some of the things you do when you're not practicing or performing—the other part of your life, when you're not involved with music.

CA / Well, I read a tremendous amount—I have this idea that one should read at least three hours a day. I go to the theater. In the summer I like to garden. I like to tidy up. [Laughs.]

JH / What are you reading at the moment?

CA / A book about Einstein and the relativity theory, which I must confess I've never been able to understand. I try again and again. What else am I reading? I just read the biography of Walt Whitman, the new one by Justin Kaplan. And I read—with *regrettable* patience—*The Executioner's Song,* by Norman Mailer, which is bad, bad, bad. I finished it out of the kindness of my heart. I thought maybe at the end there would be something to justify the effort. What else? I just finished Toynbee, *Mankind and Mother Earth,* a marvelous history of the whole planet. It's fifteen hundred pages or something. You really get an idea of what was happening not only in the Mediterranean, but in China and India and the pre-Colonial cultures. I really recommend it.

JH / Do you ever put down a book without finishing it?

CA / I usually *make* myself finish a book. I actually finish them all. I feel that I owe it to the writer.

JH / You once mentioned reading *Pickwick Papers* because you were recording the Debussy preludes, and thought it might shed light on *Hommage à S. Pickwick*. That's what, close to a thousand pages? For a five-minute piece?

CA / Less, I think. Three minutes, maybe.

JH / I know you go to the movies a lot. Do you have favorite directors? Favorite actors?

CA / I used to love Garbo. And Bette Davis—I never missed a picture of hers. Ida Lupino. Dorothy McGuire.

JH / How about the films of Ingmar Bergman? He's somebody I imagine you would like.

CA / Yes. Did you see his film with Ingrid Bergman, *Autumn Sonata*?

JH / The one about the pianist who visits her daughter, and is made to remember how she had abused and ignored her. She used to give her daughter piano lessons, and was very critical.

CA / It made me feel a little guilty—that I might have ended up the same way. It reminded me of the dangers of self-centeredness in an artist.

JH / Well, to some degree that's inevitable, if you're going to perform.

CA / It's inevitable in the beginning. It's something one has to fight against one's whole life. And it gets easier and easier to fight it. Oh, I have almost a phobia against self-centered performers.

JH / Do you think you imposed expectations on your children— that they pursue music, learn an instrument, and so on?

CA / Not at all. I accept other possibilities for human beings.

JH / If it had happened that one of them had wanted to be a pianist, how would you have reacted?

CA / Well, then I would have tried to help them, but would also have advised them to study with somebody else. To be as free as possible from my influence.

JH / Did any of your children study an instrument?

CA / Our daughter studied clarinet. And seemed to be quite musical. But then she didn't want to practice. She never took it seriously.

JH / Were you secretly disappointed in that?

CA / Oh no. I was rather relieved, because of how difficult careers are in music.

JH / One movie you've told me you particularly enjoyed was *Saturday Night Fever*.

CA / Yes. I enjoyed it because I enjoy John Travolta's dancing. I don't know whether he did the choreography himself. But whoever did it must be full of imagination and vitality.

JH / People are going to be amazed to discover that you're a John Travolta fan. Did you enjoy the music in *Saturday Night Fever?*

CA / Yes. I sort of liked it.

JH / Have you seen any other Travolta films?

CA / *Grease.* I thought it didn't show him dancing enough.

JH / I brought along an article from *The New Yorker*, from November 15, 1941, an interview with you which states: "The only thing he got excited about when we chatted with him was the dancing at the Savoy Ballroom in Harlem. 'In tropical cities I have seen wild dancing, voodoo ceremonies, and primitive African rites. But none of it was as frightening as the dancing in Harlem,' he told us solemnly."

CA / Can you imagine? I had *completely* forgotten that I used to go there to see this incredible dancing. I had *completely* forgotten.

JH / You danced yourself in those days.

CA / Yes. I was a good dancer.

JH / Did you dance the tango?

CA / I *even* danced the tango. And the maxixe. That's a Brazilian dance that was in fashion. With my wife, we danced really beautifully.

JH / Not that it has anything to do with dancing, but we haven't said a word about your teaching. Do you still teach?

CA / At the moment, very, very little. Not that I dislike teaching. On the contrary, I love it. But I have had some students who very much disappointed me. This way of playing that I try to teach has to do with a general attitude toward life. And I thought I had succeeded in giving it to them. Then I didn't see or hear them for several years. And when I did, finally, I realized there was nothing left. I still hear young people when they want to play for me—I feel this is a duty. And it's interesting, too. But the moment I notice some of this terrible vanity, I lose interest.

JH / At one time teaching was a major activity of yours.

CA / Yes, of course. In Germany, I taught at the Stern Conservatory for many years.

JH / Who were some of your outstanding pupils?

CA / One student of mine was hanged by the Nazis—Karlrobert Kreiten, a great, extraverted virtuoso who was making a tremendous career. He was not Jewish. But toward the end of the war, at a party, he said, "I don't know why people worry about the war, because it is already lost." The Nazis took him away in the middle of a concert the next day. Another one of my students who was killed was Paul Kiss, a fine musician with whom I once played a concert of Schubert four-hand music. I never taught at any other institution. For a while there was a system with Rafael de Silva as my assistant. The students would work with him and I would more or less provide the final touches.

JH / Who are some of the outstanding Arrau products since the war?

CA / There is Edith Fischer, who has quite a good career in Europe. David Lively, who has won prizes in a number of the European competitions. Philip Lorenz and Ena Bronstein, who are a two-piano duo. And William Melton, one of my favorite pupils, in whom I have great hope. Probably I will teach more in the coming years. Although Friede [Rothe] tells me I should save my strength for performing.

JH / How much performing do you do now? What's your seasonal schedule like?

CA / Well, Friede would know. I'm still under the illusion that I play about a hundred concerts a season. But I don't think it's quite a reality anymore. Maybe it's between eighty and a hundred concerts.* I don't want to cut down at all. And I'm not the one who does it. It's Friede.

JH / Why don't you want to cut down?

CA / Because it's a question of *giving in to age*. Without *reason*. If I felt weaker, that would be a reason. On the contrary, I get *strength* from *performing*. But everyone wants to *protect* me.

JH / How many concerts would you play when your schedule was at its heaviest?

CA / I used to play, I would say, up to a hundred and forty. [See Appendix B.] That was maybe twenty years ago. That was a time when fees were not as high as today. The higher the fees go, the fewer concerts one has.

JH / But you wouldn't want to play a hundred and forty concerts, would you?

CA / I think I would love to.

JH / It's rejuvenating.

CA / *Absolutely.* This concert in Chicago the other day was *so* satisfying. And there was a wonderful atmosphere in the hall.

JH / When I asked you some years ago about cutting down on your schedule, you said, "I can't imagine reducing the number of concerts I play. I might go through hell. I might get too scared to go on stage again."

*Arrau played seventy-four concerts during the 1980–81 season.

187

CA / That's true. Now, for instance, after two and a half months in Vermont, my first concerts were difficult. I really had to pull myself together psychologically. There was quite an amount of anxiety.

JH / Do you think it was too long a layoff?

CA / Yes, I do. On the other hand it was quite necessary to rest.

JH / Was two and a half months the longest you had ever gone without playing in public?

CA / I would say it was the longest period in the last thirty years. Some people decide at an advanced age to take a year off. If I would do that, I don't think I would be able to play again. Anyway, it's absolutely important to play for an *audience*. The anxiety acts like a motor, a creative push.

JH / Now that you've returned to the stage, are there any concerts coming up that you're especially looking forward to?

CA / I don't really keep track of my schedule. I don't like to be burdened with it. Sometimes I don't even know what concerts I'm going to do the following month.

JH / The reason I asked is that I thought this might be an appropriate opportunity to mention some of your present-day colleagues you particularly admire.

CA / Let's see, whom do I like? Whom do I enjoy? I enjoy Kempff. Kempff always. I enjoy Daniel Barenboim—quite a lot, actually. And then, I'm ashamed to say, nobody else occurs to me. It's awful. I'm ashamed.

JH / How about conductors?

CA / Well, there are a lot of fine young conductors now, no? Gerard Schwarz. John Nelson. Riccardo Chailly. Gary Bertini.

JH / I know you enjoy working with Colin Davis.

CA / Colin Davis I love very much. Kurt Masur is wonderful. Eugen Jochum, doing the G-major Concerto of Beethoven—I'll never forget that performance, with the Concertgebouw.

188

JH / Do you think there's more talent among the young conductors today than among the young pianists?

CA / No, I don't. There's as much *astonishing* talent among the young pianists. Talents are not missing. The conditions for *developing* the talents are questionable. The competition is so great. They are *thrown* to the public much too early. And from their angle, they have to take what they get. It's a very dangerous situation.

JH / You say there are many talents among young conductors and young pianists, both. But your list of conductors is longer than your list of pianists.

CA / It's because I'm more concerned with the development of pianists. I ask maybe too much from a young piano talent.

JH / Why should the conditions for nurturing musical talent be so different from, say, Germany in the 1920s?

CA / The amount of talent in the public eye is much more. But *much* more. I don't know whether there weren't as many talents, or whether not as many young people decided to become pianists. But the fact is there were in Germany many fewer young pianists in the public eye.

JH / The entire structure of the concert scene is different today. How would you assess the current state of music, compared to Germany in the twenties?

CA / In general, the quality of the performances is probably on a higher level. I mean, there are many more first-rate orchestras. There used to be only three or four in the world. And the quality of the programs has become much better. For instance, an all-Schubert piano recital would have been impossible twenty or thirty years ago. Even in Berlin. Schubert as a piano composer took a long time to be accepted. Also, the audience for lieder singers in the twenties was very limited. But now, for the recitals of Fischer-Dieskau or Prey, the quality of the programs is incredibly good. And Fischer-Dieskau sells out Carnegie Hall. That's *amazing*. That didn't exist before. Another thing is chamber music. Chamber music concerts used to be very rare. And they were usually played only in smaller halls. In fact, in Berlin in the twenties even Busoni and Schnabel played in the Beethovensaal, which had twelve hundred seats. The Berlin Philharmonie, which seated about two thousand people, was very difficult to fill.

JH / A skeptic might say that these changes are not necessarily beneficial—that the proliferation of music brings certain disadvantages. And you can't ignore the fact that you yourself respond most enthusiastically to certain musicians who are not of the present day. The people who really excite you, with a few exceptions, are from a previous generation.

CA / It's true that listening to music was more of an event in those days. Now it's so easily available—you can put on a record while you are taking your bath. That's something I have always been afraid of—that the enjoyment of great art would become too easy. On the other hand, now you can *live* with great works of music much more easily than before.

JH / If you had your choice of either being part of the concert world as it exists today or as it was in—

CA / [interrupting] I would pick today.

JH / In spite of all your nostalgia for Berlin, and for Busoni and Carreño and Furtwängler.

CA / Yes. I think the present historical moment is marvelous.

JH / Isn't it a temptation, late in life, to look back?

CA / Not really. I dare say, not *yet*. I still have the feeling that I have a lot of things to do in the field of performing. I think the temptation will probably be much greater the moment I start performing less.

JH / What are some of your objectives at this moment in performance?

CA / I would like to play much more Schubert. And also Debussy. I'm very much attracted by Debussy, right now. To the *spiritual* meaning of his music. Sometimes he's played just for the sound, for the atmosphere. But he was one of the great geniuses. His music is absolutely unique. It's like the music of another planet.

JH / Are you drawn to Debussy now because for a long time you didn't have an opportunity to play him? Or do you see it more directly as a function of age?

CA / I adored Debussy all my life. But then, as with Liszt, circumstances prevented me from playing him very much. I developed a reputation playing Beethoven, Brahms, and Schumann. That's how I made my success in this country in the beginning. It was necessary, due to my being born in Chile, to emphasize my training in Germany.

JH / So you wouldn't seem a rootless artist. Or perhaps a "Mediterranean" pianist, specializing in French and Spanish music.

CA / Exactly. This idea that German music can only be played by Germans, that French music can only be played by Frenchmen . . . I was left with nothing. [Laughs.] Humberto Allende. Well, that's very pretty, but . . .

JH / You've also talked of recording some Busoni and Schoenberg.

CA / I would like very much to record the Schoenberg Opus 11, which I used to play a great deal. And of Busoni, the Toccata and the *Fantasia contrappuntistica*. But things come up that people think are more important.

JH / Like the five Beethoven concertos.

CA / For the third time. I don't think it's so necessary.

JH / Friede seems to think that you're not famous enough. I think she would like to see your picture on the cover of *Time* magazine. That's one reason she wants you to re-record the Beethoven concertos in digital.

CA / From her angle, the career angle, she's probably right.

JH / Well, how do you feel about being on the cover of *Time* magazine?

CA / [Giggling.] Oh, I would like that! But I don't think that Serkin has been on the cover of *Time* magazine. I don't even think that *Horowitz* has been on the cover. I remember only Rubinstein and Beverly Sills.

JH / Are you jealous of Rubinstein and Beverly Sills?

CA / Well, *yes!* [General laughter.]

JH / You once wrote about the life of the artist being a heroic journey, like those of Odysseus, Hercules, and Perseus. And about the second half of one's life being a time of inwardness and stock-taking. You mentioned certain musicians, such as Stravinsky and Klemperer, who seemed to have achieved a greater wholeness late in life. And then you said that the final goal of this scenario was "leaving behind all vanity, which can lead into the final fusion with the All." [See pages 239–48.] Do you apply these concepts to yourself?

CA / Oh yes. I feel I am widening my cosmos more and more. As if I were breathing more deeply. I feel it actually in my playing. Where it strikes me right now is in the *Dante* Sonata. And in Debussy. Now that I have recorded all the Debussy preludes, I look forward very much to recording the etudes.

JH / They're less approachable for most people than the pre-ludes. I have the sense you thrive on the spaciousness of the Debussy pieces that are less pictorial. It's noticeable in the pre-ludes—that you seem to expand in the ones that are more ab-stract. *Des Pas sur la neige,* for example.

CA / Yes, it's true. Or for instance *Canope.* That's very sparse. It's *miraculous* that he created, from so few notes, this kind of depth.

JH / That's what I mean about the etudes. The air is thinner. There's something of that in the *Dante* Sonata, too. The religious, ecstatic, exalted Liszt. The musical fabric vaporizes. Which is related to the idea of conquering vanity, isn't it? Because the musical expression is less egocentric when it's more diffuse.

CA / The ego assertion has disappeared.

JH / Does it ever disappear entirely?

CA / Well, it's almost impossible for a performer to get rid of his desire to achieve. And at certain epochs of one's life this desire is a driving force, and necessary. Still, one should fight vanity with all one's intensity. And the older one is, and the better the personality is integrated—then, I think, certain handicaps of vanity are overcome with quite a bit of success.

JH / If you had conquered your vanity, you wouldn't be jealous of Rubinstein and Beverly Sills for having had their pictures on the cover of *Time* magazine.

CA / Actually, *that* particular idea I haven't struggled against.

# Postscript
# July 1981

My final conversations with Arrau took place in June and July of 1981. The first meeting was in Douglaston on June 6. Arrau had returned from Europe six days before, having played eleven recitals and eleven orchestral dates in just under twelve weeks. The five final concerts of the tour had been canceled on the advice of his physician in Munich.

Arrau looked tired. Since returning, he had neither touched the piano nor opened a book. He was, he said, "on strike." And he felt "depressed" and "guilty" about having curtailed his European tour, even though it had been, as he confided, "triumphantly" received. (Joachim Kaiser, an unusually discerning piano critic, had written of his Munich recital in the *Süddeutsche Zeitung:* "Claudio Arrau's capacity to submerge himself with consuming urgency and to play with scrupulous precision has for many decades earned this artist love and admiration in Munich as well as worldwide. Whoever has recently heard him play, especially when he appears to be in 'good form,' as he was recently in his concert in Hercules Hall, cannot overcome his astonishment at the truth and efficacy of great music. . . .")

Rather than broaching Chopin or Schumann—the two topics we had left for last—we primarily discussed the connecting narrative I was working on for the autobiographical conversations.

When we met again in Douglaston three days later, Arrau had still not begun practicing. He had begun reading "a little"—but not about music. He said he had decided to reduce his 1981–82 schedule. When I opened the Chopin preludes and suggested we talk about them, there was silence. Then Arrau looked up from the music and exclaimed, "Blank!" He said that, for the first time in his life, he felt "saturated" with music.

In Vermont four weeks later, Arrau looked rested and relaxed. We discussed Chopin (as transcribed in the chapter "Brahms, Chopin, Beethoven"), but this time it was Schumann that, for whatever reason, drew a blank. Before leaving Vermont, I decided to update the conversation in "Taking Stock," which had occurred the preceding December. The result is given below.

The first topic is dogs, which requires an explanation. Arrau loves large, active dogs. For decades his household has included a retinue, and when the household moves to Vermont, the dogs go, too—in the back of the family station wagon, a 1976 Ford driven by Mrs. Arrau. A visitor approaching either Arrau house invariably incites a canine riot. One dog, leaping on windows and doors with a view of the intruder, is a black German shepherd with erect tail and ears, rippling muscles, and fierce eyes; this is Congo, whose father was a national champion. The others, both older, are Tinny, a Belgian sheep dog, and Petra, a mid-sized mutt. The day of the conversation which follows, the turmoil of the dogs was unusually prolonged because Arrau, atypically, was alone in the house. From the porch, I could hear his kind voice requesting obedience: "Come here, dear . . . *Tinny* . . . *Congo* . . ." One by one, the creatures were corraled. Then Arrau appeared, wearing a metal whistle on a string around his neck like a sports referee. He used it, he explained, to call the dogs when on walks they roamed too far. No sooner had we settled ourselves in the study than the herd came bursting through a side door and careening about the room. "How did they get out?" Arrau inquired. The dogs were laboriously put away again. Not five minutes later, Mrs. Arrau pulled up in the station wagon with Christopher, the younger Arrau son, and Nicky, his frisky Samoyed. Doors were opened, and suddenly a four-dog pack was seen hurtling across the yard. "They love to play with Christopher's dog," Arrau mildly explained.

JH / When did your attachment to dogs start? Was it in Berlin?

CA / Oh yes. It had something to do with my mother, who was afraid of animals. She was once attacked by a dog when she was pregnant. Not with me—with my older brother. So she never wanted me to have a dog in the house. When I married and moved away, one of the first things I did was to get a dog. As a matter of fact, we got one as a wedding present. A wire-haired terrier.

JH / Wagner and Busoni both loved big dogs. One of my favorite stories about Wagner was his insistence on taking his Newfoundland, Robber, with him when he and Minna fled Riga. They had to sneak across a border patrolled by cossacks with instructions to shoot on sight. And Busoni once praised one of his students for being "so straightforward, so serious and intelligent—like a dear dog."

CA / I always say that dogs are nicer and more intelligent than many people are. I'm interested in how they took to human beings. It happened thousands of years ago. The dogs decided that it would be a convenient arrangement. They could defend human beings, and be fed by them.

JH / How many dogs would you say you've had in your lifetime?

CA / Maybe thirty.

JH / And you have three right now.

CA / Yes. And we will have to take our son Christopher's dog, because next year his fraternity doesn't allow dogs. Also our housekeeper owns a little dog. So actually five.

JH / Do you play favorites among your dogs?

CA / I try not to let them know I prefer one to the other. Because they notice it. They are very sensitive.

JH / Do you have favorites?

CA / Yes. Secretly.

JH / Do you have favorite breeds?

CA / No. Dispositions. In dogs, I appreciate, first, intelligence. Then kindness. And that they are good watchdogs, but that's dated. This feeling of belonging together with a dog, it's a wonderful thing.

JH / Do you miss your dogs when you're on tour?

CA / Yes. And now more than before. It has to do with the fact that I don't enjoy traveling as much as I used to. I'm really more happy at home than traveling. And traveling I can't have my dogs.

JH / I have the sense, too, that you're less social than you used to be, less interested in people. Focusing on your music and the things that are close to you, as opposed to being exploratory. That's probably one reason the dogs seem more important.

CA / Yes. Of course it has also a weak side, this attachment to dogs. It has something to do with a power drive. But I fight against that. I don't want them to obey blindly.

JH / Well, they don't. Every time I come here, it takes you at least five minutes to put them away.

CA / I want them to keep their personalities. The older black one is very obedient, but not through me. He was going to be abandoned, and we were asked whether we wanted to take him. And he was overtrained.

JH / Generally, your dogs are anything but docile.

CA / I don't like to make them do things that they don't want to.

JH / How obedient are they, actually?

CA / The younger black one, Congo—he is quite obedient, if you *insist*.

JH / You like the wildness in him.

CA / Exactly. For him to express himself.

JH / Even so, a dog is less trouble than a person.

CA / [Laughing.] Yes, it's true.

JH / If you don't feel like talking to a person, you still have to in order to be polite. If you don't feel like talking to a dog, the dog doesn't object at all.

CA / He lies down and sleeps at your feet.

JH / And you prefer that.

CA / [Laughing.] I prefer that.

JH / And I think you have a stronger preference for that now than you did twenty or thirty years ago.

CA / Yes, that's true.

JH / You enjoy traveling less than you used to. You feel more attached to your dogs. And four weeks ago, in Douglaston, you told me you had finally decided to reduce your concert schedule.

CA / Well, yes, because the doctor in Munich said my heart was a little overstressed. He thought I should take it easier. Now, probably, I will have seventy-five concerts the coming season. Friede [Rothe] would like to give me just *ten* concerts a year. You know, my heart has been always marvelous. Now for the first time it is a tiny bit strained.

JH / Well, how do you feel about it? Do you want to cut down a little, stay home a little more?

CA / I'm ambivalent. The idea of cutting down is frightening; I don't like it. And also the fact that if I cut down I will get lazy. I simply don't like it. It reminds me of *retiring*. And I just don't feel like it.

JH / There's also a practical problem that you've described to me. A psychological problem of returning to the stage after a long layoff.

CA / Yes. Now I am going to Brazil in August. And it will be over two months in which I have not played in public.

JH / When I saw you a month ago, you said you felt so saturated with music that you didn't want to hear it, talk about it, or read about it, let alone practice the piano. I take it that has changed now.

CA / Now I really have an urge to prepare new works. But playing the *Appassionata* again—that, at the moment, doesn't produce any enthusiasm.

JH / I didn't know you were planning to include the *Appassionata* on your recital program for next season.

CA / Well, yes. At first, you know, I had thought of doing a first half only of Brahms—the Opus 2 Sonata and the *Handel* Variations. Now I am a little doubtful again, because an entire half a recital of Brahms is not attractive for audiences. So I am thinking I could play just the sonata, and then end, before intermission, with the *Appassionata*.

JH / Why choose the *Appassionata* if you're tired of it? Why not choose a different Beethoven sonata?

CA / I need a *Schlager* in the middle of the program before intermission.

JH / Can't you open with a Beethoven sonata, and then do the Brahms Opus 2?

CA / No, because it fades away at the end. One has always to think of that also. One needs always some kind of climax before the intermission. And I haven't played the *Appassionata* for several years. Anyway, it isn't decided yet.

JH / What would come after intermission?

CA / Then I will do *L'Isle joyeuse* by Debussy; Ravel, *Valses nobles et sentimentales;* the E-flat Nocturne of Chopin—the third from the last [Op. 55, no. 2]. And then what Liszt I don't know. Maybe *Funérailles*, maybe the two *Legends*, maybe *Orage*.

JH / How many weeks were you away from the piano this summer after you got back from Europe?

CA / I think it was a month.

JH / For a full month you didn't touch the piano.

CA / Maybe it was four weeks. Almost a month.

JH / Is there *any* part of you that feels that it would be a relief to schedule more time away from the piano? Is it seductive at all—the idea of not having to travel and practice and play so much?

CA / Yes, to my *lazy* side.

JH / If you *were* to play fewer concerts, are there other goals you might pursue? Would you teach more?

CA / No. Teaching at the moment—I don't feel like that at all. What I would really like to do is study a lot of music that I have never played, or not played in a long time, with the idea of recording or even performing it. Although it would be *taxing* at my age. Frightening, in a way. But still a very attractive idea.

JH / What music?

CA / For instance, the three big etudes [Op. 18] of Bartók. I played them many years ago. But they're completely gone from my memory. The piano textures are different from anything else. A little bit anticipating Stockhausen, music of that type. And I would like to play again the *Diabelli* Variations. I'm scheduled to record it. But I would like to also play it a lot in concert. And I would love to play, for instance, Chabrier. I *adore* Chabrier. The *Pièces pittoresques*. And the Debussy etudes I would like to play a lot now, if I were to feel like practicing a lot, which I don't. I haven't been able to practice more than two hours a day.

JH / Isn't the Ravel *Valses nobles et sentimentales* a piece that you haven't played in a long time?

CA / In many years, yes. But it's not much work, because there are no technical difficulties or other complications. It's coming back very easily.

JH / And *L'Isle joyeuse?*

CA / *L'Isle joyeuse* is one of the pieces that I've played most in my life.

JH / It's a brilliant work. I'm struck by that aspect of your program. You know, when we discussed the Brahms Opus 2 Sonata, you said of the opening that it's such a "challenging of the world" that you couldn't understand how every young pianist didn't want to undertake it. Brahms was, what, nineteen when he wrote it. You're mainly programing heroic, exuberant music.

CA / I love *L'Isle joyeuse* because it's like a *pagan orgy.* The end is incredible. I have always loved it.

JH / You don't seem to have an impulse to play the sort of music people associate with ripeness or old age.

CA / No.

JH / Like late Brahms, or the Schubert B-flat Sonata. Music that is thought of as autumnal. I thought you were considering performing the Schubert B flat.

CA / Yes, I was considering it. I have to relisten to my recording.
I have heard only the first movement. I'll try tonight to listen to
the rest of it.

JH / How did you like the first movement?

CA / Well, I didn't like it too much, you see. But I was in a
terrible mood when I heard it. So I would like to hear the whole
thing now. My recording of the Schubert C-minor Sonata I adored;
I think it's one of my best. Anyway . . .

JH / Anticipating the coming season, are there particular concerts or trips that you're especially looking forward to? You've got
four concerts in Rio coming up in August. And then you're going
to Japan.

CA / Yes. You know, I used to love to play in Brazil. Such incredibly vibrant audiences—they go absolutely crazy if they like
something. And I'm looking forward very much to Japan. This
will be my fifth visit.

JH / I understand you will need two different recital programs
for Tokyo. Have you thought about that?

CA / *Yes.* The management and the audiences seem to have been
asking for me to repeat the Liszt sonata. So I would finish with
that. And play two Beethoven sonatas before intermission. But
somehow I'm not too happy about it. I would prefer to play—I
know it sounds funny at my age—more *orgiastic* music.

JH / Liszt isn't orgiastic?

CA / Yes, that's why I came back to Liszt. That's why I want to
play again *L'Isle joyeuse.* And also the Ravel—*incredibly* sensuous, the Ravel waltzes. At least I feel it tremendously—certain
nuances and shadings.

JH / Does the Brahms Opus 2 Sonata seem orgiastic too?

CA / Oh *yes.* The first movement. And also the *second.*

JH / But Beethoven less so.

CA / Less so.

JH / Even the *Appassionata.*

CA / The *Appassionata* is one of the Beethoven sonatas that still attracts me because of that. I would also like to play certain things of Schumann. Like the *Davidsbündlertänze*. It attracts me tremendously, the idea of picking it up again. Did I tell you that I saw the Balanchine ballet? It was beautiful. And *very well* played by this young pianist, I don't remember his name.* But the idea of the ballet was just Romantic bourgeois, with nothing of the demonic side of the music. I was very disappointed with the choreography. I have only heard in my life one really good performance of the *Davidsbündlertänze*—Gieseking, in one of his good concerts.

JH / Was that orgiastic?

CA / *Yes.* It was really *fantastic.* I mean, when he was in that mood, he swept everything away.

JH / When did you last play the *Davidsbündlertänze*?

CA / It was in New York, in the fifties, probably.

JH / But you've recorded it since then.

CA / Yes. That's one time when I was completely satisfied. I think it's one of my best recordings. . . . There are a lot of things I would like still to play. *Busoni* I would like to play.

JH / What happened with this idea of recording the Schoenberg Opus 11 together with the Busoni Toccata?

CA / That is still possible. Probably I will do it. The other day I heard a *student* in Germany—a student of a student of mine. He played the Busoni *Carmen* Fantasy *very well.* And I thought, Why don't I play it? I *adore* it! It's a piece that I used to play a lot. And I forgot completely about it. There were idiotic prejudices—not that I myself had these prejudices, but audiences and intellectuals were always against anything that was a transcription. So I stopped playing it. It would be very, very easy to pick up again. And the *Indianisches Tagebuch*—that's a marvelous piece. Those are projects. . . . I'm in a pessimistic mood today. I have actually lost a month of my life now. Of *precious* time. I

*It was Gordon Boelzner.

could have practiced, *learned* a lot of music—new things, or nearly new things. And I haven't done a thing about it.

JH / Don't you ever give yourself a break? I mean, don't you ever stop pressuring yourself?

CA / It's probably necessary. You know, Martin Krause always made a rule for his students that they had to stop playing *completely* for a minimum of a month. Every year.

JH / Did you ever do that?

CA / Oh yes. I used to do it regularly.

JH / But it only works if you consciously decide that you want to do it, so you don't feel guilty about it.

CA / I do feel guilty. *Now* I feel guilty. Because I know that time is—how do you put it?—running . . . and I should . . . As a matter of fact, when I heard that I was going to have two months off this summer, I felt a tremendous *urge* to do new things, and be creative. But I haven't really even started to work seriously.

JH / But you obviously needed to be away from music and to relax. That serves a purpose.

CA / Precisely, precisely.

JH / What happened last summer? Wasn't there a similar layoff?

CA / Last summer they actually made me cancel Australia. Because they thought I was overstrained.

JH / I mean, did you spend as much time away from the piano?

CA / Yes. The same thing happened. Here. Well . . . another thing that I would like to play—you will be surprised—is *Reger*. Reger *Bach* Variations. I always wanted to play that.

JH / Did you ever?

CA / No. It's such an effort to memorize it. Reger!

JH / If you were to record a piece like that, to what extent would you have to memorize it? To what extent could you just read it?

CA / I would demand of myself that I memorize it even if I didn't play it in concert.

JH / Don't you ever record music that you haven't memorized?

CA / Many times I have had the music in front of me. But actually I was playing from memory.

JH / Well, I'm sorry to hear that you feel so guilty about . . .

CA / It's two-sided. First of all, I feel guilty because I figure that there's not very much time left. And on the other hand I tell myself that I *deserve* time to enjoy myself in a superficial way. And do all sorts of things that I have never done in my entire life.

JH / Like what?

CA / [Laughing.] Well, I don't know.

For his remaining 1981 recitals, Arrau chose to retain the same program of Beethoven, Schumann, Debussy, Chopin, and Liszt that he had played throughout the 1980–81 season. His new recital program, unveiled in San Francisco on January 10, 1982, consisted of Beethoven's *Les Adieux* Sonata, the Liszt B-minor Sonata, the *Appassionata* Sonata, and the Liszt *Dante* Sonata.

# PART III

# Conversations
# about Arrau

# With Philip Lorenz

Of his former students, Arrau maintains a unique relationship with Philip Lorenz. Their rapport is such that Lorenz is one of the few people with whom Arrau feels he can reliably make "casual conversation." Over the years, the two have frequently traveled and socialized together. When Arrau was asked by C. F. Peters to edit the Beethoven sonatas, he asked Lorenz to be his assistant. The task took from 1969 to 1978.

The first volume of the Arrau Beethoven edition (Sonatas 1 through 15) was published by C. F. Peters in 1973. The second came out in 1978. Unlike the Beethoven sonata editions of such pianists as Hans von Bülow and Eugène d'Albert, Arrau's preserves the *Urtext* (that is, the text precisely as Beethoven wrote it). At the same time, he has inserted interpretive suggestions, using brackets and dotted slurs to set off his contributions from Beethoven's. Additional features of the Arrau edition include recommended fingerings and metronome settings. Also, as discussed below, Arrau has adopted an idiosyncratic method of drawing attention to Beethoven's subito markings—the indications of abrupt loudness or softness that abound in his music.

Philip Lorenz was born in 1935 in Bremerhaven and moved to the United States in 1950. He was brought to Arrau in 1951, and took lessons from him until 1969. During part of this period, he also studied with Rafael de Silva, for many years Arrau's teaching assistant. In 1969, Lorenz joined the faculty of California State University, Fresno, where he has been professor of music since 1974. He is also a frequent guest artist at the Universidad Veracruzana in Mexico, where he teaches a master class in the Arrau piano method.

As a performer, he has toured both as a solo recitalist and in a two-piano team with his former wife, Ena Bronstein, also a former student of Arrau and de Silva. Among his joint appearances with Ena Bronstein was an all-Busoni concert in New York in 1980. I met with Lorenz in California in July 1981. His fluent descriptions of Arrau's keyboard habits conveyed both the command of an experienced pedagogue and the zeal of a grateful disciple.

JH / How did you and Arrau go about editing the Beethoven sonatas for Peters?

PL / We set up a system of having the music in front of us on a little table, with four, five, or six editions to consult, plus the manuscript sheets which Peters supplied with some recent musicological corrections. They had taken the old Köhler-Ruthardt edition and whited out everything that was not *Urtext*. It amounted to a blank, noncommittal edition. We also meticulously consulted facsimile editions, where available. I was amazed at Claudio's ability to decipher these—it was something that came naturally to him. The first problem was starting. There was some initial reluctance and apprehension; he just didn't know where to begin. So that was my main function at first—a catalyst to get him working. I simply started asking questions: "Well, what about this here? Is this the fingering you use?" "Heavens, no! Impossible!" I kept at it, suggesting this and that, and finally he got involved. And we went measure by measure through the thirty-two sonatas, which ultimately took close to ten years.

JH / What did you have to work on most? The fingerings?

PL / It might seem that way, because at first glance the fingerings appear the most conspicuous editorial feature. But there are also suggestions for tempos, phrasings, dynamics, caesuras. Very often we used dynamic markings and accents to clarify *Stimmführung*—voice leading. And we added a little "*s*" in italics to indicate subito dynamics.

JH / That little "*s*" is certainly unique to the Arrau edition. Why did you decide to draw extra attention to every subito dynamic?

PL / Because Claudio thinks they're so essential to Beethoven's language—these abrupt changes in dynamics. He wanted to be sure that people would execute the subito dynamics without the usual tapering. Of course, there are other places where the dynamic change is more gradual. These are indicated with a diminuendo or crescendo in brackets. These are decisions he made very emphatically. He also indicated the use of the una corda and the extent of a given crescendo or diminuendo. So there are a lot of dynamic instructions which at first glance aren't so obvious.

JH / I'd like to talk in some detail about one sonata, or perhaps a single sonata movement—discussing fingerings, phrasings, and other technical and interpretive details distinctive to the Arrau edition, or to Arrau's playing style.

PL / Maybe we could choose the *Appassionata*, because it's a very popular piece, and it's something I've studied with Arrau and performed quite a bit myself. We could stick to the first movement, and go into several passages very thoroughly.

JH / Do you want to say anything about the very beginning?

PL / Well, before I played it with him, I started with the third finger in the right hand, to keep the F-minor chord under the hand. But I've changed everything, because ultimately his fingerings insure tremendous security by keeping the hand balled and totally relaxed. It's like lining up the fingers in a natal position.

The right hand makes a little circle down to the thumb; the left hand does the opposite, starting with a low thumb and circling up to the fifth. This way you don't have to play with the hands spread open, which already risks tension or nervous trembling, especially at the very beginning.

JH / His fingering of the staccato bass notes in measure 10 is characteristic.

PL / He finds that with the fifth finger you can control the sound more than with the fourth. First of all, because the fourth doesn't have a separate tendon in the hand—you can't move the fourth by itself. Also, going from the third to the fifth gives you more lateral range than going from the fourth to the fifth—you have more possibility to rotate. Throughout the edition you find very often that he goes from the third to the fifth finger, skipping the fourth. The fourth he eliminates quite rigorously for being weak and hard to control.

JH / Didn't you once tell me this use of the fifth finger was partly a function of the shape of Arrau's hand?

PL / The top joints of his fifth fingers are curved slightly inward. He says it's a result of playing too much in his early years. The right-hand fifth finger even looks a little bit misshapen. But it's totally suited to the use he makes of it. Especially on the black keys, he plays with the outside of his hand, rather than with the tip of the fifth finger, or with the finger flat. Another personal use of the fifth finger in his playing is for bass notes, where you have to leap down at a fast tempo. He lines up the left index finger pointing downward and parallel to the thumb, so that the index finger and thumb look like a prong or a clothespin. This leaves the fifth finger sticking out to the side. And then you can use the entire length of the fifth finger on black keys, rotating to the left and slapping down. And the whole weight of the hand reinforces the fifth finger.

JH / Back to the *Appassionata:* Arrau makes a point of articulating the big arpeggiated passage at measure 14.

PL / He conceives it not as a virtuoso flourish, but something totally rhythmical. Technically, he uses lateral motion as well as finger action to get the necessary power. The heavy arm weight rests in the keys. Then you shift the weight from left to right, left to right. It's a rotating of the entire arm, causing the fingers to slap, shifting the weight all the time. Once you stop the rotation, you're stuck. If you feel yourself getting nervous or tense, it's better to exaggerate the motion, rather than to try and pull it in. Stiffness doesn't help at all. I used to be so plagued by it—in the Schumann G-minor Sonata, for example. I was barely able to get through it, being so stiff and cramped because there's so much activity and speed—remember, Schumann says "as fast as possible," and then "faster still." That was before I came to Arrau. I haven't known those problems since. And, you know, when a passage *feels* good to play, there are no doors closed—you feel you can continually explore the sound and your reactions to it. It's just a joy to play that way.

Measure 28 is an example of where we use "sopra" and "sotto" to indicate whether the right hand should be above or below the left. He knows these things to perfection. I played the Brahms *Paganini* Variations for ten years without ever getting the passage in double notes in the coda to the second book. I struggled and struggled with it, but it was never clean. Once I had a session with Gina Bachauer, who said, "It's impossible to play as written. Let me show you what Rachmaninoff did, what fingerings he used." Well, as it turned out those weren't fingerings at all; they were merely arrangements, omissions of notes. Gimmicking around with the music. And then by chance I found out that where I used to go under with the right hand, Claudio goes over.* And the problem was solved. It seemed more difficult at first—to go over. But it doesn't kill me anymore, now that I've gotten used to it. Anyway—sotto and sopra.

To play the pianissimo passage effectively in measure 47, he suggests withholding the weight of the arm.

In other words, raising the upper half of the arm, so that the hand is automatically light. You simply raise the arm, but never from the hand, so that the fingers walk ever so lightly over the keys.

---

*The double notes in question are D sharp and A, in measure 18 of Variation 14.

JH / There's a similar passage in the finale. Arrau's fingering is simply one-two-one-two.

PL / Right. Again you withhold the weight of the arm and walk over the keys. It looks a little strange but it's actually very, very enjoyable, because you have the two most secure fingers, and you just rotate from one to the other, with the arm raised high.

JH / Returning again to the first movement—Arrau makes a huge sound in the passage beginning at measure 51. It's articulate— you can make out all the notes—and at the same time full. There are no percussive splinters, no unintegrated accents.

PL / Here again is a case where the fingers form two balls, rotating in opposite directions.

JH / There's a similar passage just before the prestissimo coda to the *Waldstein* in which I find the majesty of Arrau's sound even more memorable.

PL / This is a page most people can barely get through, because it's so conducive to stiffness. His use of the thumb on the sforzandos, which at first seems almost bizarre, is crucial.

It only works with a tremendously mobile wrist. By using the whole arm, and dropping on the thumb, everything is heard, and rich sounding. The thing to remember is that the entire arm weight must stay in the keys at all times. You're sort of wallowing in the keyboard. The fingers of course have to be strong enough to support the weight of the arms. With butterfingers you wouldn't be able to do this sort of thing.

JH / Did you and Arrau ever have any qualms about recommending fingerings that wouldn't work without the kind of mobility and natural weight we've been talking about?

PL / Very often he would exclaim, "How are people going to know how to do this? It will seem crazy!" So sometimes Arrau's own fingerings are the secondary suggestions in parentheses, and we've chosen a less personal fingering as the main recommendation.

JH / Can we talk a bit about your relationship with Arrau outside music? You spent ten summers practically living with him in Vermont. What did you do together besides working on the Beethoven sonatas?

PL / Well, for one thing, a lot of weeding. And we would go shopping in antique stores. Going out to restaurants, of course. And then I also would act as a guinea pig when he tried out pieces that he hadn't played in a while.

JH / What pieces did he play for you privately?

PL / The Second and Third Brahms Sonatas. Oh, it was marvelous, when his wife and I would sit and listen to him after supper. As soon as he entered the room he could have been in the Berlin Philharmonic hall. He could have been playing just for Ruth and me, or for three thousand people, because the grandeur and the gestures and the feeling were the same. And if he had a little memory problem, or a certain passage didn't come the way he had practiced it, it became a major dilemma. He could have fixed it right then and there, but that wasn't the purpose.

JH / Do you want to say anything about weeding, gardening?

PL / The weeding became a nagging competitor to working on the Beethoven edition. I think if one didn't put a stop to it he would one day disappear, he gets so engrossed in weeding, in clearing land. There's a particular weed peculiar to Vermont that spreads, and you can't take it out except by hand—with a hand sickle, and with clippers (which are very good for the hand muscles, actually). He would come in with his hands full of blisters and sores and scratches. But he never got hurt. I was the one who got hurt—I cut the top of the fourth finger of my left hand. I severed all the skin. And his reaction was "I told you, dear, talking is the root of all evil." You see, he would just as soon be cut there for hours not saying a word. But I would trail after him, pumping him about this or that. . . . And what else? In my frustration I would talk about the virtues of a *jardin anglais,* or formalized French gardens. But he dislikes nature to be manipulated for the sake of prettiness. And he's partial to trees rather than flowers. I don't think he's ever planted flowers.

JH / How about eating?

PL / He can appreciate the finest food in the most exclusive restaurants in the world but he also likes flea-bitten motel restaurants in Vermont. He'll say, "Oh, that's *marvelous,*" and it'll be some kind of breaded fried chicken. When I'm traveling with him, it's impossible not to balloon out of all proportion, because he loves to eat, and then he works it off during concerts. And he doesn't hold back when it comes to dessert. He's always dying to have dessert.

JH / In 1970 you assisted Arrau in a series of master classes in Bonn, given in Beethoven interpretation in conjunction with the Beethoven Bicentennial.

PL / He had never to my knowledge done anything comparable in public. I helped set it up, and was at his side from morning till night. That was a great experience. And he was a wonderful friend at the same time—my marriage was splitting up, and he couldn't have been kinder. The classes were a big success. There were students from Europe, Japan, America—people whose names you see now and again today. Some of the lessons were like concerts. I remember in particular one girl who played Opus 111—the way he got her to do certain things and the way he talked about the piece. Even in teaching, his personality and his emotional world came out so beautifully. His relationship to the music was projected without his playing a note. There was thunderous applause after the effect of the final measures had sunk in; I think a lot of people were moved to tears. And, as I say, it wasn't so much for her playing, although she played very well. It was for him.

JH / How did your relationship with Arrau begin?

PL / I had a teacher in Bremerhaven after the war, a lady with a name which even now he laughs at as if hearing it for the first time. Elisabeth *Stunkel.* Well, she had studied at the Stern Conservatory. And when her house was bombed, the things she wanted to rescue more than anything else were her grand piano and a portrait of Arrau. Because she was once brought by her teacher to see how the little boy played. And I remember her telling me that he did the most phenomenal things in Liszt's music—double notes and trills. Well, that's when I first heard the name. And after I moved to Washington, D.C., I don't know how, I won a competition. As a result of this, I was brought to Arrau's house. Then I played for him and he accepted me, referring me to his assistant Rafael de Silva. I worked with de Silva for a while and then played for Arrau again. He was extremely kind to me and said he would take me on himself. And it was just after that that I heard him for the first time—a Beethoven recital at Town Hall in New York. I was just shocked by this experience. It was as if Beethoven were revealed to me from the earliest sonatas to the last, a journey that just uprooted me. He opened with Opus 2, no. 3, and ended with Opus 111. It was noble, sublime, brilliant. It seemed the ideal presentation—not the personal success of a man playing, but a saintly experience at the service of music. I was stunned. I went backstage and said something that still seems true—I said it was the happiest day of my life. And his reaction—I can still see his face; it was so full of radiance and kindness and appreciation, as if it had surprised him to hear something so genuine. He smiled in a way that gave me time to express myself. Well, that was great. Little did I know that I would later wind up collaborating with him on these very sonatas. And never, ever, in all these years have I been disappointed. I've been constantly sustained by his example, by the incorruptibly high purpose of his life in music.

# With Daniel Barenboim

It is perhaps not widely known that Daniel Barenboim spent his first nine years in South America—he was born in Buenos Aires in 1942. His father, who was his first piano teacher, and who knows Arrau, arranged for Barenboim to play for Arrau when he was nine. Arrau was impressed, and remains so. Now that Barenboim has taken up the baton, Arrau has collaborated with him in concertos by Beethoven and Brahms.

Barenboim returns Arrau's admiration. In a seventy-fifth birthday tribute appearing in the Munich newspaper *AZ*, he wrote in part: "What most astonishes me in Claudio Arrau is the joining of the nineteenth and twentieth centuries. He is one of the last remaining links to the musical tradition of the nineteenth century. The ancestry of his teachers reaches back to Franz Liszt. Thus the heritage of the subjective virtuoso interpreters still lives. On the other hand, Arrau has adopted the best feature of modern piano style: absolute textual fidelity which never sets itself above the composer. . . . These elements Arrau combines like no other; he unites the best aspects of both worlds. I would be happy to learn this ideal from Arrau."

Barenboim's musical heroes also include Edwin Fischer, whose master classes he observed as a piano prodigy in 1952, and Wilhelm Furtwängler, whom, like Arrau, he reveres above all other conductors. Both as conductor and as pianist, Barenboim seeks to reinstate the warm sonority and ample yet purposeful rubatos he associates with Fischer, Furtwängler, and Arrau.

A further interpretive principle espoused by Barenboim in what follows is the application of sustained harmonic tension as a long-range organizing tool. In this, too, he looks back to Furtwängler, and to the celebrated theoretician Heinrich Schenker, with whom Furtwängler frequently conferred. In Schenkerian analysis, whole movements of sonatas and symphonies are shown to elaborate core linear and harmonic progressions.

I met with Barenboim for an hour in a New York hotel in March 1981. His busy schedule was much in evidence. The night before, he had performed an all-Beethoven recital. That evening he was to play a program of Liszt. The score of a Bruckner symphony was lying open on a table. His speech was brisk and intense. As his most recent collaboration with Arrau had been in the Brahms D-minor Concerto in Paris, I began by inviting him to comment on Arrau's interpretation of that work.

DB / Arrau gets the weight of the Brahms D minor like very few people. And somehow in spite of all the tempo fluctuations the first movement is such a unity the way he plays it. That makes a very big difference; usually it's cut up into pieces.

JH / His emotional stamina in such music is remarkable.

DB / That's one of the most important qualities he has—that when he plays a piece of music, it's obviously the result of a lot of thought and analysis, and all kinds of preparatory work; but it is also the result of this total immersion at every moment. In a psychic way and a physical way, the music really goes into his bones and his blood. I think it's one of the most appealing qualities about him.

JH / Who are some of the other people you've collaborated with who have this quality of deep and continual immersion?

DB / Fischer-Dieskau is, I think, the most obvious example. Usually the intensity of the relationship between the performer and the music varies very much from performance to performance. Very few people have it to the high degree that Arrau and Fischer-Dieskau have it. Whether you agree or disagree with what they do, there's such commitment and belief—the performance of that particular piece becomes at that moment the most important thing in their lives. I'm sure that when Arrau is playing the Brahms D-minor Concerto, at that particular moment it is really the most important thing—more than his personal or physical well-being, more than the public, more than anything else. That relationship to the music is what communicates to the audience.

JH / What's it like having Arrau as a soloist when you conduct?

DB / Wonderful. Because he's such an all-round musician, and he knows the orchestral parts so well. He doesn't play the piano part in concertos as something outside the orchestra, but really as part of it. And therefore it's really very easy to play with him. I say it's easy partly because one of the main driving forces in the way he plays is the harmonic tension. More so than the melodic beauty of a phrase; much more so even than the rhythmical impulse. And it is the speed of the harmonic change, and the degree of the harmonic tension, which drive him to play certain works much slower than one is used to hear from other people. And I think very rightly so. Because if someone were to play his tempos without having that intensity of harmonic relationships, it would be disastrous. Much better that people who haven't got that capacity should play a little faster. Because when you play very slowly, you must fill every note, you must fill every space, and you must feel the tension of the harmonies. I mean, sometimes the harmony doesn't change for four bars, and then a single harmonic change becomes terribly important. And to take the time to express that change of harmony, you must be able to bring great intensity to it.

JH / Do these observations bring Furtwängler to mind to you, and Schenker?

DB / Yes. Very much the same line of thinking.

JH / How about piano technique? Arrau is of course a great advocate of using arm and shoulder weight. Is that something that has had meaning for you, in addition to his interpretive gifts?

DB / No. I can't really say that. I mean, I greatly admire his pianistic ability, and the sound he gets out of the piano—the really orchestral sonority that he gets. I think that is so obvious when he plays Liszt, for instance. But this technical way of playing he has, it's not something that you can do half-hearted— either you use it fully or you don't use it at all. It's not something to pick up twenty percent of and leave the rest.

JH / You mentioned his sound.

DB / The first thing about his sound, I would say, is the thickness. I mean that of course in a positive sense. And that when he plays

218

chords, they always sound so full, because every chord is balanced internally so that you don't just hear a lot of the top notes and a lot of the bass notes with nothing in between. Another thing that he has, that I suppose has something to do with the way he uses the arms, is a disembodied sound, especially when he plays a thing like *Jeux d'eaux à la Villa d'Este*. This wash of sound that is so typical of Liszt's writing—the harplike sonorities, which so many so-called Liszt experts simply don't want to produce when they play; at least I don't hear it. I think that Liszt's obsession with harplike sounds, in arpeggios and things, has really rarely been brought out so well as by Arrau. And he uses *every pianistic device* for musical expression. In Liszt especially, when he plays arpeggiated chords, there are never two at the same speed. In other words, he consciously varies the speed of the arpeggios for the musical expression at that particular moment in the phrase. You know, the fact that there's an arpeggio sign doesn't mean that it automatically goes rmmmmmm! It may sometimes be expressive to do it so, very fleetingly; on the other hand, at other times, especially when there is harmonic intensity, it might be necessary to play more deliberately.

JH / You described two distinct sounds—one full-bodied and orchestral, the other disembodied.

DB / An ethereal sound.

JH / They're much different.

DB / But they complement each other. If you played everything with a thick, full sound, it would be unbearable.

JH / It seems to me these two sounds are related to the fullness of his voicing, the polish of his sound—the way it never splinters. They're both steady states—the texture is relatively even, as opposed to being jagged or scarred.

DB / Yes. Sure.

JH / I understand you once had a talk with Arrau about the *Appassionata* Sonata.

DB / He came to a concert once in New York when I played the *Appassionata* and didn't like it at all. But he was terribly, terribly nice and positive about it. I remember going to his house afterward, and he didn't just say "That was terrible," and so on. He really explained to me why he thought it was—mostly about tempo in the first movement; about the natural tendency to rush the minute it gets loud. I don't mind his dogmatism, you know. Because it's not just superimposed. I mean, that's the way he is. At the very extreme, maybe, he could be accused a little bit of being pedantic. But there is such conviction behind it, that even if what he says sounds dogmatic or pedantic, it always gives you food for thought.

JH / When were you first aware of Arrau?

DB / I met him for the first time when I was nine years old. I played for him. He was terribly nice and very complimentary. And all through my childhood and adolescence he was a source of great strength, because he always believed in me. Also at times when my professional life was not as smooth as at others—he always staunchly gave me the feeling that he supported me. And, as I say, that was always a source of great strength and satisfaction.

JH / Do you want to say anything about him as a man—how he compares to other musicians of stature?

DB / Well, the most important thing about him, I think, is his wide range of interests. He will really spend hours and hours talking about things other than music. Unfortunately, it's the exception rather than the rule. And I'm sure this is why his own playing has so much variety and character to it, because he is interested in so many other things—opera and theater and philosophy and literature; Etruscan art; pre-Columbian art—I don't know, anything that is or has been creative in life. This is what he feeds on, just as he feeds on reading the scores again and again. I greatly admire it.

JH / What have you talked about, other than music, for hours and hours?

DB / Political things—the relative merits and the necessity of democracy. About history and mysticism. I remember once in Israel, quite a few years ago, having a long conversation about Jewish mysticism in the Middle Ages. I think he has a certain fascination: on the one hand he's extremely rational; on the other, he has a type of obsession, having proved everything rationally, to find as the ultimate proof also a mystical reason for things. Oh, he's a fascinating person.

# With Garrick Ohlsson

Compared with Daniel Barenboim, who studied or performed in London, Paris, Salzburg, Tel Aviv, and Vienna as a child, and whose idols included Edwin Fischer and Wilhelm Furtwängler, Garrick Ohlsson, born in White Plains, New York, in 1948, was initially circumscribed by a postwar American arena wherein Fischer was unknown and Furtwängler was condemned as a supposed war criminal. Jascha Heifetz, Vladimir Horowitz, and Arthur Rubinstein, all under contract to RCA Victor and beneficiaries of a promotional mentality more zealous and ingenious than any known abroad, were the ranking instrumentalists. A fourth RCA artist, Arturo Toscanini, was marketed on radio and recordings as the greatest conductor in history.

Horowitz's hold on the first postwar generation of American pianists was roughly comparable to the centrality once accorded Franz Liszt in Europe. Despite instances of formidable early success, by 1970 his spiritual progeny were sidetracked, and not merely because opinions had shifted. The stressful mechanics employed to emulate Horowitz's power and turbulence tended to shorten the life span of the machine. Among the prominent American keyboard careers of the fifties and sixties, an alarming number were sabotaged by fingers that faded or even quit.

By his own account, Ohlsson, too, aspired to become a second Horowitz. But he was young enough to escape this ambition. When Sviatoslav Richter made his dramatic American debut, Ohlsson was only twelve, and still impressionable. Eventually, he came under the wing of Olga Barabini (d. 1980), whose godhead was Arrau. Though Ohlsson continued at the Juilliard School, where he studied from 1961 to 1971, Barabini was his primary mentor from 1966 to about 1972. He subsequently took about a dozen lessons with Arrau in the summers of 1973 and 1974.

Neither Arrau nor Ohlsson himself regards Ohlsson as an Arrau product. Temperamentally, they are poles apart. Arrau is anchored, Ohlsson eager, speedy. At the same time, Ohlsson's nimble adaptation to Arrau was crucial. Though he has strayed from total adherence to the principles he absorbed from Barabini and Arrau, his technical apparatus remains preponderantly indebted to Arrau's "natural weight" philosophy. His superb ability to produce resounding fortissimos without shattering the tone—especially difficult on the gentle Bösendorfers he favors—stems from his reliance on body rather than finger weight.

I talked with Ohlsson about Arrau in his New York apartment in March 1981. His speech was congenial, profuse, and so rapid the words tumbled into one another. When he wished to demonstrate a musical point—as in referring to Arrau's lesson on the Brahms B-flat Concerto—he dashed to the piano. He began by describing how he came to seek help from Olga Barabini.


GO / I had been studying with Sascha Gorodnitzki at Juilliard, and I guess that I had absorbed what you might call the Old Russian Conservatory style of playing. I was a little bundle of energy, and very much a Vladimir Horowitz imitator, like so many pianists are, especially the Juilliard competitive-type pianists. And I was quite good at it. Of course in those days I didn't have a very clear idea what made Horowitz the pianist he was— that in addition to the pianistic mastery that went into, say, his thunderous bass sonorities, he used a carefully treated piano. I didn't know that, and nobody around me knew it, and there I was flailing away. One day I was in a master class of Gorodnitzki's, probably making one hell of a racket playing Scriabin and Liszt, when I had the most excruciating pains throughout my left forearm. Now I would know what to do about that, or how to prevent it before it developed. But in those days I was playing with willpower. I must have been about seventeen. Gorodnitzki was at a loss; he didn't know what to recommend. So I was taken to an emergency room in a hospital and had some kind of muscle relaxant shot into my arm. This was quite alarming, of course. And Olga Barabini—she was like the quack doctor or acupuncturist who says they can do something when nobody else can. She said to me, "You know, you don't have to pay such a terrible price for this. You could use less energy to achieve the same results. And it would be much more satisfying musically." I didn't know what she meant, and of course I didn't believe her. Because no pianist or piano teacher I'd ever run into had ever said anything like that. And I thought, She's really a nut; this is a case for the loony bin. Not making the connection, for example, with when I'd heard Arrau play, and watched him. I didn't know why he was different. I was just aware of the immense ease and natural power of his technical apparatus. I didn't know how to look at piano playing in those days—visually, I mean. Nobody had ever taught me.

And so I wound up going to Barabini. It was in fact about a year later, if I remember correctly. I needed some work on the French repertoire. I was learning *Scarbo*, from *Gaspard de la nuit*, and Barabini said, "Oh, you're learning *Scarbo*. I have some very good fingerings. They might untie a few knots. You've noticed what a difficult piece it is." And I said, "Yes, I've noticed what a difficult piece it is." And I went to her house and was not prepared to have a three-hour lesson on *Scarbo*, but I got one. I thought she was going to give me some marvelous interpretive ideas, and a few fingerings, and leave it at that. But she dove right in at the basis of my technique as well, because that's the way she taught, and that's pretty much the way Arrau teaches. I mean, he doesn't say, "We're going to talk about technique for half an hour, and then we're going to talk about interpretation." It all goes together. And I was astonished. She taught me a few things about relaxation. She didn't do it all at once.

Then I continued to have lessons with her. We looked at some Chopin, and it was the same—she kept interfering with what I was doing technically. She kept showing me how to relax the wrist, relax the arms, how to use weight, how to move more efficiently. And I guess at some point I asked her, "How do you know about this?" And she sort of sniffed very snobbishly and said, "You know, I studied with Claudio." As if that would explain everything. Then she went on to explain his emphasis on Yogic techniques, and modern-dance techniques, the whole thing. She began to indoctrinate me, bit by bit. And I lapped it up because it solved a lot of problems. And being a naturally gifted athletic pianist anyway, it was just a joy for me to discover that you didn't have to grit your teeth and kill yourself physically in order to achieve certain effects of power, or to control very delicate passages. Because the only way I had known to do such things was through sheer force of will: you know, you feel big and you make a big noise, and you feel small and you make a small one. It was a question of mind over matter for me. When you're eighteen you can get away with that. No problem when you're eighteen. But as you get older it gets more difficult.

I would say it took me about two years, personally, to become convinced of this. About two years of study with Barabini. And I was also benefiting from her musical range. I mean, while I think Gorodnitzki's a fine pedagogue, I do feel that he's bound into being a professional teacher of the fifty-five-minute piano lesson. And, for whatever reasons, he didn't have the wide background that Olga had. She was a cultured person. She spoke many languages. She would just as soon pick out a passage from *Faust* and look at it for half an hour as start with the next Beethoven piece. It was that kind of old-fashioned relationship, and it was extremely exciting and wonderful for me.

During all of this period, Arrau became deified in my mind. I began to go hear him. I began to get his records, which were just beginning to appear in quantity on the American market. And that was my first acquaintance with him after having learned a little bit of what he was about. I discovered that he was in many ways quite outside of what I had considered to be the mainstream of music making. That of course reflected how limited my idea of mainstream was. It was a matter of context.

JH / You had been exposed to the American deities.

GO / I had been exposed to the American deities.

JH / Who were your idols before Arrau?

GO / The first one was Rubinstein. Rubinstein was the first concert pianist I fell in love with. When I was ten. Of course, I knew Horowitz from records—he wasn't playing in public. I knew that Serkin was there to be dealt with, but I never got too interested; he played all this very serious music, and I liked flashy music. And then Richter came along with an all-Beethoven program at Carnegie Hall. That was a major turning point at age twelve. I had never enjoyed a slow movement in my life. I used to wait for the fast movements to come back. And I remember being mesmerized by the slow movement of Opus 2, no. 3 when Richter played it.

J H / Were Heifetz and Toscanini important to you?

G O / Yes, simply because I had their records and I heard them. Of course, I knew from all the PR that Toscanini was the greatest conductor who had ever been conceived of in the history of seven universes. Sorry for the sarcasm, but that's the way I perceived it.

J H / Did that inculcate a certain way of hearing music?

G O / It certainly did.

J H / And was that related to the muscular tension?

G O / I think it was, yes. Toscanini, Horowitz, and Heifetz all had this kind of optimal electric excitement, which was related in many cases to fast, driving tempos and slashing sonorities. Anyway, those were the people I was listening to, along with Rubinstein and Richter. And then, when he came to New York, Gilels. Meanwhile, the inculcation I was getting at Juilliard was toward the Slavic piano style, without being anywhere nearly as grandiose as the style which had produced Horowitz. I mean, I don't think we had any Anton Rubinsteins around to listen to. But I went on with my secret passion for Arrau. And, due to Barabini, my technique began changing quite blatantly. Gorodnitzki didn't seem to mind. My playing seemed, if anything, to be improving—in terms of range of color, and expressive potential, and singing sound.

J H / When did you first play for Arrau?

G O / I was taken to play for him in 1967. The *Eroica* Variations. He was very flattering, very kind. But, you see, Barabini did not want me to study with Arrau. Because I'm afraid that she knew that if I went to study with him it would minimize her hold over me. To make a long story short, by the time I was twenty-five I had begun to hear that various people I knew were going and playing for Arrau. And I thought, If these people can play for him, I can bloody well play for him, too. I called him up one day and I asked him. And he said, "Would it be all right with Olga?" And she very huffily said yes. So I did study with him, and it was a very good experience.

JH / What did you study with him?

GO / The first thing I did with him was the Brahms B-flat Concerto. It was invaluable. I mean, absolutely an invaluable experience on all kinds of levels. Because whereas Olga was very good with the philosophy, she didn't have the practical experience that he has, needless to say. And I was amazed what a practical man he could be. One thing he was absolutely floored by, that I got from Olga, was that I was just a little Arrau in terms of fingering. I would use fingerings that were more extreme than the ones he used. And at one point in the opening cadenza of the Brahms he said to me, "Marvelous fingering. But, you know, you've only been on stage for a moment. You're getting used to the sound of the piano, the hall. I myself would not risk such a fingering. Why don't you use this?" And I thought, Oh, my idol's a human being. He worries about the same things I worry about. I mean, for Olga he walked three feet off the ground and was not made of flesh. I remember feeling a great sense of relief at that. And I remember the power of his personality. And the range of expression he drew from me. And the incredible impact of his attention. I mean, he didn't miss *anything*. I mean, *nothing*. He was inexorable, as a teacher, and that was fabulous. Because I knew that was what the greatest teachers had to be. And I had never had a teacher that inexorable and powerful. At the same time, he always told me that if I had other opinions I should speak up. But I was slightly paralyzed because of the nature of my own personality, especially in those days. And besides, I'm fairly good at seeing things in other people's contexts if they present them well. I'm a fairly tolerant person in that respect, among musicians. Many of my colleagues—you try to suggest something and they say, "No, that's not my way." But I was always an absorber first. I mean, I'm a suggestible person. So I began to fear. Arrau feels so many things so absolutely strongly—there wasn't any other way to hang that painting on the wall; once you got it, that was it. This was something I couldn't tell Arrau at the time, because I was too afraid of him. So, much as I revered everything he did, I was also ambivalent and having conflicts.

JH / Did you have the same conflicts regarding technique?

GO / Not while I was with him. At one point I made the acquaintance while I was on tour of a rather eccentric Russian gentleman in Vancouver called Jan Cherniavsky. He was a funny old geezer who used to harass every pianist who came through town with his individual thoughts on music making. And I was intrigued. He wanted to change certain things in my technique, and I wasn't sure he was right but I was willing to try. And Arrau heard me during that period and he was quite appalled, and I don't blame him a bit. Because there was a lot of confusion in my mind. And then he was also amazed when I played for him later that summer. Because I knew that it would do no good to play for Arrau using anybody else's system, I sort of got myself working back in his system, and he was amazed that I was able to be that much of a chameleon. And he said, "You know, you mustn't play with my technique if you're not really convinced of it."

JH / After the Brahms B flat, what were the pieces you studied with him?

GO / The Beethoven First Concerto, the Mozart C-minor Concerto, the Schumann F-sharp minor Sonata. That was all. But that represented about twelve sessions.

JH / Do you remember any interpretive insights that you'd care to mention?

GO / There are millions. Here, in the second movement of the Brahms, for example:

Arrau talked very much about tilting the left hand all the way to the extreme right side, so that the thumb functions almost in a vertical position, bringing out the melodic notes. And then doing something similar in the corresponding spot two octaves above in the right hand, where the middle fingers play the same line that the thumb plays in the left hand. He said that one must place the middle fingers of the right hand almost vertically, like spikes, and one must relax the thumb and fifth finger, so that they will not overwhelm the melodic line contained within this chordal passage. And then he suggested that it's rather like a mallet player choosing mallets of different hardness to delineate the notes of a chord. That stood for me as a paramount technical lesson. That's what he thinks about. That's the kind of mastery he shows all the time. And of course I ran home and listened to his recording with Giulini. And of course he was as meticulous making the points in performance as he was in the lesson.

Another time I had a lesson on the Schumann F-sharp minor Sonata. And I remember how he was trying to get me to use a certain kind of push-pull rubato, a very typical Arrau rubato, in the second subject of the main body of the first movement. As always, he was going at it from the inside. He wouldn't just say speed up here and slow down there; he wanted you to feel certain surges and certain pulls of resistance in the line. And I guess I really got it, because Arrau sat back and said, "You know, when I hear you play like that I almost have an *orgasm!*" That was fabulous. I mean, he's so bloody serious that when he comes up with something like that, you really howl.

JH / Did your artistic personality change, would you say, purely as a function of the technical changes? Did your refurbished technique affect the sound you were producing and the type of interpretations you were conceiving?

GO / I suppose basically you could say that I changed from being an attack-oriented pianist to a flow-oriented pianist. In other words, I became concerned more with the progress of notes in a line. The sense of flow—that, for me, is the most valuable part of Arrau's playing, his titanic sense of flow. There's something organic about his playing, something living that seems to harness itself to natural forces. The first time I heard Furtwängler's recordings, I had a similar feeling—that whatever nourishes this music making comes from someplace very deep. It can be a crushing emotional experience.

JH / Are there certain Arrau performances or interpretations that you particularly admire?

GO / I always think of his recording of Liszt's *Bénédiction de Dieu dans la solitude*. I think it's colossal. That anyone can get such a liquid, nonpercussive sound out of a modern Steinway concert grand in a recording studio with the microphones practically inside the strings; that he can still make a wash of sound which is yet specific—it's not just a color; it has structure and it has shape. Not to mention the way he builds up the great climaxes of the piece in the most terrific way. Although I can imagine him giving an even greater performance in concert. I also love the old Columbia Debussy records. That's glorious playing, sensuous in the extreme. That was another quality that was new to me when I first heard Arrau—the sensuous component. Which, actually, I don't find him emphasizing these days—the luxurious, shall we say the Latin side of his nature. I also remember that incredible first Liszt record he made for Philips, with the two *Petrarch Sonnets* and *Jeux d'eaux à la Villa d'Este*, among other things. It was in 1970 that I got that record. I remember it so vividly—I sort of lived with it for half a year. It is so radiantly beautiful. It's funny: when the Arrau "historic recordings" came out on Desmar, a number of my piano colleagues liked the old *Jeux d'eaux* better. And I don't. The later performance has added depth and spaciousness and a real trueness of color. I mean, if you wanted to be a record reviewer: it's almost as if you can see each different jet and each different fountain in the shape of the arpeggios he's creating. I'm not sure that he was thinking about that. Knowing what I do about him, I think he probably was.

JH / Has he influenced your Liszt?

GO / Yes, considerably. Probably more than anything else, actually. My general conception of Liszt was very much influenced by his spaciousness, and his *extreme*, unabashed, unembarrassed passion. I loved those qualities very much. But I can't always carry them across as much as I'd like to.

JH / I remember your *Funérailles* recording as being unusually spacious.

GO / If you wanted to look back at me stylistically, that would be my "High Arrau" period. Definitely. I had never heard him play the piece. But I was definitely operating under the impression that his ideas would include the same pushings and pullings and agonies. And ecstasies, I hope. I still like that record of mine very much.

# With Sir Colin Davis

In contrast to his ebullient podium manner, Sir Colin Davis is a gravely composed conversationalist. He does not gesticulate. His searching pale green eyes are seldom crinkled by a smile. His voice is gentle and implausibly soft; to emphasize a word, he makes it softer still. His presence is uncommonly absorbent, his address uncommonly direct.

Our meeting, in a New York hotel, took place several weeks after I had met with Daniel Barenboim, and under similar circumstances. Davis had conducted the Boston Symphony at Carnegie Hall the night before, and was to repeat the concert that evening. The score of *Die Meistersinger*, which he was first learning, beckoned, open, on a table. But though our time was short, he dedicated himself to the subject matter with such completeness that no pressure was felt. He asked that I begin. My first question elicited less an answer than a succinct panegyric of five or six points, to most of which we returned in the ensuing conversation.

JH / When did you first collaborate with Arrau?

CD / It goes back many years. Compared with him, I was a total beginner. But he was always very nice to me. I regret in those days I didn't have the experience that I have now. Because I'm now able to serve him in a way I couldn't before.

He is representative of another kind of musician than most of those we have today. He and Serkin and Clifford Curzon. And Kempff. (I played with him only once, and he said he would never play with me again because I sang; and he had been one of my heroes.) These men have a connection to Busoni and to the Berlin of the 1920s. Which gives them a connection to a whole nine-teenth-century tradition. When you think that Arrau studied the Grieg concerto with Mrs. Grieg—there is something there which is missing today.

Arrau has, first of all, a sound which is entirely his. It's almost organ-like. At the same time it possesses an astonishing clarity. He *woos* the instrument; he doesn't beat it into submission. That makes the sound. And it is also that he produces an operatic cantabile—the imitation of the human voice, which lies behind all music. He can do that. He also has a sense of rubato that is unsurpassed.

His devotion to Liszt is extraordinary. Most people would not regard Liszt as one of the most important composers. He does, and he ennobles that music in a way which nobody else in the world can do.

I think the first time I ever felt *equal* to giving him all I was trying to convey was in Amsterdam in 1975. He came there to play the *Emperor* Concerto. As ever, I asked him if he wanted to see me beforehand. And he hardly said anything. (He has never talked to me a great deal. And I've always felt very shy; he's not a man who gabbles.) And then, at the concert, he played . . . I shall never hear the piece sound like that again. *Technically,* it was absolutely perfect. He played it like a piece of chamber music. He took what we did, and instead of correcting it, as so many pianists do, he made sense and logic of it. It was an experience of music making which I shall never forget. And I think that somehow that established something, certainly on my part. That I was able to provide a framework in which he could flourish.

And then there was the suggestion that he should make some more concerto records; would I like to do it? I said I would like to do it if he would accept. We began in Boston with the Tchaikovsky B-flat minor. I went to see him at his hotel. He had countless editions of the piece, and he said, "I haven't played this in twenty years," and so forth. He began to talk to me in a way that he had never done before. I spent a delightful hour with him; he didn't play anything, we just talked. And I think he was pleased with that.

Then we did the Schumann concerto. In the recording session, after the orchestra had gone, he recorded the cadenza, and I did something for him which I had never done for anyone else.

He gets so intensely involved in what he is doing that, in recording, when the telephone rings, he doesn't really want to answer it, but he knows he has to because people don't interrupt unless there's something wrong. I asked him, "Would you like me to sit next to the piano bench during the cadenza and answer the telephone, so you don't have to move?" And he said yes. So I did that. And then afterward he said, "I think perhaps I have found a friend." You can imagine what it meant to me.

JH / You mentioned his exposure to Busoni and to the Berlin of the twenties. Is it possible to specify what it was that he—or Serkin or Curzon or Kempff—imbibed from that environment?

CD / I'll try. Of course I wasn't there. But Clifford Curzon knew Busoni. And when Clifford—who's a totally different kind of man from Arrau, with a wicked twinkle in his eye—plays K. 537, in the first movement development he perks up and says, "Busoni called this *'piano tempestuoso.'* " And one gets a feeling of the *leisure* that these men had when they were studying. I mean, Claudio Arrau was a prodigious musician from a very early age. He had no technical problems, really; if any man has had command of the piano, he has. But I think beyond that he and others in Berlin had the leisure to examine music in a way which I don't think people do now. There would have been so many minds around, and so much could be taken from these minds. There wasn't this whizzing about. These musicians stayed in one place. Now a man doesn't stay more than two days in one place. And certainly there is no city in which the giants of the musical profession are assembled, and can exchange views, and discuss music late into the night.

JH / As you know, Arrau studied with Martin Krause, who was a student of Liszt. Perhaps we could talk a bit about Liszt.

CD / Perhaps a dozen times in my life I have conducted some Liszt. I've done the *Faust* Symphony—that's a very powerful piece; the Gretchen movement is one of the most beautiful pieces to come out of the nineteenth century. But he's a perplexing composer. And it's really only in the piano music that the richness of his imagination is entirely manifest. The textures are extraordinary—when they're played with the kind of Mozartian clarity which Arrau brings to that music.

JH / You recorded both concertos with him. Did you do them in concert with him as well?

CD / We did the A-major Concerto. We recorded it and played it in concert, as we did with the Schumann in Boston. That was a great thrill. The E-flat Concerto we only recorded.

JH / Did you experience these pieces in a new way?

CD / Well, *completely.* I mean, these two concertos can sound utterly preposterous, like one damned thing after another. They can sound like a vehicle for a pianist who's trying to make a huge impression, but musically gibberish. The main problem is to make them grow logically from one thing to another, so that one feels the unity that is built into them in a most unusual and original way. And that is what Arrau manages to do.

JH / You mentioned the *Emperor* in Amsterdam as a watershed in your relationship with Arrau. What were some of the details that made that performance so memorable?

CD / The whole problem of performing a piano concerto is that the pianist and conductor must make the piece something other than a battle, so that the music weaves into the solos and out again. That is the ideal in my head. There is a spot in the first movement, for instance, where the pianist has a lyric passage leading into a march for the orchestra [measure 166], at which point it's very easy for it to sound as if you've started the piece all over again. It depends entirely on how your soloist goes into this lyric dream, and brings you out again. And Arrau is fantastic at it.

JH / I find that his insistence on the importance of every note— even in, say, arpeggio figures—helps him to make such transitions, because no matter what he's playing there's a continuous melodic thread. When he performed the *Emperor* this season in New York, the piano part seemed to have two or three times as many notes as I had ever heard in it before.

CD / That's what I mean. Even in passage-work of any kind, the notes are still on the breath.

JH / He makes an amazing moment of the onset of the double octaves in the first movement development section.

CD / Ba-barooooom! That's one of his specialities. That kind of noise which he can make is unique to him. It's as though the whole concert hall were involved in it. If you watch his hands, they're like great paws. They're not steel. He sort of plunges his hands into the keys, and out come these sonorities. It's all to do with his theory, of course, that you play the piano with your whole body.

JH / I have never heard anybody make the little first-movement cadenza as eventful as he makes it. Which again is a matter of giving every note its due. Because part of that cadenza is just passage-work.

CD / You can hear *everything*. And yet it is never technique for its own sake. He has the most *astounding* technical control. *Every note* is, as it were, a drop of rain hanging on the branch of a tree when the sun comes up.

JH / Does this make him unusually easy to accompany?

CD / Of course. Because he doesn't throw any of it away, you see. He's not absent. And he's not absent from anything the orchestra does either. And what I love so much about him is if we do do something especially well together, he delights in the joy of having *shared* it. I remember one lovely moment in one of the Liszt concertos when I was able to get the orchestra to answer a particular rubato. And he looked up with a twinkle and said, "Who said orchestras can't play rubatos?" And we had such fun with the slow movement of the Schumann. "Which of us is Robert and which is Clara?" It's a very domestic little piece, isn't it? I think I enjoyed this movement as much as I've ever enjoyed anything. Because we never did the same thing twice. The delay before a pizzicato, for example. A pizzicato is such a tricky thing. You've got to make a breath, and then direct the orchestra to play. You've got somehow to anticipate the pianist's rubato. But with him . . .

JH / You always know where he's going.

CD / Of course. Because never, never—not for a moment does it lapse into routine. What else can one say?

JH / When I spoke to you yesterday on the phone, you said, "I'd do anything for that man." Is there anything we haven't mentioned that accounts for his inspiring such loyalty in you?

CD / Many things. I'm reading this biography of Beethoven, by Maynard Solomon. I'm learning an awful lot of things from it, about Beethoven and about myself. Not that I think I'm in any way comparable; I'm unworthy to untie his shoes. I wasn't born into a professionally musical family, as Beethoven was. I wasn't a child prodigy, as he was; I didn't start studying an instrument until I was twelve. I don't have that kind of musical background. I am therefore full of reverence for those who do. And I have— which is something I don't notice much in other people today— a natural respect for older people. So when I meet a man of Arrau's background, and a man of his integrity, *and* a man after my own heart . . . what do you think is going to happen? And the fact that he accepts me as a musician gives me exactly what I lacked as a child. You understand? I feel a devotion to him.

# PART IV

# A Performer Looks at Psychoanalysis

*The following article by Claudio Arrau appeared in*
*the February 1967 issue of* High Fidelity.

Friends and pupils often have heard me say that in my ideal music school, psychoanalysis would be a mandatory part of the general curriculum. That and the art of dancing.

Psychoanalysis to teach a young artist the needs and drives of his psyche; to make him come to know himself early rather than late and thus sooner to begin the process of fulfilling himself, which until the end of his life must become his main driving force as a human being and as an artist. Indeed, only insofar as this will be his goal, his conscious or unconscious goal, will he grow as an artist and become worthy of the name. I would include the art of modern dance for the use of its liberating, expressive movements in the release of psychophysiological blocks, tensions, and inhibitions and for the greater awareness and projection of feeling.

We have all heard of psychic blocks; of musicians suffering breakdowns, of fingers, muscles, and memory suddenly collapsing and refusing to function, of fear so acute that high notes in singers vanish and all technique and mastery seem to evaporate. At such dire times, we say that he or she needs psychoanalysis. Yes, indeed, but at such time analysis usually comes too late. Only the most aware, the most intensely driven by the will to live and the courage to be, ever make it to full light and health. Others flounder in a perpetual half-light of suffering, the mind's real Purgatorio.

In my ideal school, a young artist would never be driven to

such an impasse. Learning and guidance would light the way from the beginning, the same as in ancient times the Mysteries helped initiate the Greek neophyte into the stream of life. But, unfortunately, in our own society today, with its insistence on the competitive and material aspects of life above all else, growth and development are not the natural order of things. Although, as Jung pointed out over and over, life often does take matters into its own hands and carries us along, sometimes to our good fortune, life can also play us terrible tricks—putting out stumbling blocks when we are not looking, or bringing us to dangerous precipices down which we sometimes fall, and from which only the most heroic ever find the way back.

Psychoanalysis has come a long way since Freud published *The Interpretation of Dreams* in 1900. We know today that there are many ways to self-knowledge and self-fulfillment, which in the end is the cure of any neurosis (or at least must be the aim of any cure), whether it be lengthy analysis going back to the age of one, or Tillich, or Buber, or Zen, or sheer life-giving everyday good sense. But to me, the most pertinent way for the life of the artist is a return to the ancient knowledge and wisdom as embodied in the writings of Jung and expounded in his idea of the Collective Unconscious.

This, as distinguished from the personal unconscious, is the sum of man's total psychic history from the beginning of time, which has come down to us in mythology, fairy tales, religion, and ancient customs and rituals. As man's mind and soul evolved, as he fought his psychological battles of attainment, renewal, realization, and conscious awareness and gave them concrete form and symbol in his learning, art, and literature, so was formed the whole mystical and mythological store of our entire psychic past. Individually, in our own time and lives, we go through the same psychic battles as recorded in mythology, only without the aid of the Wise Old Man to guide us (save when we find one in the guise of the analyst in time of need); we undertake heroic journeys just as the great heroes of mythology—Hercules, Perseus, and Theseus—did, and sometimes we are even helped in our tasks by similar miraculous advice, forewarnings, and assistance. And like Prometheus, we challenge the Gods, courting disaster, which we sometimes reap and sometimes triumph over. Over and over again, we repeat what Man in his short and dangerous passage from birth to death has undergone consciously and unconsciously from the beginning of his history.

In the course of a lifetime of struggle and achievement, the artist, creative and recreative, as society's culture bearer, carries out the patterns of individual growth and development, and sometimes final realization, more clearly than other people (or we see the patterns more clearly, if for no more reason than that the life of the artist is more often recorded).

If the artist's gifts are exceptional, he will often show in his early years the qualities symbolized in the archetype of the Divine Child, which, as Jung describes it, "is a personification of vital forces quite outside the limited range of our conscious mind: of a wholeness which embraces the very depth of Nature. It represents the urge, the strongest, the most ineluctable urge in every being, namely the urge to realize itself. It is, as it were, an incarnation of the *inability to do otherwise* [Jung's italics], equipped with all the powers of nature and instinct, whereas the conscious mind is always getting caught up in its supposed ability to do otherwise."

This is the unconscious power of the child prodigy. But passing over from the divine innocence of unconscious security to the young manhood of conscious responsibility takes an act of supreme courage and heroism. For the young artist, it represents one of the most difficult periods of his life. He must pass through a great test in which he wins his standing in society (the first prize in a competition usually as his reward) along with the Princess, even as Tamino does in his Rite of Initiation in Mozart's *Magic Flute*. First he must slay the terrible dragon (attain conscious understanding), then he must pass through the test of fire and water (with Sarastro, the force of conscious knowledge and commitment, as guide), and only then does he attain Pamina (his soul), and his heart's desire. In doing so, the dark, terrible forces of the unconscious (Queen of the Night), which always seek to drag him down, sink into the deepest layers of his psyche from where he can then begin to draw his creative power, but this time mastered by his conscious mind.

If passing the heroic test—usually preceded by such depression, discouragement, and fear and trembling that the young artist often contemplates suicide—were all that had to be achieved, life would be comparatively simple. But in the life of the artist, as well as life in general, it is only the first of many essential tasks that he must accomplish.

From the age of twenty to forty or fifty, man is in the full flush of his life force. Eros is behind him and in him. His work makes strides, he wins success and recognition, and he usually marries at this time. But even with Eros within him and the drives of ego-attainment running instinctively, each accomplishment, each success, must be a conscious labor. No less than Ulysses, the artist must pass trial after trial, until little by little he reaches his life's goal and finds his soul in the guise of Penelope waiting for him.

This is if all goes well. Most of the time, as life goes, it doesn't. Eros may be within us, but so is the Death Wish (in the Jungian sense of the symbolic fear or urge to slip back into the dark unconscious state of an earlier stage of development), and we do the most inexplicable things. We frustrate ourselves constantly. Out of fear—fear of failure and, strange as it may seem, fear of success as well—we artists suddenly fall sick before major appearances. We create frightful emotional upsets, we risk losing what we hold dearest. We fall and break an arm. We have car accidents. Singers suddenly become hoarse, can't make their high notes, and often tighten their neck muscles into such a vise that it is amazing that their vocal cords can function at all. Instrumentalists suddenly lose the use of some fingers or suddenly can't play the simplest (or the most difficult) passages. Or out of competitiveness and the wish for almightiness, as it were, the least sign of imperfection can cause one to give up in the middle of an otherwise fine performance. Worst of all, the struggle may suddenly lose all meaning, and the artist, lost in a terrible maze of conflict and despair, may give up performing altogether. This giving up is a real death, the death of the soul. One descends into the abyss and the return takes the most heroic battle with the Furies (the dark aspect of the unconscious) which man is ever called upon to make and which requires all the remaining power of his soul to overcome. If he wins, he is a true hero who accomplishes his own rebirth.

The no less terrible, if less dramatic, effects arising from the failure to deal with psychoneurotic blocks are the blocks of communication. The blocks of emotional life and feeling which hinder the flow of communication and expression are often the result of teaching and upbringing, but more basically of the fear of commitment, the fear of putting one's stamp on an interpretation, so to speak. In the end the failure of communication is the failure of psychic growth and development in general. Most often, communication is blocked through unawareness and often through sheer vanity, where the artist becomes the victim of his own success and, disconnecting himself from his essential being, becomes increasingly isolated from the source of his creative powers.

Fortunately, in young artists emotional blocks of communication frequently can be broken through with the right kind of teaching. I have been astonished many times to see pupils with seemingly nothing to express, virtual emotional blanks, suddenly experience an inner emotional explosion through the sheer means of playing with the whole body instead of stiffly with only the fingers, arms rigidly at the sides. It is as if the newfound freedom of movement works back on the psyche to awaken and release the dormant creative imagination and enable it to begin to grow and blossom. It goes without saying that the potentialities of creativity must be there to begin with. Where there are no such potentialities, a good psychic and physical shaking-up will be a stimulant but only for the moment.

As the first half of an artist's life is dominated by Eros and the outward driving instinct for work and attainment, so the second half of life must be a time of stocktaking, a turning inward to the essence of one's being where unessentials fall away and only the most meaningful and deepest sides of our nature and gifts are fulfilled. This period of life can be as much a crisis in an artist's life as the very first gropings for the identity of self and purpose. Then there is the fear before the demands and dangers of life. Now there is the terror of the dissolution of life and the oncoming night of nothingness and death.

This does not mean that from the age of fifty or so an artist begins to flag and accomplish less. Just the contrary happens if everything in his psychic development has gone well. His energy is as enormous as ever. Only now, if, as Jung describes it, the full process of individuation has taken place, or is taking place—the process by which a man, through ever greater consciousness, effort, and wisdom finally attains his complete selfhood in harmony with the cosmos—does he do his best and most meaningful work. If this last task is achieved, it produces a new wave of creativity arising from still deeper sources than anything before.

In our time, Picasso, Stravinsky, Chagall, Casals, Klemperer, Rubinstein, Ansermet, among many other great old men, are the best examples of the power of individuation, of what I call continuous and endless evolvement, where the limits of one's persona begin to break down and evaporate, leaving behind all vanity, which can lead into the final fusion with the All. In the creative field, the continuous invention, active imagination, endless curiosity, and the wisdom of concentrated expression are wondrous facts in Picasso and Stravinsky particularly. Only the greatest creative spirits ever attain so far—the saying of more through less.

In creative life, or in the recreative, there are all kinds of levels of realization and fulfillment and at all stages of development. Mozart died not quite thirty-six, Schubert at thirty-one, and Beethoven at fifty-seven. Yet each fulfilled himself creatively in the fullest sense if quite differently. Mozart shows a creative power of such magnitude from *Idomeneo* to *The Magic Flute* that one can virtually say that he tossed out of himself one great masterwork after another. Schubert's creative forces toward the end of his life grew in depth and richness (the *Great* C-major Symphony, the Quintet, Op. 163, and the three Op. Post. piano sonatas among other major works) so that had he lived, I feel he would have gone on to give us still more masterworks. Beethoven underwent many rebirths and finally a complete transfiguration at the end. Sometimes he even tried to fight the early battles over again (on a higher level), as in Opus 106 when (probably tempted by the new Broadwood piano under his hands) he tried to go back to the time of the *Appassionata* in an attempt to give birth to yet another heaven-storming sonata. But he was now beyond such things and far on the way to a spiritual transformation of the highest order, and the attempt after the fiery opening proclamatory bars seems to break up under his fingers. Instead, he goes on to the profoundest slow movement of his entire *corpus* and then concludes—the virtuoso once more to the fore—with the most ragingly difficult fugue imaginable, as if to say, "Now that will show you." Beethoven always won every battle. That is why his message to mankind and especially to young people is still so powerful today.

Closer to our time, Mahler showed the same ability to overcome the dark night of the soul and over and over again to transcend the death wish, achieve rebirth and renewal on ever higher levels, and win through to the final exaltation and apotheosis of the last symphonies. We know today that Mahler consulted Freud about some of his most personal problems and we can be certain that he was helped, at least to some extent (even one good talk with a wise person can open a window to self-understanding), for toward the end of Mahler's life his anguish and fear of death had given way to a firm belief in the indestructibility of the human soul and the divine possibility of man's fulfillment on earth.

When Jung wrote that life takes care of us, he uttered an often basic truth, but only for those most positively and consciously oriented. When we have the drive and courage to enter contests (never mind that not everyone can win—it's taking the risk that counts), when we take on the responsibility of marriage and family, when we overcome obstacles and win successes, that is life taking care of us. (At this point, what with the renewed interest in contests vis-à-vis our political competitiveness with the Soviet Union, it is most important to remind young artists that contests are only a practical means in the launching of a career and, while important psychologically as a test of endurance and courage, are not the meaning of art. In my ideal school, young artists would compete but there would be no first prizes, only many prizes for different gifts.) When we need a guide and mentor most (our own private Merlins) is when we come to crossroads and crises. Only the most informed and aware get help out of their own beings. The rest are fortunate if they have the luck to come across a helping hand.

From the time I was fifteen, when my teacher Martin Krause died, until I was twenty, I went through the most difficult and unhappy years of my life. I continued to work. I won the Liszt Prize twice in succession at sixteen and seventeen, but hardly a day passed when I didn't think of death. Then at twenty–twenty-one, after my first United States tour and my return to Berlin, I was overwhelmed by the difficulties of the struggle before me and wanted to give up then and there. But a friend brought help. This friend had heard of how much analysis had helped Edwin Fischer to continue to play (Fischer's problem was a stage fright of paralyzing proportions—when he was able to overcome it, he gave some of the most demonic never-to-be-forgotten performances I have ever heard), and since Fischer was Krause's older and more famous pupil, I decided to go to an analyst too. Actually, at that time I would have gone to a witch doctor if help had been promised. My analyst, Dr. Hubert Abrahamsohn, not only helped me (in three years I had enough interest in life to enter the Geneva Concours of 1927 and win First Prize) but he has remained my friend and mentor to this day. His help and teaching (he started out as a Freudian and came to Jung and finally to what today is called Existential Psychology) opened so many windows for me that I could finally interpret my own dreams—or at least recognize them as dreams of anxiety, forewarning, and, sometimes in moments of despair, of a foretelling of fulfillment. Over a period of thirty years, analysis helped clear my personal psychic jungle until my full creative forces could flow freely. Layer after layer of covering and unessentials were stripped away in a process which must continue until one's death. In this sense the old saying that "when one stops growing one dies" is literally true.

If so far I have not mentioned women artists, it is not an oversight. The psychology of woman differs from man's as wholly as her sex. The woman artist in today's world is not only confronted by the problems of her own individual feminine psychological development but with making her way in a man's world. Since man's goal is to achieve his total personality through work, attainment, and family, a career is his natural state—nay his necessity. A woman artist must also fulfill herself as a woman. If she can do that and succeed in her career as well, without ambivalence, she is indeed blessed. But since a woman artist's career can be no less demanding, no less ego-centered than a man's— the more demanding it is indeed, the greater will be the conflict which will arise in the fulfillment of her personal life. Due to her many ambivalences, a woman artist's chance to win through to a great career is consequently more difficult than a man's. She has to battle twice as hard, I think, and fairy tale and myth are rarely on her side. (Patriarchally grounded, they are usually concerned only with the princess who has no other aim in life than to live happily ever after with her prince charming.)

Even in this day of rather waning patriarchy, when we seem to be on the threshold of a new society based on the equally strong personalities of both sexes, the normal man shuns the strong, independent woman; he has no need of her. It takes an exceptional man to effect a happy marriage with a woman artist, and lucky she is if she finds such a man. But more often she doesn't find him; she wins him, as Psyche, through trials of patience, courage, and love, finally wins back Amor.

In the Jung canon of the Collective Unconscious, the archetypes of the Anima and the Animus figure prominently. The anima is man's womanly aspect, the part of himself which he must not reject as unworthy but which he has to absorb and integrate into his psyche to become a total man. The less of this integration he accomplishes, the more of a child he remains. The woman must absorb her animus, her masculine aspect, in order to achieve full femininity.

The creative artist, I think, is among the few happy ones most able to achieve the union of opposites into the total whole which is the goal of the process of individuation—the attainment of the unity of the total self. In the artist, the tensions to be overcome may be greater, but the union—the whole—can become more perfect. The dragon slaying done with and the hero battles won, the artist can now allow himself to remain open to the sources of his imagination, divination, and creativity—his unconscious—which now no longer will appear as an aspect of the dark dread but of beneficial wisdom. Without that source, no amount of intellect, reason, ego-stability, and control would ever have enough meaning in art.

One last thought. I am often asked by friends and pupils: isn't psychoanalysis dangerous to artists, isn't it important for artists to have conflicts and neuroses and problems and to suffer? Yes, absolutely. But then psychoanalysis or self-analysis or group psychotherapy doesn't do away with conflicts and suffering. It is the finding of a *modus vivendi* with conflict and suffering—of how to deal with them and live with them—that matters. For the artist, tensions and handicaps, once understood, conquered, or sublimated, are important and need not be erased, for it is these very

247

tensions that give the creative process its intensity and are a vital source of creative power. But what psychoanalysis can do is to eliminate the handicaps of fear—the fear of being unique, or of not being unique. For the truth is that every artist, who in a greater or smaller way is a true artist, is unique.

# PART V

# Conclusion
# Arrau on Records

Arrau has been lavishly served by the phonograph. With over two hundred listings, ranging from Albéniz to Weber, his discography (see Appendix C) is unusually full. The earliest listings are piano rolls of a Schubert impromptu and of a waltz written for him by Sophie Menter, both made in London in 1922. Following his victory in the 1927 Geneva competition, he was invited by German Polydor to make his first 78s. He subsequently recorded for a variety of German and British labels before moving to the United States and recording for RCA Victor, beginning in 1941. Five years later, invited by Goddard Lieberson, he joined the roster at Columbia. He moved on to American Decca in 1952. In 1955 Walter Legge lured him to EMI,* where his output was prolific. His present association with Philips dates from 1964 and has been even more productive, fulfilling, among other things, his ambition to record all the Beethoven sonatas.

To some degree, Arrau's extensive discography is a mixed blessing. Not only does a recording fix a misleadingly permanent impression of a given interpretation, it tends to fix an impression somewhat different from impressions fostered in concert. This is because the increasingly sophisticated gadgetry of the studio has pried open an increasing gap between "live" and "recorded." A double standard is now in effect: in Carnegie Hall, wrong or vague notes are to be expected; on disc, precision and clarity are the rule. Generally, the studio standard is enforced less by the artist than by producers and engineers. Microphones are positioned to insure maximum definition; tapes are edited to insure

*Britain's Columbia label, on which Arrau recorded while with EMI, was an EMI affiliate. Some of these recordings were issued in the United States on EMI's Angel and Seraphim labels.

maximum accuracy. Too often, the spontaneity and urgency of a concert performance are less successfully fabricated.

With rare exceptions, Arrau's Philips recordings are note-perfect. His EMI recordings are often note-perfect. His 78 rpm recordings, which mainly predate the use of editable magnetic tape, contain more split notes than his EMI recordings, which do not. This progression reflects less on Arrau's marksmanship than on the increasing intervention of control-room surgeons.

Arrau himself believes that a recording, intended for repeated home listening, serves a distinct nonconcert purpose. He rebels at the thought of preserving wrong notes as an affront to the text he serves. He is in any case too much the perfectionist to overlook opportunities to "improve."

Naturally, there is no preventing private tapings of Arrau concerts with hidden equipment or, when they are broadcast, off the air. The biggest individual collections of noncommercial Arrau tapes are far more voluminous than his commercial output. In many instances, unadulterated pirate tapes surpass the intricately manicured studio products. Certainly nothing in Arrau's official discography adequately documents the abandon with which he applies himself to the Liszt sonata or the *Mephisto Waltz*. According to Amy Fay in *Music-Study in Germany*, "Liszt sometimes strikes wrong notes when he plays, but it does not trouble him in the least."* Such works as the B-minor Sonata were not intended to be scrutinized by electronic wrong-note detectors.

Concertos are especially susceptible to the pitfalls of the studio. With a hundred musicians, including two primary interpreters, on hand, there are extra egos to coordinate, and extra mistakes to correct. Arrau's concerto recordings often disappoint. In the Beethoven *Emperor* under Bernard Haitink, the opening cadenza and opening tutti sound as if they have been extracted from different performances. In Beethoven under Alceo Galliera, Arrau's cadenzas are better integrated, but the piano sounds louder when it plays alone—presumably as a result of knob-fiddling and splicing.

A further cost is exacted by close studio pickups. Arrau's sound is more luminous, more liquid from afar, as in concert. The stereo era has seen the resonating space surrounding recorded piano

*Amy Fay, *Music-Study in Germany*, p. 242.

tones expand, which is to the good. But—with proliferating microphones swarming, insect-like, nearly into the guts of the instrument—so have the individual tones expanded. If their impact and definition are thus enhanced, their collective properties are debatably altered. Piano color congeals more firmly from a distance, as a comparison of Arrau's Debussy on Columbia and Philips will show. The constant play of light and shade demanded in a work such as Beethoven's Fourth Piano Concerto is similarly compromised when every keyboard texture is made to comprise a thicket of foreground detail, as in Arrau's recording with Haitink; the less detailed, less vivid Galliera recording reproduces his hovering pianissimos more credibly, and his fortissimos have more body.

Fortunately, many of Arrau's recordings manage to minimize these risks. While it is worth remembering that his playing is sometimes more precariously inflamed in concert, his technical fluency generally allows him to record right notes without dousing the fire. While the shortcomings of his concerto recordings are unignorable, his solo recordings thrive on his ability, so evident in rehearsal, to plunge deeply the moment he enters the musical current. And while his sound can seem exaggeratedly chiseled on disc, it still emerges with a distinctive signature that in fact suits the studio better than most: like the microphones, Arrau scrutinizes every note.

The final proof of the reliability of his phonographic legacy lies in its consistency. To the degree that the young Arrau resembles the Philips artist of today, the recordings document a core of fundamental traits. To the degree that he does not, they document coherent patterns of change.

Describing an Arrau performance of the Chopin F-minor Concerto in 1954, Neville Cardus wrote: "His every note was a perfect pearl of tone and execution; any one of them could have been put on a plush tray and given as a present to any other living pianist. Any falling phrase of ornamentation could have been caught in the air and made into a rope of pearls to grace the neck of any other living pianist's wife."*

*\*Manchester Guardian*, September 3, 1954.

Precise articulation even where the dynamic is muted or the tone veiled; evenness and clarity even at mercurial speeds— judging from his recordings, these were always part of Arrau's apparatus. If the German 78s are to be trusted, his tone did not always have the uniform depth it later acquired; there are suggestions of brittleness in agitated passages. But in none of Arrau's recordings does he skim the tops of the keys, or strike phantom notes in the manner of Gieseking's Debussy or Ravel. The left hand is never neglected, nor are the insides of chords, nor are the specific harmonic and melodic ingredients of subsidiary figures. The polyphonic dimension is constant.

These aspects of his sound bespeak Arrau's grounding in *The Well-Tempered Clavier*. Though no samples of his Bach playing were ever released commercially, he did set down the *Goldberg* Variations, the *Chromatic* Fantasy and Fugue, and some of the inventions for RCA in 1942 and 1946, and copies of these performances circulate privately. Here Arrau's polyphonic gift is revealed in its purest state: the ability to "follow" diverse voices, to highlight obscure entrances and subsidiary threads without violating the poise of the whole. A taste of these accomplishments, for those with access to the 1952 recording, may be found in his haunting traversal of the fughetta (Variation No. 24) of the Beethoven *Diabelli* Variations, in which he furnishes a legato so seamless and a tone so velvet that the contrapuntal transparency emerges almost as a paradox.

In fact, with his other Decca/Brunswick releases from the same period (the *Eroica* Variations and a two-record Chopin set), this *Diabelli* arguably reproduces the beauty of Arrau's pianism more seductively than any of his more recent recordings. Whether applied to a Chopin impromptu or the knotty culminating fugue of the *Diabelli*, the combination of power and sheen captured by Decca's engineers is memorable. Arrau's Philips recordings, by comparison, are more massive, detailed, and brilliant. In the earliest of these—including most of the Beethoven and Schumann releases—the extreme proximity of the piano generates a relatively hard, even claustrophobic acoustic. Subsequently, Philips's engineers contrived to combine closeness with warmth, creating an acoustic unlike any to be encountered in concert, yet conducive to very handsome results. The notes are full and burnished throughout the range of the keyboard, and at every speed and dynamic. That is what Arrau's sound is about.

. . .

Many of Arrau's earliest recordings—the Chopin Tarantelle (ca. 1930), for instance—make no secret of the speed and precision of his fingerwork. Still, there are no obtrusive stunts. Similarly, his tonal signature is an integrated basis for interpretation, not a peripheral feat. His attention to immediate structure—the notes placed like building blocks in sturdy vertical and horizontal formations—fosters attention to the larger architecture. The statuesque luster of the shapes confers an inherent dignity.

This framework of sound and structure generates a given interpretation the way wine ages. "Such things should simply ripen," Arrau says. (See page 128.) The plan, once fixed, changes not so much in detail as in depth. Arrau has recorded the Chopin Ballade in A flat three times—in 1939, 1953, and 1977. The essential phrasings and rubatos hardly vary. But the weight and scope of the performances do. On the surface, the steady interpretive blueprint organizes an ever more turbulent interior.

I have already mentioned in this regard Arrau's two recorded versions of the Chopin preludes—performances similar in outline but different in effect. (See page 128.) A close examination of these similarities and differences reveals much about how Arrau's art has evolved.

The First Prelude, in C, already summarizes the change. In the 1973 performance, on Philips, the interpretive plan is stretched to occupy a larger frame than on Columbia (1950–51). While the stress points are identically located, and in both instances signaled by hesitations, the increased harmonic tension of the 1973 performance mandates grander distensions of the pulse.

The sighing rise and fall of the melody of the E-minor Prelude (No. 4) is stressed by Arrau in both recordings. In the B-minor Prelude (No. 6), the sighing pairs of eighth-notes in the right hand are similarly stressed on both occasions. But on Philips the tensile resistance stiffens mightily, making Arrau's exhalations more anguished. In the E-minor Prelude, moreover, the anguish is underlined by weights applied to the falling left-hand chords. The same impression of arduous progress is conveyed in miniature in Arrau's second version of the F-sharp minor Prelude (No. 8). Here he italicizes crucial downbeats by minutely retarding the right hand's octave leaps, each lasting the barest fraction of a second.

Such playing crams every crevice with expression. The sheer emotional density is stunning. Its source, beyond Arrau's agitation, is again his sound, especially when reproduced as vividly as by Philips. Arrau clarifies, as few pianists can, the twisting, rocketing passage-work of the B-flat minor Prelude (No. 16)—without telescoping the scales or cheating on the left hand. In the D-minor Prelude (No. 24), his fortissimo trills are fastidiously spun. Such sustained linear detail accumulates an intensity of its own. The same holds true of chording: to strike each member cleanly, to balance the voices as even-handedly as Arrau does, is to assemble energy payloads in which every molecule stands ready to chart its own course. Even in the G-sharp minor Prelude (No. 12), where the octaves and triads must be located and struck at a breakneck pace by the bounding left hand, Arrau's are clean and full-bodied: both as harmonic girders, and as a sprinting counterpoint to the right hand's spitfire rhetoric, they are packed with energy.

Arrau's discography, over all, reflects a tendency toward the brave scale and disquieting intensity of the 1973 Chopin preludes. His earliest recordings, extending into the forties, are his most mercurial, and are buffed with the glistening tonal refinements mentioned in his early New York reviews. His recorded performances of the following decade or so are more majestically paced; given room to maneuver, he is more likely to linger than to bolt. He excels equally in passages of lustrous power and mesmerizing stillness; at the same time, his purity can make him seem aloof. Then, sometime around 1960, the recordings document a different kind of change. An emerging undercurrent of raw feeling not only dictates yet slower tempos and grander rubatos, but adds to the dignified architecture of Arrau's sound a steady projection of human frailty. It is as if a flame that leaps and recedes through his earliest recordings were consigned to a bedrock of blazing coals. Or, to use his fifties recordings as the yardstick, as if blood had begun coursing under marble.

How did this change come about? Arrau speaks of learning to "use" anxiety rather than trying to expunge or suppress it, of applying nervous energy to the "creative stream" in order to cultivate a fuller and more vivid empathy. (See pages 56–7.) At the risk of resorting to cut-rate psychology, I am tempted to cite, as well, the event Arrau recalls as "the greatest shock in my life":

his mother's death in 1959. Perhaps mourning opened new emotional pathways. Perhaps the disappearance of a pervasive authority figure freed or emboldened him to make a more vulnerable
statement in his art.


Of Arrau's pre-LPs, at least two seem to me among the finest
recordings he has made—Schumann's *Carnaval* (1939) and Weber's Sonata in C (1941).

One could do worse, in describing the *Carnaval*, than cite
what Noel Strauss and Robert Lawrence wrote when Arrau played
the work at Carnegie Hall on February 19, 1941—the recital that
inaugurated his American success. (See pages 60–3.) The unity
and sincerity they observed, the "spurts of whimsicality, defiance, caprice," are all apparent in the dazzling recorded performance.

Arrau's account of the Weber C-major Sonata also elicited fa-
vorable critical comment in New York in 1941. Reviewing the
Carnegie Hall recital of November 14, Olin Downes wrote in the
*New York Times* of the "courtliness, wit, scintillation, the chival-
ric flourish" of Arrau's Weber. The recording documents pianism
of unpretentious brilliance. The perpetual-motion finale, marked
Presto and leggiermente, is a fabulous tour de force. (A second
Weber 78, the 1946 Konzertstück, is a blistering performance
sluggishly accompanied.)

The most accessible of Arrau's 78s are to be found, transferred
to LP, in the two-disc *Claudio Arrau: The Historic Recordings* on
Desmar. Of chief interest are ten Liszt selections: two song transcriptions, four of the *Paganini* Etudes, the F-minor Concert
Study (*La leggierezza*), the *Spanish Rhapsody, Au bord d'une
source,* and *Les Jeux d'eaux à la Villa d'Este.* The execution, often
at hair-raising speeds, is superbly athletic and—if the term is
understood to designate German conservatory rather than French
salon breeding—elegant. As always, Arrau's virtuosity is lent dignity by the firmness and honesty of his declamation. Compared
to the slightly later *Carnaval,* however, his manner at times seems
brusque. And in comparison to his later Liszt, including second
recordings of *La leggierezza* and *Les jeux d'eaux à la Villa d'Este,*
the depths and heights of the Lisztian cosmos are compressed.

.   .   .

A convenient yardstick for "Middle Arrau," because it is the second recorded version out of three, is his 1953 recording of the Chopin A-flat major Ballade. The conception is broader and more deliberate than in 1939, less agitated than in 1977. The ballade's contrasting episodes are distinctly characterized, yet unified by an unbroken line mounting toward the passionate final pages. The first two fortissimo climaxes are poised to anticipate the third, at which point, characteristically, Arrau relies on tonal depth and bold rubatos to drive home the weight of the passage without shattering the architecture with explosive attacks. In the 1977 performance the climaxes are comparably calibrated, but the line writhes from the start, asking for a more feverish emotional investment. The embattled drive toward the final stretto is in 1977 viewed, close up, as a hand-to-hand affair; in 1953, the combat is commanded from a height.

Decca envisioned Arrau's Chopin set as the first installment of an exhaustive Chopin series, but the American critical reception was so mild that the project was abandoned. One can see why the critics balked: Arrau's Chopin lacked both the heartiness of Rubinstein and the complex display of Horowitz. Without inquisitive listening, not only was the scope of Arrau's interpretations not likely to be received as a virtue, but the detailing—so different from Horowitz's—was likely to pass unnoticed.

A case in point is the più lento section of the C-sharp minor Scherzo, which Arrau charges with mystery. His method is itself mysterious. Rather than dramatizing the modulation to the minor with pathetic inflections and smeared pedalings showing the dejection of the filigree, the meaning of the passage is uncovered at a depth. The muted chords are weighted to retain their majesty. The filigree is softened without diluting its poise. The smorzando (measure 533) is underlined by an imperturbably steady ritardando. The effect is of tragedy dissolving, just before the healing surge of the coda, to a searching calm rarely found in Chopin, and certainly not normally associated with the C-sharp minor Scherzo.

The highest achievement in the Decca Chopin set may be the F-minor Ballade, in which a similar inwardness and simplicity help fashion a reading of rare unity and scope. The sighing phrases of the opening pages are subdued, but not achingly so, as in Arrau's 1977 recording. Even the first big accelerando is restrained, making the transition to the dolce melody in B-flat major (measure 84) ravishingly gentle. As the density of the writing increases, Arrau's patience serves to expose the inner parts, which, clarified, accumulate momentum on their own. Following the cadential flourish at measure 134, the overlapping melodic threads of measures 135–151 do not expire upon unveiling the familiar melody at measure 137, but, through stresses applied to the inner right-hand voices, spin an ongoing polyphonic web.

Nor does the tortuous reprise at measure 152 unravel the process of steady growth. When Arrau does begin to press, following the a tempo at measure 169, the entire structure is carried forward. The coda for once completes the assemblage rather than imposing an extra climax.

Arrau's concerto recordings from the fifties and early sixties are, on the whole, his best. Carlo Maria Giulini and Alceo Galliera furnish incisive, imaginative support. The Philharmonia Orchestra plays superbly, with distinctive contributions from the solo winds. Under Giulini, Arrau gives warm, poetic accounts of the two Brahms concertos, both culminating in blazing sunlight. Galliera and the Philharmonia are at their best accompanying Arrau in the Grieg concerto, a reading combining demonic strength with gorgeous repose in the lyric sections. The Schumann concerto, on the flip side of the Grieg, receives a radiant, relaxed performance. Near the end, as Joachim Kaiser observes in his book *Great Pianists of Our Time*, Arrau uncovers a charming waltz fragment in the left hand.

"And this," Kaiser goes on to comment, "is not done in the tri-fling manner of some Chopin players, who by arbitrarily accen-tuating particular notes in a richly-scored passage suddenly spell out quite new melodies, because wherever there are a hundred notes, it is naturally possible to pick out 'Baa-baa black sheep' or a national anthem. Arrau's discovery is not the outcome of an intense passion for originality, but the result rather of curiosity, of desire for change, and of an inner poise that allows him to concentrate on the particular because he can in any case be sure of the obvious."*

Significantly, Arrau's most exciting concerto recording of the period was made in concert: the Chopin E minor with Otto Klemperer (1954). The performance, which happens to be the one Arrau identifies as Klemperer's first Chopin (see page 125), is flawed by an occasional hardening of sentiment and tone in the heat of the moment; one does not find, as Neville Cardus did in Arrau's Edinburgh Festival account of the F-minor Concerto of the same year, "every note a perfect pearl." But there are pearls enough to make a point. And Arrau performs with a frank pa-nache, even a playfulness, rarely to be heard when he is en-sconced in the studio. The virility of the passage-work; its easy power in the face of the thinly scored climaxes; its firmness and clarity of design; its sheer stamina and security, underlined by a more propulsive, less searching overview than in his 1970 record-ing with Eliahu Inbal—all this is simply thrilling.

In the late fifties and early to mid-sixties, around the time of Arrau's peak identification with Beethoven on the concert stage, Beethoven also dominated his studio activities at EMI and Phil-ips. The core undertaking was his 13-disc sonata cycle on Philips, recorded from 1962 to 1966.

Accounts of Beethoven's own playing stress his brilliance and expressive fervor; other pianists were tidier and clearer. In our century, some of the most fervent Beethoven players have had to scramble through parts of Opuses 101 or 106 or 111. Arrau, by comparison, is the pianist who most thoroughly commands the

*Joachim Kaiser, *Great Pianists of Our Time* (New York: Herder and Herder, 1971), p. 90.

notorious patches of dense texture or tangled polyphony. March-
ing through the fiendish scherzo of Opus 101, or sorting out the
voices in the finale's fugal development, he has no peers. His
passage-work, too, combines power with extreme clarity; he
seemingly enunciates more notes than anyone else. The lucid
polyphony stiffens the harmonic tug. The linear articulation promotes lyric continuity. One outcome, and perhaps the most
characteristic feature of Arrau's Beethoven, is a synthesis of intensity and luminous breadth. Thus, in the *Waldstein*, Arrau
generates huge, coiled climaxes from the swirling scales and
arpeggios, yet traverses the whole with such rippling fluency and
dark majesty of sonority that the perspective is as much epic as
dramatic.

On another listening plane, Arrau's probing left hand, with its
narrative ease and declamatory power, is unusually informative
throughout the cycle. As good an example as any is offered by the
big Opus 7 Sonata, in which the grandeur of Arrau's reading owes
as much to the virile, two-handed chording as to the generous
ground plan. In the coda to the cavernous slow movement, six
measures from the close, Arrau sings the rising tenor line with a
striving eloquence suggesting Florestan's dungeon aria.

If another pianist tried piercing the darkness here in the same
manner, the effect would be of a spotlight aimed at selected
notes. Under Arrau's left hand, the tenor's song is discovered,
like the waltz theme in the Schumann concerto, as an uncontrived result of ongoing polyphonic investigation.

In terms of foreground detail, Arrau exhaustively explores the
diverse meanings of Beethoven's subito dynamics and ornaments. In particular, he commands an extraordinary spectrum
of trills—sparkling, steel-spun, caressing. In the coda to the

finale of the *Moonlight* Sonata, where a sustained trill emblazons the dynamic crest, he does not interpolate the customary (though unmarked) diminuendo, but stirringly intensifies the trill by retaining volume while slowing the pulse—as a Busch or Szigeti might heighten a climax with broadened vibrato.

In the complex discourse of the late sonatas, Arrau's immersion in polyphony, linear articulation, and ornament dictates grueling rubatos; even in the *Hammerklavier*'s monstrous fugue, he refuses to skim. Here, or in the opening movement of Opus 111, the combined impact of emotional entanglement and lucid textual exposition truly reflects, in Richard Osborne's phrase, "a quality of discipline and selfless involvement . . . Dostoyevskian in its intensity."* Such performances can be heard again and again, and remain a challenge to the listener.

With all this said, I do not find that the Philips cycle conveys Arrau's full stature as a Beethoven player. The problem, and a listening challenge of another sort, is the reproduction, which, as I have suggested, is claustrophobic. The piano seems larger than life and encased in dead air. The dynamics are compressed and hardened, exaggerating midrange fluctuations and canceling pianissimos and veiled tones. In the second movement of Opus 111, the big trilled crescendo (measures 114–116), an Arrau specialty, is miniaturized, and the shimmering ascents, which he pedals to perfection, sound inscribed in barbed wire.

Philips has recently reissued three Beethoven sonata performances—of *Les Adieux*, the *Waldstein*, and the *Tempest*—in warmer, subtler Festivo pressings that do fuller justice to Arrau. More than the Philips, the Festivo *Waldstein* registers Arrau's Jovian thunder.† But it is the earlier EMI *Waldstein*, with its thin yet plausible sound, that more truly reproduces the penumbra he confers on the sempre pianissimo episode (measures 251–284) preceding the finale's main reprise, and in which the broken chord figures preceding the coda attain a tonal effulgence unique in my experience of the work. Arrau's Opus 111 on EMI, regally declaimed and quiescent at the close, is equally distinguished.

---

*"Arrau's Beethoven Pilgrimage," *New York Times*, June 10, 1973.
†Philips plans to remaster many of its older Arrau recordings for the "Arrau Edition" planned in conjunction with his eightieth birthday.

Of Arrau's two Beethoven concerto cycles, the performances on EMI with Galliera eclipse the performances on Philips with Haitink. In particular, the Arrau-Galliera Fourth Concerto is an exceptional reading. More than Haitink, or Leonard Bernstein on the DGG concert recording, Galliera shares Arrau's melancholic vision of the opening tutti. (See page 165.) Arrau's application of the four-note knocking motif he associates with the grieving Orpheus casts a veil over the entire movement so that it ends poised on the brink of the pivotal lamentations to come.

After the Beethoven sonata and concerto sets were finished in 1966, Arrau for a time mainly recorded Schumann for Philips. To some extent, the reproduction again suffers from a dearth of sunlight and air. Of the big cycles, I admire most the *Humoreske*. Philips's pickup is marginally less cramped than in *Carnaval* or the C-major Fantasy, and Arrau is in particularly impetuous fettle. His interpretation combines unfeigned emotional diversity— Schumann's inner and outer personae are equally served—with a rare grasp of overall structure. Specifically: the *"mit einigen Pomp"* episode is the sonorous capstone, leading, via a finely gauged transition, to a leavetaking (*"zum Beschluss"*) of Mahlerian magnitude. The flavor of the performance also owes much to pianistic detail. More than comedy, Schumann's title implies a gamut of rapidly changing moods. To this end, Arrau dramatizes displaced accents, intertwining inner parts, contrasts in articulation between the hands. The second page (*"sehr rasch und leicht"*) is already distinctive: by seizing the interior arpeggios Schumann hurls in contrary motion to the top voice, Arrau achieves an unnervingly active texture, suggesting, in his own words, "grotesque joy—really something [E.T.A.] Hoffmannesque."

This is typical of Arrau's Schumann method and the vision behind it. The restless polyphony is unstintingly extracted, conveying the restless imbalance of Schumann the man. "Schumann's music," Arrau says, "is never quiet. There is always, even in the lyrical sections, an undercurrent of turbulence. People make the mistake of dividing it into the ardent and the sentimental. They forget that Florestan and Eusebius were part of the same personality." In the late pieces, with their obsessive patterning and compressed registration, Schumann's world contracts to a shadowy cubicle. In Arrau's recording of the Opus 111 *Fantasiestücke*, written four years before Schumann's confinement to an insane asylum, the swarming arpeggios and contorted melodic scraps of No. 1 distill a harrowing night of the soul.

The best engineered of Arrau's solo Schumann recordings is the most recent (1976), comprising *Kinderszenen, Papillons,* the Opus 28 Romances, and the *Blumenstück.* Philips's acoustic is warmer than before. The playing, too, is somewhat altered: gentler, more settled. Partly, this reflects the quieter repertoire— *Kinderszenen,* Schumann's refuge from adult tumult, is glowingly confided. But there may also have been a change in Arrau. Generally, I find his recordings from this period his most inspiring and diversified. The principal composers are Liszt, Chopin, and Brahms.

"It is a peculiarity of Liszt's music that it faithfully and fatally mirrors the character of its interpreter," writes Alfred Brendel in his valuable *Musical Thoughts and Afterthoughts.* "When his works give the impression of being hollow, superficial, and pretentious, the fault lies usually with the performer, occasionally with the (prejudiced) listener, and only very rarely with Liszt himself."[*]

To Liszt, Arrau brings his immunity to sham and capacity for high regard. Few Liszt interpreters, even great ones, project an understanding of the composer so devoid of condescension. Arthur Rubinstein has said of Busoni that he made Liszt's compositions "sound even more important than they actually were." If anything, Arrau makes Liszt seem nobler than he was.

Arrau's 1969 Liszt recital on Philips—his first solo Liszt recording in seventeen years—consists of the B-minor Ballade; the *Valse oubliée* No. 1; and, from *Années de pèlerinage,* the *Vallée d'Obermann,* the *Petrarch Sonnets* Nos. 104 and 123, and *Les Jeux d'eaux à la Villa d'Este.* His playing throughout justifies his unswerving faith in the composer.

In Vladimir Horowitz's 1966 recording, the *Vallée d'Obermann* is memorable for two episodes of febrile extroversion: the recitativo and the climactic final pages. In Arrau's performance,

---

[*]Alfred Brendel, *Musical Thoughts and Afterthoughts* (Princeton: Princeton University Press, 1976), p. 78.

the recitativo and climax are integrated into a striving narrative the whole of which fastens his attention. Twenty-six measures into the piece, where the brooding eighth-notes of the first theme give way to sighing phrases in half-notes and quarters, Horowitz accelerates. Arrau observes Liszt's più lento, unfolding a vista of spires, chasms, and oceanic calm; the rhetoric of Etienne Pivert de Sénancour's *Obermann* ("Vast consciousness of a Nature everywhere overwhelming and impenetrable . . .") is rescued from cliché. When the soliloquizing first theme returns, Arrau's delivery is shrunken and dazed. Later, in the dolcissimo C-major episode, the humbling landscape inspires a healing ecstasy. The recitativo's contortions and the progressive exaltation of the climax advance and complete the argument. The victorious epilogue begs for silence, not applause.

Even in terms of pianism, Arrau's performance is an act of faith. Where Horowitz rescores passages and adds sforzandos, Arrau trusts Liszt. He approaches the text with the same respect he might lavish on a Mozart sonata, and obtains a rendering of Mozartean polish. As a technical feat, however unadvertised, it is astounding. Even the rapid-fire repeated chords of the closing pages, sometimes approached by leaps of an octave or more, are never smudged, simplified, percussive, or undernourished. If Liszt were unworthy of such consideration, Arrau's diligence would be as perverse as another pianist's (I do not mean Horowitz's) interpolations. But the architecture, detail, and plush colors his diligence secures are anything but perverse. More: in serving the text so honestly, he underscores the emotional integrity of his reading.

There is a danger in taking Liszt's musical descriptions too literally; Liszt himself warned against it. But Arrau's performance of the B-minor Ballade (on the flip side of his *Vallée d'Obermann*), with its tender inner life, leaves little doubt that the Hero and Leander myth he applies (see pages 142–6) was present in Liszt's imagination: the story, score, and performance correspond point by point. The appassionato statement of the love theme directly following Leander's death, for instance, is cloaked in mourning.

The twelve *Transcendental* Etudes and three Concert Studies (G. 144), on a two-disc set, are also vintage Arrau. Where Liszt is swashbuckling, as in *Mazeppa* or *Wilde Jagd*, Arrau is epic. In *Chasse-neige*, where Liszt is visionary, Arrau's combination of

passion and pianistic integrity—the tremolos are thick with inci-
dent—is shattering. His pacing is so lavish, and his visceral investment so extreme, that one break in the fabric would be fatal.
Normally, even the most dedicated performers must struggle
against falling back on an emotional automatic pilot. With Arrau,
this is not part of the struggle.

Arrau's recent recordings of the two Liszt concertos with Sir
Colin Davis are among his best with orchestra; the E flat, in
particular, is arguably the best concerto recording he has made.
The complex textural interpenetration of piano and orchestra—a
fascinating feature of both works—is appreciated not only by the
performers, but by the engineers, who situate piano and orchestra in a single, plausible acoustic space. In his 1952 version of the
E-flat Concerto, Arrau's phenomenal pianism is sabotaged by a
tinsel accompaniment. Here, Davis's shaping of the opening motto
in its various guises is always sincere. In particular, the motto's
pivotal recapitulation three-quarters through the second movement is as triumphant as I have ever heard it. The Arrau-Davis
interpretation of the A-major Concerto commands the same high
ground. But the crucial cello solos are blandly taken, and an
audible splice some minutes from the close (measure 456) inter-
cepts the current; afterward, the performance never regains its
full electric charge.

The summit of Liszt's keyboard output, and of Arrau's Liszt, is
the B-minor Sonata. Here Arrau enshrines his protean image of
the composer, a concatenation of striving, softness, and negation,
the whole of which finds consolation in God. His recording, made
shortly after he restored the sonata to his active repertoire, falls
short of documenting the terrifying experience he makes of it in
concert. Even as a dry run, however, the recording demonstrates
the veracity of Arrau's interpretation. His integrity is not made a
pretext for modernizing burning Romantic truths. Nor does he
try grasping the satanic and macabre through bold applications of
makeup. His method is that of the great actor he insists every
great interpreter must be: self-transformation. In the opening
pages, he embodies Mephistopheles, then Gretchen. The first
inhabits a sound world of stark staccatos and fortissimos. The
second, all innocence and tenderness, seems glimpsed through
gauze. The contest of pleading and rebuff preceding the slow
movement is a comparable tour de force of crossed antinomies.

The scope of Arrau's realization is not the result of applying personal feelings and, as it were, stretching them to match the extravagance of the dialectic, but of stretching, organically, to uncover feelings already big enough to fit.

According to the English Chopin scholar Arthur Hedley: "Chopin is a tragic, not a merely pathetic, figure. Owing to his almost impenetrable reserve where all but his Polish intimates were concerned, scarcely any of those who have described his character ever penetrated beneath the charming and polished exterior. The gentle, amiable, and ineffectual Chopin of a thousand legends never really existed."* And: "In unguarded moments he could be swept by strong waves of anger or contempt, which found expression in language far removed from that of the elegant salons he frequented in Warsaw or Paris. His letters (in Polish) show this constantly, as do the confidences of friends who saw him in some boisterous or passionate mood. With strangers the lid of the pot had to be firmly held down, and George Sand for one has described how he sometimes almost choked in keeping a tight hold over his temper."†

To warn against sentimentalizing Chopin may seem unnecessary. But in the early years of this century, when Arrau was a student in Berlin, images of Chopin as a drawing-room mannequin or accomplice to pianistic display were more respectable than today. The real Chopin could not stand to hear pianists tinkering with or otherwise belittling his scores. He was a meticulous, self-critical workman, bent on refining his febrile muse.

Arrau's disavowal of Chopin as salon or circus entertainment is absolute. Beyond charm and surface excitement, he finds, as in Liszt, striving and repose. Neville Cardus once called Arrau's Chopin "Chopin plus." Chopin the pianist produced a relatively fragile sound, and was not given to strenuous rubatos. Arrau honors the strenuous heroism of Chopin the composer, of whom it was repeatedly said that his spirit seemed to consume his flesh.

Breadth and idealism are constant features of the Chopin recordings Arrau made between 1950 and 1960. In addition to

---

*Arthur Hedley, *Chopin* (London: L. M. Dent, 1947), p. 73.
†Hedley, "Chopin: The Man," in *The Chopin Companion*, ed. Alan Walker (New York: Taplinger, 1967), pp. 6–7.

the preludes on Columbia and the two-record Decca set, both of which I have discussed, these include, on EMI, dimly reproduced yet unusually lucid performances of the complete etudes, and a performance of the B-minor Sonata distinguished by its hypnotic slow movement and granitic finale. Arrau's Chopin performances on Philips are all the more weighty. The Twenty-four Preludes, the second time around, prove an ideal vehicle. As I have suggested in comparing his two versions of the cycle, the added density of emotional detail in Arrau's 1973 performance enables him to pack each small berth with a world of feeling. Equally stirring is his 1977 recording of the F-minor Fantasy.

The further Chopin strays from the muscle and compression of the preludes, the fantasy, and the ballades, the more Arrau's Philips recordings violate conventional understandings of the composer. In the nocturnes, as opposed to melancholic night-songs, he proposes a series of charged monologues. The Twelfth Nocturne in G (Op. 37, no. 2), usually suggests the peaceful flux of waves; the second subject is practically a barcarolle. In Arrau's performance, the second subject is practically a lament. And yet Arrau uncoils Chopin's cantilenas so skillfully that every interpretive convolution is explained. The embellishments are fused to the line as in Mozart, or the slow movement of the *Hammerklavier*. (Chopin himself, in one of his letters, praises the soprano Constantia Gladkowska for articulating ornamental sixteenths not as "rapid *gruppetti*," but with every note "fully sung.") More than once the depth and darkness of the vocal filament suggest Callas, a singer Arrau reveres.

Another unconventional Chopin performance is of the F-minor Concerto, a work Furtwängler once described as "that autumnal masterpiece."* With Eliahu Inbal, Arrau gives a ripe, infinitely patient account of the slow movement, caressing the fioriture with such tender wisdom that to call the music "charming" or "dreamy" would be out of place. The nineteen-year-old Chopin's moonlit reverie is revealed to intimate a lofty equanimity.

In the music of Brahms, plush textural upholstery results not from padding but from agglomerations of motivic fibers. The per-

*Furtwängler, *Concerning Music*, p. 17.

former is challenged to produce the proper warmth, even thickness, without obscuring omnipresent contrapuntal and rhythmic detail. This is already an essential accomplishment of Arrau's sound. Few pianists so majestically project the insides of Brahms's massive chordal structures—the juicy but awkward thirds and sixths. He extracts the hemiolas and other irregularities of rhythm and phrase with equal thoroughness. There is no fuzz, no gray fog.

Arrau's recording of the *Handel* Variations—the Brahms solo work he has performed more than any other—is a case in point. Polyphony and sonority are so well served that even in the twenty-fifth variation, where both hands are hurled toward distant fortissimo chords for sixteen consecutive measures, the text is never muddied and the sonority never chipped. (Arrau tells his students the hands must become like "wool" in order to yield and adjust to Brahms's thankless configurations.) Earlier, the legato octaves of the sixth variation furnish an excellent example of the inherent creativity of a fluent technique: the gliding smoothness of Arrau's octaves insinuates suspense. For that matter, his pianistic command throughout facilitates a magisterial overview: patiently prepared, the final variations drive toward the fugue with irresistible cumulative fury.

Arrau's avoidance of Brahms's late piano pieces, with their autumn rustlings, is suggestive. He is drawn, instead, to the hot-blooded rapture of the early F-sharp minor and F-minor Sonatas. His recordings of both works are splendidly representative—the declamation is exalted, never bombastic. His recordings of the *Paganini* Variations and the Opus 10 Ballades are revelatory. The *Paganini* Variations is a notorious test piece for virtuosos. That Arrau eschews display is predictable. The result, not predictable, is a rendering whose continuity, concision, and poignant alternation of light and shade evoke nothing so much as the Chopin preludes as Arrau conceives them. (See pages 158–62.) Capitalizing on Brahms's dark registration, and on disorienting gaps within the chords and wide-flung arpeggios, he evokes troubled nightscapes, then wafts the *Paganini* theme aloft. Never have the gentle fourth and twelfth variations of Book II sounded so benedictory.

Arrau's towering traversal of the Opus 10 Ballades is again surprising. In Wilhelm Kempff's inspiring recording (DG 2530321), the ballades are sung by the hearth; the gifted singer is sweet-voiced and untrained. Arrau, by comparison, is hugely sonorous and portentous, suggesting a Kipnis or Hotter in full concert regalia. Where Kempff's songs narrate their somber stories, Arrau's conjure up immediate experience. In the Second Ballade, which reminds Arrau of the slow movement of the F-minor Sonata (see page 155), the love motif swells to mythic proportions. In the Fourth Ballade, where Kempff spins a Schumannesque reverie, Arrau burrows within the dense, palpitating più lento sections to strike a solitary, interior note. The decelerating close, rather than a stock invitation to recede and resolve, is understood to herald an ecstatic apotheosis, frozen in time and streaming with light. (See page 156.)

This is not the only music in which Kempff and Arrau emerge as antipodes. Comparable instances may be found in Liszt (the *Petrarch Sonnets*) and in much of Schumann and Beethoven. Schiller's celebrated distinction between *naiv* and *sentimental-isch* is not irrelevant. As often as Kempff's unstudied artistry conceals itself, Arrau is found striving and embattled, stricken or triumphant.

According to Arrau: "Schubert is the final problem in interpretation—to get to a point of maturity and depth where you can bring together the different elements in his music. These are, in the first place, his dramatic power—Beethoven was his idol. And then his folklore simplicity. And then his Viennese background. And his proximity to death, especially in the last sonatas. To bring all this to a synthesis is very difficult, especially for a young person. In Schubert I don't think you can even mention vanity or ego—it would be completely out of place."

Of the classical masters, Schubert is the great equivocator. He is innocent and experienced, calm and conflicted. He moves swiftly from Elysium to the corner tavern. Especially in his piano sonatas, where the sprawling ground plans and quasi-orchestral textures are additionally controversial, his extreme mutability has delayed his acceptance. Even such masterworks as the Opus Posthumous Sonatas in C minor (D. 958) and A (D. 959) lack a performance tradition long or firm enough to establish interpretive norms. Poised between classical decorum and Romantic effulgence, their language throbs with ambiguities.

For artists who can unfold his epic paragraphs without pressing, and accept his frequent disregard for surface effect, Schubert's piano music can seem more saturated with variegated feeling than anyone else's. More than Beethoven, with his guiding ego, Schubert, with his ambiguities, molds himself to accommodate the probing, unselfish interpreter. This is what one realizes in listening to Schnabel's Schubert recordings, or to Kempff's landmark set of the Schubert sonatas, or to the Schubert recordings Arrau has undertaken late in his career, beginning with the C-minor Sonata in 1978.

Excepting an early piano roll of the first F-minor Impromptu from D. 935 (Op. 142), Arrau's first Schubert recordings were for EMI in the fifties. His *Moments musicaux* are formal, sincere, quiescent. His *Wanderer* Fantasy is sonorous and poised. But it is his 1956 recording of the Drei Klavierstücke (D. 946) that already documents an extraordinarily pregnant Schubert vision. The music itself, from Schubert's awesome final year, offers something more than the *Wanderer* or *Moments musicaux*. Some commentators derogate the Drei Klavierstücke as a long-winded pastiche. But their peculiar diversity of style and tone defeats easy classification. Arrau, in a program note from the fifties, uses words like "otherworldly," "tender," and "profound" to describe them, and his recorded performance is all of these. In particular, his recording of the second piece, in E flat, is one of his finest for EMI. Maintaining a slowish tempo (the marking is Allegretto) and taking every repeat (the timing is 15'40" as against Alfred Brendel's 9'33" on Philips 6500928), Arrau unites the contrasting episodes in a stream of trance-like concentration. Thus distilled, the menacing double trills and slithery chromatics of the C-minor episode, rather than specifying a finite disturbance, insinuate the tempered upper reaches of an inferno.

Arrau's Schubert recordings for Philips preserve the range and polyvalence of the EMI Drei Klavierstücke, but the textures are more detailed, the contrasts more extreme. Normally, such intensification would risk a narrower, more explicitly personal conception. But Arrau's intensification, rather than imposing surface detonations and other inflammations of the will, is typically interior.

Objectively, the impression of a charged undercurrent results partly from the treatment of arpeggios and other supportive figures. Arrau represents the opposite of the melody-plus-accompaniment school of Schubert interpretation. A case in point is the C-minor Impromptu from D. 899 (Op. 90), which he presents as a *Winterreise* whose eventfulness is underscored by the fullness and variety of the piano fabric. In the opening measures, the alternation of the wanderer's lonely tones and the diversified answering chorus is already dramatic. Later, the left-hand triplets that power the journey's first leg are made a distinct strain of experience. When the triplets give way to sixteenth-notes, Arrau's active articulation suggests a new, nervously alert awareness, susceptible to every passing shadow or shaft of light.

Arrau makes his most important Schubert statement in a mightier C-minor work—the D. 958 Sonata. In his article "Schubert's Illness Re-examined," Eric Sams reconstitutes a harrowing medical history of Schubert's final five years.* Like Sams, Arrau believes Schubert knew he was suffering from a prolonged fatal illness. He floods the C-minor Sonata with visions of stalking, two-faced Death. In the twisting chromatic scales of the finale (measure 131) and first movement development, which he truly renders "as something skeletal, macabre—without any flesh" (see page 126), Arrau finds a motif for existential terror. In the Scherzo, the winding, wandering right-hand passage-work is made to evoke a graveyard wind. Elsewhere, chiefly in the second movement, Schubert's morbidity is as profoundly revealed in its benign guise: the beckoning *Lindenbaum*, the brook of *Die schöne Müllerin*. In the finale, the two faces of Death mingle or compete as speeding shadows. "A ghost dance," Arrau calls it, and comments in a program note that the grim rondo theme "returns over and over . . . as if Schubert wanted to impress its terrible inevitability on the mind."

Yet another C-minor work, the D. 915 Allegretto, fills out the disc with the C-minor Sonata. Here the same twin countenance is condensed to an alternation of arpeggios in C minor, rising from piano to fortissimo, and in C and E-flat major, always pianissimo. Arrau's 1959 recording traverses a wider dynamic range, but it is his 1978 recording that encompasses far-flung spiritual realms. Here the fortissimos are absorbent, worn with experience. The pianissimos, gently dispersed with the pedal, touch heaven and the hereafter.

*Eric Sams, "Schubert's Illness Re-examined," *Musical Times*, January 1980.

. . .

A recurring motif of Arrau's earliest Berlin reviews is his resistance to artifice. "He does not exhibit the fatal precocity which is unbearable in the playing of most child prodigies: although his playing is phenomenal, it is always youthful, naïve, and uncontrived." (See page 45.) To survey his recordings is to arrive at the same conclusion: Arrau does not simulate. The eagerness of his 1939 *Carnaval* recording, the fatalism of his 1978 Schubert C-minor Sonata document stages in a talent which has ripened truthfully.

In an important sense, Arrau's creativity is unwilled. The music filters through visceral pathways and finds its own way to new goals; pictures and words come later, if at all. For Arrau, interpretation is a process not of thinking out but of playing through. He does not begin by asking what tempos and inflections drama or profundity require. He does not test brainstorms, but peers deeper with sights fixed. Versus the skeptical modern mind, Arrau's is a credulous intelligence, actually susceptible to exaltation or diablerie.

These are the aspects of Arrau's art Garrick Ohlsson identifies when he calls Arrau's playing "organic." They are linked to his principles of piano technique, which rely on the wisdom of the body, and to his principles of psychology, which rely on the wisdom of the subconscious. They pervade his Douglaston study, with its womb-like seclusion and primitive artifacts.

The early circumstances of his life focused his ambition and secured a nurturing insularity: his prodigy feats subsidized his education; Krause's intense tutelage honed his gifts and instilled a sense of high purpose; Berlin illustrated and celebrated the call to art. Today's young pianists are less fortunate. The prodigy syndrome is defunct, or nearly so; daily personal tutelage, bent on transferring received tradition, lies outside the modern conservatory regime; the concentrated cultural life of Arrau's Berlin has given way to culture blurred and dispersed. Now even the least worldly of young musicians know airplanes and phonographs.

In a letter to Princess Marie Wittgenstein, Richard Wagner once described the creative state as he knew it: "Complete absorption—forgetfulness of self and the world about me, a capacity to saturate all my being unreservedly with my subject, which, thus protected from trivial contacts, grows in depth and intensity."* Today's weight of practice and opinion leans toward less individualized norms, toward a suprapersonal scheme in which concert pianists are no longer likely supermen (and in which all individual acts of audacity, unless practiced by governments or corporations, are less potent than before).

Part of what we honor in Arrau is the fortitude of a survivor. In Beethoven's Fourth Piano Concerto, as the pleading Orpheus; in Liszt, as Faust or as Hero's Leander; in Brahms, as the ecstatic pantheist he finds in the Opus 10 Ballades, he is the enduring protagonist in rituals of quest and redemption.

*Letter No. 348 (February 8, 1858), *Letters of Wagner*, Vol. 1, ed. Wilhelm Altmann, trans. by M. M. Bozman (New York: Dutton, 1927), p. 342.

# Appendices
# Index

# Appendix A

# Sample Programs

## 1. THE MEXICO CITY CYCLE, 1933–34

Between October 11, 1933, and January 11, 1934, Arrau gave fifteen recitals and four concerts with orchestra in Mexico City. The recital programs, reflecting the extent of his solo repertoire, are given below. Some listings (e.g., the Schumann *Novelette* in D on the first program) are ambiguous—Schumann wrote four *Noveletten* in D—and impossible to clarify at this late date.

### 1

| | |
|---|---|
| Variations in F minor | HAYDN |
| Sonata in E flat (Op. 81a) *(Les Adieux)* | BEETHOVEN |
| | |
| *Novelette* in D | SCHUMANN |
| Intermezzo in B-flat minor [*sic*] | BRAHMS |
| Capriccio in B minor | |
| Rhapsody in B flat [*sic*] | |
| | |
| Ballade in B minor | LISZT |
| Two Elegies | BUSONI |
|    *Turandots Frauengemach* | |
|    *All'Italia* | |
| *Islamey* | BALAKIREV |

### 2

| | |
|---|---|
| Four Ballades (Op. 10) | BRAHMS |
| *Paganini* Variations, Book I | |
| | |
| Sonata in F-sharp minor | SCHUMANN |

| | |
|---|---|
| Toccata | PROKOFIEV |
| *La maja y el ruiseñor* | GRANADOS |
| *Soirée dans Grenade* | DEBUSSY |
| *Golliwog's Cakewalk* | |

3

| | |
|---|---|
| Rondo in A minor | MOZART |
| *Eroica* Variations | BEETHOVEN |
| Sonata in B-flat minor | CHOPIN |
| *Valses nobles et sentimentales* | RAVEL |
| *El Albaicín* | ALBÉNIZ |
| *Triana* | |

4

| | |
|---|---|
| Variations in F | BEETHOVEN |
| Sonata in D | MOZART |
| *Carnaval* | SCHUMANN |
| *Ondine* | RAVEL |
| *Navarra* | ALBÉNIZ |
| *Almería* | |
| *El pelele* | GRANADOS |

5

| | |
|---|---|
| Rondo in D | MOZART |
| Sonata in D (Op. 10, no. 3) | BEETHOVEN |
| *Pictures at an Exhibition* | MUSSORGSKY |
| *Funérailles* | LISZT |
| Two Etudes | |
| Scherzo in C-sharp minor | CHOPIN |

## 6

| | |
|---|---|
| Impromptu in B flat | SCHUBERT |
| Sonata in E flat (Op. 31, no. 3) | BEETHOVEN |

| | |
|---|---|
| Ballade in A flat | CHOPIN |
| Impromptu in F sharp | |
| Etude in E | |
| Scherzo in E | |

| | |
|---|---|
| *Idylle* | CHABRIER |
| *Scherzo-valse* | |
| *Jeux d'eau* | RAVEL |
| *Caprice italien* | POULENC |

## 7

| | |
|---|---|
| Sonata in C-sharp minor (Op. 27, no. 2) *(Moonlight)* | BEETHOVEN |
| Sonata in D (Op. 28) *(Pastoral)* | |

| | |
|---|---|
| *Waldstein* Sonata in C (Op. 53) | BEETHOVEN |
| Sonata in E (Op. 109) | |

## 8

| | |
|---|---|
| Sonata in F sharp (Op. 78) | BEETHOVEN |
| Sonata in A flat (Op. 110) | |

| | |
|---|---|
| *Wanderer* Fantasy | SCHUBERT |

| | |
|---|---|
| Four *Transcendental* Etudes | LISZT |
|     *Mazeppa* | |
|     *Harmonies du soir* | |
|     *Eroica* | |
|     F minor | |

9

Twenty-four Preludes                                   CHOPIN

Sonata in B minor                                      CHOPIN

Ballade in G minor                                     CHOPIN
Nocturne in E
Polonaise in A flat (Op. 53)


10

Three *Moments musicaux*                               SCHUBERT
Sonata in A (Op. 120, D.664)

Sonata in G minor                                      SCHUMANN

*Petrarch Sonnet 104*                                  LISZT
*Paganini* Etude No. 2
*Petrarch Sonnet 123*
*Paganini* Etude No. 4
*Paganini* Etude No. 5
*Paganini* Etude No. 6


11

Prelude and Fugue in C sharp                           BACH
Rondo in G                                             BEETHOVEN
*Handel* Variations                                    BRAHMS

Sonata in B minor                                      LISZT
*Three Movements from Petrushka*                       STRAVINSKY


12

*Variations sérieuses*                                 MENDELSSOHN
Sonata in A flat                                       WEBER

## Appendix A: Sample Programs

| | |
|---|---|
| *Symphonic Etudes* | SCHUMANN |
| Ballade in F minor | CHOPIN |
| *Les Jeux d'eaux à la Villa d'Este* | LISZT |
| *Mephisto Waltz* | |

13

| | |
|---|---|
| *French Suite* in E | BACH |
| Sonata in E flat (Op. 7) | BEETHOVEN |
| *Waldszenen* | SCHUMANN |
| Barcarolle | CHOPIN |
| Scherzo in B minor | |
| *El puerto* | ALBÉNIZ |
| *La maja y el ruiseñor* | GRANADOS |
| *Dance of Terror* | FALLA |
| *Gypsy Dance* | ERNESTO HALFFTER |

14

| | |
|---|---|
| Two Preludes and Fugues from *The Well-Tempered Clavier* | BACH |
|     F major, Book I | |
|     C-sharp minor, Book II | |
| *Paganini* Variations, Book II | BRAHMS |
| Fantasy in C | SCHUMANN |
| *Allegro barbaro* | BARTÓK |
| *Jardins sous la pluie* | DEBUSSY |
| *Feux d'artifice* | |
| *Los requiebros* | GRANADOS |

15

| | |
|---|---|
| Partita in G | BACH |
| Sonata in E flat (Op. 27, No. 1) | BEETHOVEN |

Fantasy in F minor                          CHOPIN
Nocturne in B
Scherzo in B-flat minor

Toccata                                     PROKOFIEV
Danse (*Tarantelle styrienne*)              DEBUSSY
*Voiles*
*L'Isle joyeuse*


## 2. THE BERLIN BACH CYCLE, 1935–36

Arrau's twelve-concert Bach survey, at Berlin's Meistersaal, was announced as encompassing the complete *Klavierwerk* of J. S. Bach. Given
the existence of incomplete compositions and compositions of doubtful
authorship, there is no definitive list of Bach's solo keyboard output. If
Arrau's twelve programs are checked against the Bach Gesellschaft edition, in common use at the time, the only notable omission, excluding
various lesser-known works, is the G-major Toccata. Yet he feels certain
he performed it. As with the Mexico City programs, some listings are
unavoidably ambiguous.


1

*The Well-Tempered Clavier*, Book I,
Preludes and Fugues Nos. 1–12


2

*The Well-Tempered Clavier*, Book I,
Preludes and Fugues Nos. 13–24


3

*The Well-Tempered Clavier*, Book II,
Preludes and Fugues Nos. 1–12


4

*The Well-Tempered Clavier*, Book II,
Preludes and Fugues Nos. 13–24

## 5

Six *French Suites*

## 6

Six *English Suites*

## 7

Fantasy in C minor
Fifteen Sinfonias [Three-Part Inventions]
Toccata in C minor
Capriccio in B flat
(*on the Departure of His Most Beloved Brother*)
Prelude and Fugue in A minor
Fragment from a Suite in F minor
*Three Pieces in the Form of a Suite*
(Allemande-Courante-Gigue)
Fugue in A minor

## 8

Fantasy and Fugue in A minor
Fifteen Inventions
Toccata in F-sharp minor
Sonata in D minor
Adagio in G
Suite in E minor
*Italian* Concerto

## 9

Six Partitas

## 10

*Ouvertüre nach französischer Art* in B minor
Four Duets
*Goldberg* Variations

## 11

*Aria in the Italian Manner*
Twelve Little Preludes
Capriccio in D
Little Fugue in C minor
Fugue in C
Fugue in C
Fugue in D minor
Fugue in D minor
Fugue in E minor
Fugue in A minor
Fugue in A
Toccata in E minor
Suite in A minor
Suite in E flat
Three Minuets
Toccata in D

## 12

Prelude, Fugue, and Allegro in E flat
Six Little Preludes
Fantasy in C minor
Fantasy in G minor
Fantasy in A minor
Toccata in G minor
Prelude and Fughetta in D minor
Prelude and Fughetta in E minor
Prelude and Fugue in E flat
Prelude and Fugue in A minor
Toccata in D minor
Overture in F
Fugue on a Theme by Albinoni
*Chromatic* Fantasy and Fugue

# Appendix B

# Sample Itinerary

Once Europe opened up after World War II, Arrau began to play well over a hundred concerts per season. In 1954–55, one of his busiest seasons, he had 130 engagements. His itinerary indicates the pace and extent of his travels.

July   5   Robin Hood Dell (Philadelphia Orchestra)—Beethoven Concertos Nos. 4 and 5

        11   Berkshire Festival (Boston Symphony)—Beethoven Concerto No. 5

        15   Cali, Colombia—Beethoven Concertos Nos. 4 and 5

        16   Medellín, Colombia—Recital

        18   Bogotá—Recital

        20   Bogotá—Beethoven Concertos Nos. 4 and 5

        21   Quito—Recital

        23   Lima—Recital I

        24   Lima—Recital II

        28   Santiago—Recital I

   30, 31   Santiago—Mozart Concerto K. 595, Brahms Concerto No. 2

Aug.   1   Santiago—Recital II

         3   Córdoba, Argentina—Recital

         5   Buenos Aires—Recital I

         6   Buenos Aires—Radio recital

        10   Buenos Aires—Schumann concerto

        13   Buenos Aires—Radio recital

        16   Buenos Aires—Recital II

        19   Buenos Aires—Recital III

        21   Montevideo—Recital

        31   Edinburgh Festival (Hamburg Radio Symphony)—Chopin Concerto No. 2

Sept.  4 Edinburgh Festival—Recital
     6 Edinburgh Festival (Philharmonia Orchestra)—Schumann concerto
  10–21 Singapore Musical Society—six concerts
    23 Ceylon—Recital
    25 Bombay—Recital
    28 London (Royal Philharmonic)—Beethoven Concerto No. 3
    29 London—BBC-TV Recital
    30 London (Royal Philharmonic)—Schumann concerto

Oct.  3 Brighton—Recital
    5 Liverpool—Beethoven Concerto No. 3
    7 London—Recital
    9 Bristol—Recital
   11 Swansea Festival, Wales—Recital
   15 Amsterdam—Recital
   18 Lübeck—Beethoven Concerto No. 5
   19 Hamburg—Recital
   20 Berlin—Recital
 21–22 Düsseldorf—Brahms Concerto No. 1
   24 Essen—Recital
   25 Cologne—Chopin Concerto No. 1
   27 Cologne—Recital
   28 Vienna—Recital I
   29 Vienna—Recital II

30, 31⎫
    ⎬ Berlin (RIAS Orchestra)—Brahms Concerto No. 1
Nov.  1⎭
    3 Luxembourg—Recital
  5, 6 Milan (La Scala Orchestra)—Brahms Concerto No. 2
    8 Paris—Recital
   14 Newark, N.J.—Recital
   17 Baltimore—Beethoven Concerto No. 3
   22 Houston—Brahms Concerto No. 2
   29 Dallas—Chopin Variations on "Là ci darem" and *Andante spianato;* Liszt Concerto No. 2
   30 Fort Worth (Dallas Symphony)—Repeat November 29 program

Dec.  4 Mount Vernon, N.Y.: Recital
    6 Hazleton, Pa.: Recital
  10, 11 Cincinnati—Beethoven Concerto No. 3

13 Omaha—Recital
15 Norman, Okla.—Recital
30 Detroit—Weber Konzertstück; Liszt Concerto No. 2


Jan. 6, 7, 9 New York (New York Philharmonic)—Chopin Concertos Nos. 1 and 2
11 Harrisburg, Pa.—Recital
14 Ithaca, N.Y.—Recital
16, 18 Buffalo—Brahms Concertos Nos. 1 and 2
25 Denver—Beethoven Concerto No. 5
31 El Paso—Beethoven Concerto No. 5


Feb. 2 Marysville, Calif.—Recital
4 Modesto—Recital
7 Walla Walla, Wash.—Recital
9 Spokane—Recital
14 Milwaukee (Chicago Symphony)—Brahms Concerto No. 2
17, 18 Chicago—Brahms Concerto No. 2
22, 24 Rochester: Beethoven Concertos Nos. 4 and 5


March 4, 5 St. Louis—Chopin Concerto No. 1
11 New York (Carnegie Hall)—Recital
19 Summit, N.J.—Recital
22 New Haven, Conn.—Recital
25, 26 Boston—Beethoven Concerto No. 3


April 4 Bangor, Me.—Recital
17, 18 Miami—Brahms Concerto No. 2
19 Tampa—Recital
24, 25 Frankfurt—Beethoven Concerto No. 4
26 Stuttgart—Recital
27, 28, 29 Munich (Munich Philharmonic)—Beethoven Concerto No. 5


May 2 Dortmund, Germany—Recital
3 Detmold, Germany—Recital
5–29 Nine concerts with Israel Philharmonic in Tel Aviv, Haifa, and Jerusalem, playing Brahms Concertos Nos. 1 and 2 and Beethoven Concertos Nos. 4 and 5; also four recitals in Tel Aviv, Haifa, and Jerusalem

June 1 London (BBC Symphony)—Chopin Concerto No. 1
    4 Dublin—Recital
  11 Vienna (Vienna Philharmonic)—Brahms Concerto No. 2
  13 Vienna—Recital
  15 Munich—Recital
  17 Florence—Recital
  18 Milan—Recital
(20–27 Served on jury for Long-Thibaud Competition in Paris)
 29, 30
       Holland Festival—Brahms Concerto No. 2
July 4

# Appendix C

# Discography

by T. W. Scragg

This discography, a version of which first appeared as a seventy-fifth-birthday tribute in *Records and Recording*, February 1978, is part of a comprehensive work for which I have been collecting material for nearly nine years. This has been done with the knowledge and express permission of Mr. Arrau, whose kindness and hospitality I gratefully acknowledge. The ultimate aim is an authoritative retrospective listing of all commercially made discs (issued and unissued), rolls, films, and recorded tapes and videotapes, both in private hands and in the archives of broadcasting companies throughout the world. I am greatly in debt to many individuals who have given their time and advice. For the purpose of this publication, which deals only with commercially published recordings, I acknowledge particularly the pioneer work of Messrs. F. F. Clough and G. J. Cuming, and express my thanks to Miss Friede Rothe (New York), Mr. Bruce Carr (Detroit Symphony Orchestra), Mr. John S. Edwards (Chicago Symphony Orchestra), Mr. Joseph Horowitz (New York), Mr. Eric Hughes (British Institute of Recorded Sound, London), Mr. John Jae Jones (Texas), Mr. Alfred Kaine (Polydor International GmbH,

Hamburg), Mr. Derek Lewis (BBC, London), Mr. Leonard Petts (EMI Music Archives, Hayes), Mr. Earl Price (CBS Records, New York), Mr. Hans Ritter and Mr. C. F. van Vliet (Phonogram International B.V., Baarn), Mr. Seymour L. Rosen (Philadelphia Orchestra), Mr. Greville Rothon (Munich), Mr. Gerald Stonehill (London), Mr. Peter Warwick (New Jersey), Mr. John Watson (EMI Ltd, London), and Mr. Wiktor Weinbaum (Société Frédéric Chopin, Warsaw).

The information given includes wherever possible the precise year in which the recording was made, together with details of accompanying orchestra and conductor or artists, as relevant. In a few cases, I have revised the dates of recordings which appeared in my 1978 discography with the benefit of information which has come to light in the past three years. It is now virtually certain that all the German Polydor recordings date from 1928. It seems almost certain that the German Electrola and HMV recordings come from an earlier period than was originally thought. Some sections of EMI's archives have been inaccessible for some time until a recent move to a new site in Hayes. A search there early in 1981 has revealed recording sessions in February and August 1928 and January 1929. These most likely all took place in Berlin. An appropriate note will be found at the end of the discography where a change has been made. The documentation at Hayes is incomplete and somewhat fragmentary. The responsibility for the dates I have indicated throughout the discography is entirely mine.

Basically only British and American issue numbers are indicated except for some of the early recordings, where German numbers are used. There are four specific exceptions to this rule: one Australian (HMV) issue number is given for Weber's Sonata No. 1; one Italian (Cetra) issue of a unique recording of a historic performance with Klemperer is listed; and there are two French pressings, one a Harmonia Mundi disc of reissued recordings of Beethoven Sonatas Nos. 22 and 23 and the 32 Variations, specially labeled in English and specifically made for English and American markets, the other a French RCA reissue of 1941 recordings of sonatas by Mozart and Weber. I have not included a videodisc of a recital given on November 6, 1981, in Venice; the program comprises Beethoven's Sonata in E flat (Op. 27, no. 1), Schumann's *Symphonic Etudes*, Debussy's *Jardins sous la pluie*, Chopin's F-minor Fantasy, and Liszt's *Dante* Sonata.

For the purpose of this publication, the many alternative numbers for various recordings in other countries have been omitted and no attempt has been made to indicate couplings. Commercially made recordings which have not been published are not listed. In some cases (e.g., Beethoven's sonatas), the multiplicity of issue numbers for Philips discs is very confusing, even in the British and American markets alone.

There are many instances where the same number applies to both countries although other numbers may also have been assigned for an individual country at an earlier time. Where this happens the numbers are not repeated. A similar problem arises with the numbering of cassettes which have appeared in some markets without having been formally listed as being available. Fortunately, a standard internationally accepted number is now generally being accorded in most of the recent releases, and this is presumed the case where no country of issue is given before the specific Philips number. The only other internationally standard number is the DGG issue of Beethoven's Piano Concerto No. 4.

ABBREVIATIONS

*Countries of issue*

(indicated in the following order, which is not necessarily chronological)

| | | | |
|---|---|---|---|
| GB | Great Britain | Ital | Italy |
| US | United States | Fr | France |
| Ger | Germany | Austral | Australia |

*Record labels*

| | | | |
|---|---|---|---|
| Ang | Angel | Ev | Everest |
| Bru | Brunswick | HMV | His Master's Voice |
| Cam | Camden (RCA) | Harm | Harmonia Mundi (France) |
| Cet | Cetra (Italy) | | |
| CFP | Classics for Pleasure (EMI-GB) | IGr | I Grandi Interpreti (U.S.) |
| Col | Columbia | IPA | International Piano Archive (N.Y.) |
| Dec | Decca | | |
| Des | Desmar (N.Y.) | Od | Odeon |
| DGG | Deutsche Grammophon Gesellschaft | Odys | Odyssey |
| | | Opus | Opus (Cleveland, Ohio) |
| Elec | Electrola | | |
| EMA | Educational Media Associates (Berkeley, California) | Parl | Parlophone |
| | | Phi | Philips |

Appendix C: Discography

| Pol | Polydor | Tel | Telefunken |
|---|---|---|---|
| Qui | Quintessence | UNO | United Nations |
| RCA | Radio Corporation | | Organization |
| | of America | Van | Vanguard |
| Ser | Seraphim | Vic | Victor (RCA) |

Record prefixes

| C | cassette | T | tape (open reel) |
|---|---|---|---|
| C8 | cartridge (8-track) | 33 | 33⅓ rpm |
| m | monophonic | 45 | 45 rpm |
| PR | piano roll | 78 | 78 rpm |
| s | stereophonic | | |

## ALBÉNIZ

*Iberia*, Books I and II (complete) (1946–47)[1]—US Col (78) 72583-87D, set MM757, (33m) ML4194; Odys (33m) 7464-35229-1.

## BALAKIREV

*Islamey* (1928)[2]—GB Dec (78) CA8165; US Des (33m) GHP4001-2; Ger Pol (78) 95113.

## BEETHOVEN

Bagatelle in A minor *(Für Elise)*, G. 173 (1947)—US Col (78) 1309OD; set MM917.

Piano Concerto No. 1 in C (Op. 15) (1958)—Philharmonia O./Alceo Galliera—GB Col (33m) 33CX1625; US Ang (33ms) 35723; Qui (33s) PMC-7071.

Piano Concerto No. 1 in C (1964)—Concertgebouw O./Bernard Haitink—GB Phi (33m) BAL20, (33s) SBAL20, SAL3712, 6580122, 6566026, 6770014, (C) CPC0085, 7317142, 7650013; US Phi (33s) 839749LY, PHS5-970, SC71AX501, 6570167, (C) 18242CAA, 731067.

291

Piano Concerto No. 2 in B flat (Op. 19) (1958)—Philharmonia O./Alceo Galliera—GB Col (33m) 33CX1696, (33s) SAX2346; US Qui (33s) PMC-7072.

Piano Concerto No. 2 in B flat (1964)—Concertgebouw O./Bernard Haitink—GB Phi (33m) BAL20, (33s) SBAL20, SAL3714, 6580123, 6566027, 6770014, (C) 7317142, 7650013; US Phi (33s) 839751LY, PHS5-970, SC71AX501, 6570173, (C) 7310173.

Piano Concerto No. 3 in C minor (Op. 37) (1947)—Philadelphia O./ Eugene Ormandy—GB Col (33m) 33CX1080, Phi (33m) SBR6252; US Col (33m) ML4302, Odys (33m) Y-34601.

Piano Concerto No. 3 in C minor (1958)—Philharmonia O./Alceo Galliera—GB Col (33m) 33CX1616; US Ang (33ms) 35724; Qui (33s) PMC-7073.

Piano Concerto No. 3 in C minor (1964)—Concertgebouw O./Bernard Haitink—GB Phi (33m) BAL20, (33s) SBAL20, SAL3735, 6580078, 6770014, (C) 7650013; US Phi (33s) PHS5-970, SC71AX501, 6570104, (C) 7505006, 7310104.

Piano Concerto No. 4 in G (Op. 58) (1955)—Philharmonia O./Alceo Galliera—GB Col (33m) 33CX1333; US Ang (33m) 35300; Qui (33m) PMC-7074; GB Col (Tm) CBT557.

Piano Concerto No. 4 in G (1964)—Concertgebouw O./Bernard Haitink—GB Phi (33m) BAL20, (33s) SBAL20, SAL3736, 6580060, 6770014, (C) 7317101, 7650013; US Phi (33s) PHS5-970, SC71AX501, 6570106, (C) 018029CAA, 7310106.

Piano Concerto No. 4 in G (1976)—Bavarian R.S.O./Leonard Bernstein—DGG (33s) 2721153.

Piano Concerto No. 5 in E flat (Op. 73) *(Emperor)* (1958)—Philharmonia O./Alceo Galliera—GB Col (33m) 33CX1653, (33s) SAX2297; US Ang (33ms) 35722; Qui (33s) PMC-7075.

Piano Concerto No. 5 in E flat (1964)—Concertgebouw O./Bernard Haitink—GB Phi (33m) BAL20, AL3567, (33s) SBAL20, SAL3567, SAL3835, 6580094, 6527055, 6768231, 6770014, (C) CPC0019, 7317141, 7311055, 7650013; US Phi (33s) 839600, PHS5-970, SC71AX501, 6570086, (C) PCR4-915002, 7505006, 7310086, (C8) PC8-915002, 7750024.

Concerto for Violin, Piano, and Cello in C (Op. 56) (1970)—Henryk Szeryng (vln), Janos Starker (cel), New Philharmonia O./Eliahu Inbal—Phi (33s) 6500129, 6570070, 6527121; (C) 7300092, 7310070, 7311121.

Rondo for Piano in G (Op. 51, no. 2) (1963)—GB Phi (33m) AL3517, (33s) SAL3517; US Phi (33m) A02335L.

Piano Sonata No. 1 in F minor (Op. 2, no. 1) (1964)—GB Phi (33m) AL3568, (33s) SAL3568, SAL3714, 6580123, 6747009, (C) 7317145; US Phi (33s) 839751LY, PHS3-913, 6747035.

Piano Sonata No. 2 in A (Op. 2, no. 2) (1964)—GB Phi (33m) AL3566, (33s) SAL3566, 6747009; US Phi (33s) PHS4-914, 6747035 (Scherzo only GB Phi [C] 7317101).

Piano Sonata No. 3 in C (Op. 2, no. 3) (1964)—GB Phi (33m) AL3566, (33s) SAL3566, 6747009; US Phi (33s) PHS4-914, 6747035.

Piano Sonata No. 4 in E flat (Op. 7) (1964)—GB Phi (33m) AL3568, (33s) SAL3568, 6747009; US Phi (33s) PHS3-913, 6747035.

Piano Sonata No. 5 in C minor (Op. 10, no. 1) (1964)—GB Phi (33m) AL3550, (33s) SAL3550, 6747009; US Phi (33s) PHS3-915, 6747035.

Piano Sonata No. 6 in F (Op. 10, no. 2) (1964)—GB Phi (33m) AL3550, (33s) SAL3550, SAL3712, 6580122, 6747009, (C) CPC0085, 7317142; US Phi (33s) 839749LY, PHS3-915, 6747035, (C) 18242CAA.

Piano Sonata No. 7 in D (Op. 10, no. 3) (1951)—GB Col (78) LX1540-42.

Piano Sonata No. 7 in D (1958–59)—GB Col (33m) 33CX1696, (33s) SAX2346.

Piano Sonata No. 7 in D (1964)—GB Phi (33m) AL3550, (33s) SAL3550, 6747009; US Phi (33s) PHS3-915, 6747035.

Piano Sonata No. 8 in C minor (Op. 13) *(Pathétique)* (1963)—GB Phi (33m) AL3517, (33s) SAL3517, 6599308, CXL15001, 6747009, 6768231; US Phi (33s) PHS3-907, 6747035, (C) 7300029, (C8) 7750026.

Piano Sonata No. 9 in E (Op. 14, no. 1) (1966)—GB Phi (33m) AL3611, (33s) SAL3611, 6747009; US Phi (33s) PHS3-913, 6747035.

Piano Sonata No. 10 in G (Op. 14, no. 2) (1966)—GB Phi (33m) AL3611, (33s) SAL3611, 6747009; US Phi (33s) PHS3-913, 6747035.

Piano Sonata No. 11 in B flat (Op. 22) (1962)—GB Phi (33m) AL3581, (33s) SAL3581, 6747009; US Phi (33m) A02260L, (33s) PHS4-914, 6747035.

Piano Sonata No. 12 in A flat (Op. 26) (1962)—GB Phi (33m) AL3580, A02259L, (33s) SAL3580, 6747009; US Phi (33m) 500028, PHS4-914, 6747035.

Piano Sonata No. 13 in E flat (Op. 27, no. 1) (1962)—GB Phi (33m) AL3580, A02259L, (33s) SAL3580, 6747009; US Phi (33m) 500028, PHS4-914, 6747035.

Piano Sonata No. 14 in C-sharp minor (Op. 27, no. 2) *(Moonlight)* (1950)— GB Col (78) LX8772-73.

Piano Sonata No. 14 in C-sharp minor (1962)—GB Phi (33m) AL3580, A02259L, (33s) SAL3580, 6599308, 6599987, 6747199, 6747009, 6768231; US Phi (33m) 500028, (33s) PHS4-914, 6747035, (C) 7300029, (C8) 7750026 (1st mov. only GB Phi [33s] 6833179).

Piano Sonata No. 15 in D (Op. 28) *(Pastoral)* (1962)—GB Phi (33m) AL3581, (33s) SAL3581, 6747009; US Phi (33m) A02260L, (33s) 802742LY, PHS3-915, 6747035.

Piano Sonata No. 16 in G (Op. 31, no. 1) (1966)—GB Phi (33m) AL3603, (33s) SAL3603, 6747009; US Phi (33s) PHS4-914, 6747035.

Piano Sonata No. 17 in D minor (Op. 31, no. 2) *(Tempest)* (1965)—GB Phi (33m) AL3603, (33s) SAL3603, 6747009, 6570190, (C) 7310190; US Phi (33s) PHS3-913, 6747035.

Piano Sonata No. 18 in E flat (Op. 31, no. 3) (1947)—GB Col (78) LX1039-41.

Piano Sonata No. 18 in E flat (1965)—GB Phi (33m) AL3600, (33s) SAL3600, 6747009; US Phi (33s) PHS3-913, 6747035.

Piano Sonata No. 19 in G minor (Op. 49, no. 1) (1966)—GB Phi (33m) AL3611, (33s) SAL3611, 6747009; US Phi (33s) PHS3-915, 6747035.

Piano Sonata No. 20 in G (Op. 49, no. 2) (1966)—GB Phi (33m) AL3611, (33s) SAL3611, 6747009, (C) 7317145; US Phi (33s) PHS3-915, 6747035.

Piano Sonata No. 21 in C (Op. 53) *(Waldstein)* (1947–49)[3]—US Col (33m) ML2078.

Piano Sonata No. 21 in C (1956)—GB Col (33m) 33CX1513.

Piano Sonata No. 21 in C (1963)—GB Phi (33m) AL3517, (33s) SAL3517, 6747009, 6580301, 6570190, (C) 7310190; US Phi (33s) PHS3-907, 6747035, 6570173, (C) 7301073.

Piano Sonata No. 22 in F (Op. 54) (1960)—GB Col (33m) 33CX1742, (33s) SAX2390; Fr Harm (33s) HM 10060, (C) HM 40060.

Piano Sonata No. 22 in F (1965)—GB Phi (33m) AL3605, (33s) SAL3605, 6747009; US Phi (33s) PHS3-907, 6747035.

Piano Sonata No. 23 in F minor (Op. 57) *(Appassionata)* (1957–60)— GB Col (33m) 33CX1742, (33s) SAX2390; Fr Harm (33s) HM10060, (C) HM40060.

Piano Sonata No. 23 in F minor (1965)—GB Phi (33m) AL3605, (33s) SAL3605, 6599308, 6768231; US Phi (33s) PHS3-907, 6747035, (C) 7300029, (C8) 7750026.

Piano Sonata No. 24 in F sharp (Op. 78) (1958)—GB Col (33m) 33CX1625.

Piano Sonata No. 24 in F sharp (1965)—GB Phi (33m) AL3600, (33s) SAL3600, 6747009, 6580104, 6833245, 6570055, (C) 7310055; US Phi (33s) 6833145, PHS3-907, 6747035.

Piano Sonata No. 25 in G (Op. 79) (1966)—GB Phi (33m) AL3611, (33s) SAL3611, 6747009; US Phi (33s) PHS3-907, 6747035.

Piano Sonata No. 26 in E flat (Op. 81a) *(Les Adieux)* (1957–58)—GB Col (33m) 33CX1616.

Piano Sonata No. 26 in E flat (1966)—GB Phi (33m) AL3600, (33s) SAL3600, 6747009, 6580301; US Phi (33s) PHS4-914, 6747035, 6570167, (C) 7310167.

Piano Sonata No. 27 in E minor (Op. 90) (1966)—GB Phi (33m) AL3605, (33s) SAL3605, 6747009; US Phi (33s) PHS3-907, 6747035.

Piano Sonata No. 28 in A (Op. 101) (1956–57)—GB Col (33m) 33CX1513.

Piano Sonata No. 28 in A (1965)—GB Phi (33m) AL3577, (33s) SAL3577, 6747009; US Phi (33s) PHS3-915, 6747035.

Piano Sonata No. 29 in B flat (Op. 106) *(Hammerklavier)* (1963)—GB Phi (33m) AL3484, (33s) SAL3484, 6580104, 6747009, 6570055, (C) 7310055; US Phi (33m) A02330L, (33s) PHS3-915, 6833145, 6780020, 6747035.

Piano Sonata No. 30 in E (Op. 109) (1965)—GB Phi (33m) AL3577, (33s) SAL3577, 6780020, 6747009; US Phi (33s) PHS3-907, 6780022, 6747035.

Piano Sonata No. 31 in A flat (Op. 110) (1957)—GB Col (33m) 33CX1610.

Piano Sonata No. 31 in A flat (1965)—GB Phi (33m) AL3576, (33s) SAL3576, 6747009; US Phi (33s) PHS3-913, 6780022, 6747035.

Piano Sonata No. 32 in C minor (Op. 111) (1957)—GB Col (33m) 33CX1610.

Piano Sonata No. 32 in C minor (1965)—GB Phi (33m) AL3576, (33s) SAL3576, 6747009; US Phi (33s) PHS4-914, 6780022, 6747035.

Sonatas for Violin and Piano Nos. 1–10 (complete) (1944)—Joseph Szigeti (vln)—GB RCA Van (33m) SRV300-03; US Van (33m) 4-Van 1109-12, 4-Van SRV 300-03.

Sonata for Violin and Piano No. 1 in D (Op. 12, no. 1) (1975)—Arthur Grumiaux (vln)—Phi (33s) 9500055, (C) 7300473.

Sonata for Violin and Piano No. 2 in A (Op. 12, no. 2) (1976)—Arthur Grumiaux (vln)—Phi (33s) 9500263.

Sonata for Violin and Piano No. 4 in A minor (Op. 23) (1976)—Arthur Grumiaux (vln)—Phi (33s) 9500263.

Sonata for Violin and Piano No. 5 in F (Op. 24) *(Spring)* (1975)—Arthur Grumiaux (vln)—Phi (33s) 9500055, (C) 7300473.

Sonata for Violin and Piano No. 7 in C minor (Op. 30, no. 2) (1976)—Arthur Grumiaux (vln)—Phi (33s) 9500220.

Sonata for Violin and Piano No. 8 in G (Op. 30, no. 3) (1976)—Arthur Grumiaux (vln)—Phi (33s) 9500220.

6 Variations in F (Op. 34) (1941)—US Vic (78) 11-8130-31, set MM892.

6 Variations in F (1968)—GB Phi (33s) SAL3764, 6580300, (C) 7317200; US Phi (33s) 839743LY.

15 Variations (Op. 35) *(Eroica)* (1941)—US Vic (78) 11-8130-31, set MM892.

15 Variations (1952)—GB Bru (33m) AXTL1024-25; US Dec (33m) DX122, DL4067.

15 Variations (1968)—GB Phi (33s) SAL3764, 6580300, (C) 7317200; US Phi (33s) 839743LY.

32 Variations in C minor (WoO80) (1960)—GB Col (33m) 33CX1742, (33s) SAX2390; Fr Harm (33s) HM10060, (C) HM40060.

32 Variations in C minor (1968)—GB Phi (33s) SAL3764, 6580300, (C) 7317200; US Phi (33s) 839743LY.

33 Variations (Op. 120) *(Diabelli)* (1952)—GB Bru (33m) AXTL1024-25; US Dec (33m) DX122.

# BRAHMS

Ballades Nos. 1–4 (Op. 10) (complete) (1977)—Phi (33s) 9500446, (C) 7300652.

Piano Concerto No. 1 in D minor (Op. 15) (1947)—Philharmonia O./ Basil Cameron—GB HMV (78) DB6596-601, DB9250-55.

Piano Concerto No. 1 in D minor (1960)—Philharmonia O./Carlo Maria Giulini—GB Col (33m) 33CX1739, (33s) SAX2387, CFP40028; US Ang (33ms) 35892, Ser (33s) 60264.

Piano Concerto No. 1 in D minor (1969)—Concertgebouw O./Bernard Haitink—Phi (33s) 6700018; GB Phi (33s) 6747270, 6580302, 6570014, (C) 7317201, 7310014; US Phi (33s) 6500018, (C) 7300051.

Piano Concerto No. 2 in B flat (Op. 83) (1962)—Philharmonia O./Carlo Maria Giulini—GB Col (33m) 33CX1822, (33s) SAX2466; CFP40034; US Ser (33s) 60052.

Piano Concerto No. 2 in B flat (1969)—Concertgebouw O./Bernard Haitink—Phi (33s) 6700018; GB Phi (33s) 6747270, 6570052, (C) 7310052; US Phi (33s) 6500019, (C) 7300052.

Scherzo in E-flat minor (Op. 4) (1971)—Phi (33s) 6500377.

Piano Sonata No. 2 in F-sharp minor (Op. 2) (1973)—Phi (33s) 9500066, (C) 7300476.

Piano Sonata No. 3 in F minor (Op. 5) (1971)—Phi (33s) 6500377.

Variations on a Theme of Handel (Op. 24) (1977–78)—Phi (33s) 9500446, (C) 7300652.

Variations on a Theme of Paganini (Op. 35) (1974)—Phi (33s) 9500066, (C) 7300476.

# BUSONI

Elegy No. 5 (*Die Nächtlichen*) (1928)—US Des (33m) GHP4001-2; Ger Pol (78) 90025.

Sonatina No. 6 (*Carmen* Fantasy) (1928)[4]—US Vic (78) 9340; Ger Elec (78) EH162.

# CHOPIN

*Allegro de concert* in A (Op. 46) (1956)—GB Col (33m) 33CX1443; US Ang (33m) 35413.

*Andante spianato and Grande Polonaise* in E flat (Op. 22) (1947)—Little
Orchestra Society (N.Y.)/Thomas Scherman—GB Col (78) LX1267-
68; US Col (78) 72728-29D, set MX307.

*Andante spianato and Grande Polonaise* in E flat (1972)—London P.O./
Eliahu Inbal—Phi (33s) 6500422, 6747003; (C) 7300198.

Ballades Nos. 1–4 (complete) (1953)—GB Bru (33m) AXTL1043; US
Dec (33m) set DX130.

Ballades Nos. 1–4 (1977)—Phi (33s) 9500393, 6768233, (C) 7300605.

Ballade No. 3 in A flat (Op. 47) (1939)[5]—GB Parl (78) R20443; Ger Od
(78) 177264, 121180.

Barcarolle in F (Op. 60) (1953)—GB Bru (33m) AXTL1043; US Dec
(33m) set DX130.

Barcarolle in F (1980)—Phi (33s) 9500963, (C) 7300963.

Piano Concerto No. 1 in E minor (Op. 11) (1954)—Cologne (W.D.R.)
S.O./Otto Klemperer—Ital Cet (33m) L0507.

Piano Concerto No. 1 in E minor (1970)—London P.O./Eliahu Inbal—
Phi (33s) 6500255, 6747003, 6768300; (C) 7300109.

Piano Concerto No. 2 in F minor (Op. 21) (1950)—[New York P.O.]/
Fritz Busch—US EMA (33m) IGI371.

Piano Concerto No. 2 in F minor (1970)—London P.O./Eliahu Inbal—
Phi (33s) 6500309, 6747003, 6768300; (C) 7300110.

Etudes Nos. 1–27 (complete) (1956)—GB Col (33m) 33CX1443-44; US
Ang (33m) 35413-14 (No. 3 only US Ser [33s] 60207).

Etude No. 3 (Op. 10, no. 3) (1929)[6]—Ger HMV (78) EH386.

Etude No. 4 (Op. 10, no. 4) (1928)[7]—Ger HMV (78) EH386.

Etude No. 4 (1929)[8]—US Dec (33m) GHP4001-2; Ger Elec (78) EG1500.

Etude No. 8 (Op. 10, no. 8) (?1930)[9]—GB Parl (78) R2588; US Dec (78)
20425; Ger Od (78) 0-11855.

Etude No. 9 (Op. 10, no. 9) (1928)[10]—Ger HMV (78) EH386.

Etude No. 13 (Op. 25, no. 1) (1929)[11]—US Des (33m) GHP4001-2; Ger
Elec (78) EG1500.

Etude No. 14 (Op. 25, no. 2) (1929)[12]—US Des (33m) GHP4001-2; Ger
Elec (78) EG1500.

Fantasy in F minor (Op. 49) (1960)—GB Col (33m) 33CX1755, (33s) SAX2401.

Fantasy in F minor (1977)—Phi (33s) 9500393, 6768233, (C) 7300605.

Fantasy impromptu in C-sharp minor (Op. 66) (1953)—GB Bru (33m) AXTL1044; US Dec (33m) set DX130.

Fantasy impromptu in C-sharp minor (1980)—Phi (33s) 9500963, (C) 7300963.

Fantasy on Polish Airs (Op. 13) (1972)—London P.O./Eliahu Inbal—Phi (33s) 6500422, 6747003; (C) 7300198.

Impromptus Nos. 1–3 (complete) (1953)—GB Bru (33m) AXTL1044; US Dec (33m) set DX130.

Impromptus Nos. 1–3 (complete) (1980)—Phi (33s) 9500963, (C) 7300963.

*Krakowiak*—Concert Rondo (Op. 14) (1971)—London P.O./Eliahu Inbal—Phi (33s) 6500422, 6747003; (C) 7300110.

Nocturnes Nos. 1–21 (complete) (1977–78)—Phi (33s) 6747485, 6768233, (C) 7300697-8 (Nos. 2, 5, 8, 9, 15 and 19 only [33s] 6570326, (C) 7311326).

Polish Song (Op. 74, no. 12) ("My Joys") (arr. Liszt) (1950)—GB Col (78) LX8792; US Des (33m) GHP4001-2.

Preludes Nos. 1–24 (Op. 28) (complete) (1950–51)[13]—GB Phi (33m) GBL5503; US Col (33m) ML4420 (Nos. 15 and 23 only US Col [45] 4-73261D).

Preludes Nos. 1–24 (complete) (1973)—Phi (33s) 6500622, 6527091, 6768233), (C) 7300335, 7311091 (Nos. 15 and 16 only [33s] 6833245).

Prelude No. 23 in F (c. 1934)—US Des (33m) GHP4001-2; Ger Elec (78) EG1500.

Prelude No. 25 in C-sharp minor (1973)—Phi (33s) 6500622, 6527091, 6768233, (C) 7300335, 7311091.

Prelude No. 26 in A flat (1973)—Phi (33s) 6500622, 6527091, 6768233, (C) 7300335, 7311091.

Scherzos Nos. 1–4 (complete) (1953)—GB Bru (33m) AXTL1044; US Dec (33m) set DX130.

Scherzo No. 3 (Op. 39) (1939)[14]—GB Parl (78) R20469.

Piano Sonata No. 3 in B minor (Op. 58) (1960)—GB Col (33m) 33CX1755, (33s) SAX2401.

Tarantelle in A flat (Op. 43) (?1930)[15]—GB Parl (78) R2588; US Dec (78) 20425; US Des (33m) GHP4001-2; Ger Od (78) 0-11855.

Variations on "Là ci darem la mano" (Mozart) (1972)—London P.O./ Eliahu Inbal—Phi (33s) 6500422, 6747003, (C) 7300198.

Waltzes Nos. 1–14 (complete) (1979)—Phi (33s) 9500739, 6768233, (C) 7300824 (Nos. 2, 3, 7, 9, and 14 only [33s] 6570326, [C] 7311326).

Waltz No. 1 in E flat (Op. 18, no. 1) (1947)—GB Col (78) LX1268; US Col (78) set MX307.

Waltz No. 4 in A minor (Op. 34, no. 3) (1928)[16]—US Vic (78) 4101, Des (33m) GHP4001-2; Ger Elec (78) EG833.

Waltzes Nos. 15–17 (complete) (1980)—Phi (33s) 9500963, (C) 7300963.

DEBUSSY

*Estampes* (complete) (1949)—US Col (78) 72886-88D, set MM872; (33m) ML2086, ML4786.

*Estampes* (complete) (1980)—Phi (33s) 9500965, (C) 7300965.

*Estampe* No. 3 *(Jardins sous la pluie)* (1939)[17]—GB Parl (78) R20476; Ger Od (78) 177262.

*Images*, Books I and II (complete) (1949)—US Col (78) set MM971, (33m) ML2162, ML4786.

*Images*, Books I and II (complete) (1979)—Phi (33s) 9500965, (C) 7300965.

*Pour le piano* (1949)—US Col (78) 72886-88D, set MM872, (33m) ML2086, ML4786.

Preludes, Book I (complete) (1979)—Phi (33s) 9500676, (C) 7300771.

Preludes, Book II (complete) (1979)—Phi (33s) 9500747, (C) 7300832.

Prelude No. 3 (Book II) *(La puerta del vino)* (1951)—GB Col (78) LX1550; US Des (33m) GHP4001-2.

*Tarantelle styrienne* (Danse) (1939)[18]—GB Parl (78) R20476; Ger Od (78) 177262.

## GRANADOS

*Goyescas* No. 4 (*Quejas o la maja y el ruiseñor*) (1951)—GB Col (78) LX1550, (45m) SEL1523.

## GRIEG

Piano Concerto in A minor (Op. 16) (1957)—Philharmonia O./Alceo Galliera—GB Col (33m) 33CX1531; US Ang (33m) 35561.

Piano Concerto in A minor (1963)—Concertgebouw O./Christoph von Dohnanyi—GB Phi (33s) SAL3452, 6580108, 6570170, (C) 7310170; US Phi (33m) 500047, (33s) WSS9122, 900047.

Piano Concerto in A minor (1980)—Boston S.O./Colin Davis—Phi (33s) 9500891, (C) 7300891.

## LISZT

*Aida* (Verdi) Concert Paraphrase (G. 436) (1971)—Phi (33s) 6500368.

*Années de pèlerinage* (First Year: Switzerland) (G. 160) No. 4 (*Au bord d'une source*) (1928)—US Des (33m) GHP4001-2; Ger Pol (78) 95112.

*Années de pèlerinage* (First Year: Switzerland) No. 6 (*Vallée d'Obermann*) (1969)—GB Phi (33s) SAL3783; US Phi (33s) 802906LY.

*Années de pèlerinage* (Second Year: Italy) (G. 161) No. 5 (*Petrarch Sonnet 104*) (1969)—GB Phi (33s) SAL3783; US Phi (33s) 802906LY.

*Années de pèlerinage* (Second Year: Italy) No. 6 (*Petrarch Sonnet 123*) (1969)—GB Phi (33s) SAL3783; US Phi (33s) 802906LY.

*Années de pèlerinage* (Third Year) (G. 163) No. 4 (*Les Jeux d'eaux à la Villa d'Este*) (1929)[19]—GB Parl (78) E10871; US Dec (78) 25175, Des (33m) GHP4001-2; Ger Od (78) 0–6743.

*Années de pèlerinage* (Third Year) No. 4 (1969)—GB Phi (33s) SAL3783; US Phi (33s) 802906LY.

Ballade No. 2 in B minor (G. 171) (1969)—GB Phi (33s) SAL3783; US Phi (33s) 802906LY.

3 Concert Studies (complete) (G. 144), No. 1 (*Il lamento*); No. 2 (*La leggierezza*); No. 3 (*Un sospiro*) (1974–76)—Phi (33s) 6747412, (C) 7505081.

3 Concert Studies, No. 2 (1928)—US Des (33m) GHP 4001-2; Ger Pol (78) 95112.

2 Concert Studies (G. 145), No. 1 (*Waldesrauchen*); No. 2 (*Gnomenreigen*) (1970)—Phi (33s) 6500043, 6833245, 6570345 (C) 7300402, 7310345.

Piano Concerto No. 1 in E flat (G. 124) (1952)[20]—Philadelphia O./Eugene Ormandy—GB Phi (33m) GBR6511; US Phi (33m) ML4665, Odys (33m) Y-34601.

Piano Concerto No. 1 in E flat (1967)—Danish R.S.O./Militiadis Caridis—US Opus (33m) MLG79.

Piano Concerto No. 1 in E flat (1979)—London S.O./Colin Davis—Phi (33s) 9500780, (C) 7300854.

Piano Concerto No. 2 in A (G. 125) (1953)—[N.Y.P.S.O.]/Guido Cantelli—US EMA (33m) IGI371.

Piano Concerto No. 2 in A (1970)—London P.O./Bernard Haitink—US Opus (33m) MLG79.

Piano Concerto No. 2 in A (1979)—London S.O./Colin Davis—Phi (33s) 9500780, (C) 7300854.

*Don Carlos* (Verdi) Concert Paraphrase (G. 435) (1971)—Phi (33s) 6500368.

*Ernani* (Verdi) Concert Paraphrase (G. 432) (1971)—Phi (33s) 6500368.

*Etudes d'exécution transcendante* (G. 139) (complete) (1974-76)—Phi (33s) 6747412, (C) 6505081.

*Etude d'exécution transcendante d'après Paganini* (G. 140) No. 1 in G minor (1928)—US Des (33m) GHP4001-2; Ger Pol (78) 95111.

*Etude d'exécution transcendante d'après Paganini* No. 2 in E flat (1928)—US Des (33m) GHP4001-2; Ger Pol (78) 95110.

*Etude d'exécution transcendante d'après Paganini* No. 5 in E (1928)—US Des (33m) GHP4001-2; Ger Pol (78) 95110.

*Etude d'exécution transcendante d'après Paganini* No. 6 in A minor (1928)—US Des (33m) GHP4001-2; Ger Pol (78) 95111.

Fantasy on Hungarian Folk Tunes (G. 123) (1952)[21]—Philadelphia O./ Eugene Ormandy—GB Phi (33m) GBR6511; GBL5583; US Col (33m) ML4665.

*Harmonies poétiques et religieuses* (G. 173) No. 3 (*Bénédiction de Dieu dans la solitude*) (1970)—Phi (33s) 6500043, (C) 7300402.

*Hungarian Rhapsody* (G. 244) No. 8 in F-sharp minor (1951 or 1952)—US (IPA) Des (33m) DSM1003.

*Hungarian Rhapsody* No. 9 in E flat (1951 or 1952)—US (IPA) Des (33m) DSM1003.

*Hungarian Rhapsody* No. 10 in E (1951 or 1952)—US (IPA) Des (33m) DSM1003.

*Hungarian Rhapsody* No. 11 in A minor (1951 or 1952)—US (IPA) Des (33m) DSM1003.

*Hungarian Rhapsody* No. 13 in A minor (1951 or 1952)—US (IPA) Des (33m) DSM1003.

*I lombardi* (Verdi) Concert Paraphrase (G. 431) (1971)—Phi (33s) 6500368.

*Rigoletto* (Verdi) Concert Paraphrase (G. 434) (1971)—Phi (33s) 6500368, 6599988, 6747199.

*Simon Boccanegra* (Verdi) Concert Paraphrase (G. 438) (1971)—Phi (33s) 6500368.

Piano Sonata in B minor (G. 178) (1970)—Phi (33s) 6500043, (C) 7300402.

*Spanish Rhapsody* (G. 254) (c1929)[22]—US Opus (33m) MLG79; Des GHP4001-2 Ger Tel (78) E1629.

*Il trovatore* (Verdi) Concert Paraphrase (G. 433) (1971)—Phi (33s) 6500368.

*Valse mélancolique* (G. 210) (1928)[23]—US Vic (78) 4102; Ger Elec (78) EG836.

*Valse oubliée* (G. 215, No. 1) (1969)—GB Phi (33s) SAL3783; US Phi (33s) 802906LY, (C) 7300402.


## MENDELSSOHN

Andante and *Rondo capriccioso* in E (Op. 14) (1951)—GB Col (78) LX1515, (45m) SEL1523.


## SOPHIE MENTER

Valse (1922)—GB (PR) Aeolian Duo Art Roll 019 (produced but probably never officially released).

## MOZART

Fantasy in C minor (K. 475) (1973)—Phi (33s) 6500782.

Fantasy in D minor (K. 397) (1973)—Phi (33s) 6500782, 6833245.

Rondo in A minor (K. 511) (1973)—Phi (33s) 6500782, 6833245.

Piano Sonata No. 5 in G (K. 283) (1941)—US Vic (78) 18279-80, set M842; Fr RCA (33m) GM43679, (C) GK43679.

Piano Sonata No. 14 in C minor (K. 457) (1973)—Phi (33s) 6500782.

Piano Sonata No. 16 in B flat (K. 570) (1951)—GB Col (78) LX1551-53.

Piano Sonata No. 17 in D (K. 576) (1941)—US Vic (78) 18280-81, set M842; Fr RCA (33m) GM43679, (C) GK43679.


## SCHUBERT

Allegretto in C minor, (D. 915) (1959)—GB Col (33m) 33CX1709, (33s) SAX2363.

Allegretto in C minor (1978)—Phi (33s) 9500755, (C) 7300836.

Fantasy in C (*Wanderer*) (D. 760) (1957)—GB Col (33m) 33CX1569; US Ang (33m) 35637, Des (33m) GHP4001-2.

"Hark, hark, the lark" (D. 889) (arr. Liszt) (1928)[24]— US Vic (78) 4101, Des (33m) GHP4001-2; Ger Elec (78) EG833.

Impromptus Nos. 1–4 (complete) (D. 899) (1978)—Phi (33s) 9500641, (C) 7300806.

Impromptu No. 5 in F minor (D. 935, no. 1) (1922)—GB (PR) Aeolian Duo Art Roll 010 (erroneously labeled as being in A flat).

Klavierstücke Nos. 1–3 (complete) (D. 946) (1956)—GB Col (33m) 33CX1569; US Ang (33m) 35637.

March in E (D. 606) (1959)—GB Col (33m) 33CX1709, (33s) SAX2363.

*Moments musicaux* (D. 780, nos. 1–6) (complete) (1956)—GB Col (33m) 33CX1709, (33s) SAX2363, (Nos. 1, 2, and 3 only GB Col [45m] SEL1680, [45s] ESL6285) (No. 1 only GB HMV [33s] YKM5010).

Piano Sonata No. 13 in A (D. 664) (1980)—Phi (33s) 9500641, (C) 7300806.

Piano Sonata No. 19 in C minor (D. 958) (1978)—Phi (33s) 9500755, (C) 7300836.

Piano Sonata No. 21 in B flat (D. 960) (1980)—Phi (33s) 9500928, (C) 7300928.

SCHUMANN

*Arabesque* in C (Op. 18) (1947)[25]—US Col (78) 72362D, set MM716.

*Arabesque* in C (1967)—GB Phi (33s) SAL3690, 6768084, 6570320,(C) 7310320; US Phi (33s) 900181, 839709LY.

*Blumenstück* in D (Op. 19) (1976)—Phi (33s) 6500395, 6833245, 6768084.

*Carnaval* (Op. 9) (1939)[26]—GB Parl (78) R20448-50, SW8062-64; US Vic (78) set M1009, (33m) DL7502; Ger Od (78) 177276-78.

*Carnaval* (1966)—GB Phi (33s) SAL3630, 6768084; US Phi (33s) 802746LY.

Piano Concerto in A minor (Op. 54) (1944)—Detroit S.O./Karl Krueger—GB HMV (78) DB6373-76, DB9095-98; US Vic (78) 11-8852-55, set M1009.

Piano Concerto in A minor (1951)—New York P.S.O./Victor de Sabata—US IGr (33m) IGI297.

Piano Concerto in A minor (1957)—Philharmonia O./Alceo Galliera—GB Col (33m) 33CX1531; US Ang (33m) 35561.

Piano Concerto in A minor (1963)—Concertgebouw O./Christoph von Dohnanyi—GB Phi (33s) SAL3542, 6580108, 6570170, (C) 7310170; US Phi (33m) 500047, (33s) WSS9122.

Piano Concerto in A minor (1980)—Boston S.O./Colin Davis—Phi (33s) 9500891, (C) 7300891.

*Davidsbündlertänze* (Op. 6) (1971)—Phi (33s) 6500178, 6768084.

Fantasy in C (Op. 17) (1966)—GB Phi (33s) SAL3630, 6768084, 6570319, (C) 7310319; US Phi (33s) 802746LY.

*Fantasiestücke* (Op. 12) (complete) (1972)—Phi (33s) 6500423, 6768084 (*Aufschwung* only [33s] 6570345, (C) 7310345).

*Fantasiestücke* No. 2 (*Aufschwung*) (c1962)—US Ev (33m) 3128/2; UNO (33m) UNM2.

*Fantasiestücke* No. 5 (*In der Nacht*) (c1962)—US Ev (33m) 3128/2; UNO (33m) UNM2.

*3 Fantasiestücke* (Op. 111) (1968)—GB Phi (33s) SAL3663, 6768084; US Phi (33s) 802793LY.

*Faschingsschwank aus Wien* (Op. 26) (1967)—GB Phi (33s) SAL3690, 6768084; US Phi (33s) 900181, 839709LY.

*Humoreske in B flat* (Op. 20) (1968)—GB Phi (33s) SAL3690, 6768084; US Phi (33s) 839709LY.

*Kinderszenen* (Op. 15) (1976)—Phi (33s) 6500395, 6768084, 6570320, (C) 7310320 (No. 7 ["Träumerei"] only 6833245).

*Kreisleriana* (Op. 16) (1946)—US Col (78) 72362-66D, set MM716.

*Kreisleriana* (1972)—Phi (33s) 6500394, 6768084.

*4 Nachtstücke* (Op. 23) (1971)—Phi (33s) 6500178, 6768084.

*Noveletten* (Op. 21) (1973)—Phi (33s) 6500396, 6768084.

*Papillons* (Op. 2) (1976)—Phi (33s) 6500395,6768084.

3 Romances (Op. 28) (1976)—Phi (33s) 6500395, 6768084.

Piano Sonata No. 1 in F-sharp minor (Op. 11) (1967)—GB Phi (33s) SAL3663, 6768084; US Phi (33s) 802793LY.

Piano Sonata No. 2 in G minor (Op. 22) (1972)—Phi (33s) 6500394, 6768084.

*Symphonic Etudes* (Op. 13) (1970)—Phi (33s) 6500130, 6768084.

Theme and Variations (Op. 1) *(ABEGG)* (1970)—Phi (33s) 6500130, 6768084, 6570320, (C) 7310320.

*Waldszenen* (Op. 82) (1972)—Phi (33s) 6500423, 6768084, 6570320, (C) 7310320.

## RICHARD STRAUSS

*Burleske* in D minor (1946)[27]—Chicago S.O./Desiré Defauw—US Vic (78) 12-0279-80, 12-0283-86, set M1216; US Cam (33m) CAL191 (issued anonymously as "Century Symphony Orchestra").

## STRAVINSKY

*Petrushka—Danse Russe* (arr. Stravinsky) (1928)—US Des (33m) GHP4001-2; Ger Pol (78) 90025.

TCHAIKOVSKY

Piano Concerto No. 1 in B-flat minor (Op. 23) (1960)—Philharmonia O./ Alceo Galliera—GB Col (33m) 33CX1731, (33s) SAX2380; US Ser (33s) 60020.

Piano Concerto No. 1 in B-flat minor (1979)—Boston S.O./Colin Davis— Phi (33s) 9500695, (C) 7300783.

WEBER

Konzertstück in F minor (J. 282) (1946)—Chicago S.O./Desiré De-fauw—US Vic (78) 12-0281-82, 12-0283-86, set M1216; US Cam (33m) CAL191 (issued anonymously as "Century Symphony Orchestra").

Konzertstück in F minor (1960)—Philharmonia O./Alceo Galliera—GB Col (33m) 33CX1731, (33s) SAX2380; US Ser (33s) 60020.

Piano Sonata No. 1 in C (Op. 24, J. 138) (1941)—US Vic (78) 18521-23, set M884; Austral HMV (78) ED500-02; Fr RCA (33m) GM43679, (C) GK43679.

TALK BY CLAUDIO ARRAU

Narration Record—"Thoughts on Beethoven's Sonatas" (1969)[28]—US Phi (33s) PHS3-915.

NOTES

1. This recording is believed to date from 1946–47, not 1950, as previously indicated.
2. This recording is now believed definitely to date from 1928, not possibly 1927, as previously thought.
3. This recording is believed to date from 1947–49, not 1950, as previously indicated.
4. The matrix numbers of this recording are remarkably close to those of a session believed to date from February 1928. Accordingly, this date is given rather than 1930, as previously indicated.
5. This recording was made in England on April 4, 1939, not in 1938, as previously indicated.
6. This recording is believed to date from January 1929, not 1930, as previously indicated.

7. This recording is believed to date from February 1928, not 1930, as previously indicated.
8. These recordings are believed to date from January 1929, not 1930, as previously indicated.
9. There is some doubt about the date of this recording. Although the disc was not catalogued in Britain until 1938, it is believed to have been made earlier, probably in 1930, not 1928, as previously indicated.
10. See note 7.
11. See note 8.
12. See note 8.
13. These recordings are believed to date from 1950–51, not 1950, as previously indicated.
14. See note 5.
15. See note 9.
16. This recording is believed to have been made in August 1928 (the 19th?), not in 1930, as previously indicated.
17. See note 5.
18. See note 5.
19. This recording is believed to have been made on April 8, 1929.
20. This recording was made on February 17, 1952, not in 1951, as previously indicated.
21. See note 20.
22. For some years it has been felt that this recording dated from 1936, and has been indicated as such in two recent LP transfers. However, it seems clear that it comes from an earlier period, certainly not later than 1935. Mr. Arrau considers it is one of his earlier recordings, dating probably from 1929. It comes from a period when he was desperately short of money and it was for this reason that he agreed to make the recording, omitting a number of bars so as to fit the work on a 78 disc. This is something he would never normally have agreed to do.
23. This recording is believed to have been made on August 19, 1928, not in 1930, as previously indicated.
24. See note 16.
25. This recording is believed to date from 1947, not 1946, as previously indicated.
26. This recording was made in England on the 3rd and 4th of April 1939, not in 1936, as previously indicated. Mr. Arrau considers that he may have made an earlier recording of *Carnaval* in 1929 or 1930. Unfortunately, no trace of such a recording has been found, and it certainly never appears to have been issued.
27. This recording was made on April 13, 1946, not possibly in 1945, as previously indicated.
28. This recording was made in 1969, not 1970, as previously indicated.

# Index

*(Numbers in italics refer to music examples.)*

# Index

# Index

311

# Index

# Index

# Index

# Index

# Index

A NOTE ON THE TYPE

This book was set via computer-driven cathode ray tube in Caledonia, a face originally designed by W. A. Dwiggins. It belongs to the family of printing types called "modern face" by printers—a term used to mark the change in style of type letters that occurred about 1800. Caledonia borders on the general design of Scotch Modern but is more freely drawn than that letter.

Composed by Centennial Graphics, Inc., Ephrata, Pennsylvania.
Printed and bound by The Haddon Craftsmen, Inc., Scranton, Pennsylvania.

Designed by Judith Henry.